Research Method

Research Methods

*Designing and Conducting
Research With a Real-World Focus*

Carrie A. Picardi, University of Bridgeport

Kevin D. Masick, Krasnoff Quality Management Institute,
a division of the North Shore-LIJ Health System

Los Angeles | London | New Delhi
Singapore | Washington DC

Los Angeles | London | New Delhi
Singapore | Washington DC

FOR INFORMATION:

SAGE Publications, Inc.
2455 Teller Road
Thousand Oaks, California 91320
E-mail: order@sagepub.com

SAGE Publications Ltd.
1 Oliver's Yard
55 City Road
London EC1Y 1SP
United Kingdom

SAGE Publications India Pvt. Ltd.
B 1/I 1 Mohan Cooperative Industrial Area
Mathura Road, New Delhi 110 044
India

SAGE Publications Asia-Pacific Pte. Ltd.
3 Church Street
#10-04 Samsung Hub
Singapore 049483

Copyright © 2014 by SAGE Publications, Inc.

Library of Congress Cataloging-in-Publication Data

Picardi, Carrie A.

Research methods : designing and conducting research with a real-world focus / Carrie A. Picardi, University of Bridgeport, Kevin D. Masick, Krasnoff Quality Management Institute, a division of the North Shore-LIJ Health System.

pages cm
Includes bibliographical references and index.

ISBN 978-1-4522-3033-7

1. Psychology—Research—Methodology. I. Masick, Kevin D. II. Title.

BF76.5.P53 2013
150.72—dc23   2013017900

Acquisitions Editor: Reid Hester
Editorial Assistant: Sarita Sarak
Production Editor: Olivia Weber-Stenis
Copy Editor: Beth Hammond
Typesetter: C&M Digitals (P) Ltd.
Proofreader: Theresa Kay
Indexor: Sheila Bodell
Cover Designer: Anupama Krishnan
Marketing Manager: Shari Countryman

13 14 15 16 17 10 9 8 7 6 5 4 3 2 1

Brief Contents

Detailed Contents

6   Construct and External Validity   73

8 Quasi-Experimental Research Designs

9 Nonexperimental Research Designs

Preface

Research methods is a course that encompasses a variety of concepts ranging from the simple, such as understanding the purpose of a hypothesis and writing in APA format, to the complex, such as determining the appropriate statistical calculations to conduct a study's data analysis and identifying a study's potential threats to validity. In addition, a research methods course often explores various research elements and methodology design options suitable for answering a research question in a specific setting and context. Because we are not only professors and researchers but also field practitioners, we consider a course successful if we can equip students with all the necessary tools for conducting sound research, the knowledge to determine *which tools in the toolbox* to select for various research needs, and the understanding of why the methodology selected is appropriate as well as its strengths and limitations in real-world settings.

While these objectives may sound quite reasonable, it has proven to be a challenge for us to find a comprehensive resource that connects the dots between concepts and application. When we were developing research methods courses geared toward graduate or advanced level undergraduate students, we found ourselves adopting one book for the course but supplementing with multiple other textbooks, current research in the field, and real life examples to provide the in-depth practitioner focused methodology we believe is critical for current students and professionals. Based on our many years of experience teaching research methods, we believe these additional techniques provide students with the "Ah ha!" moment where they can begin to connect the dots between a conceptual understanding and practice. In our experience, we have found that students appreciate the practical experience that current professionals in the field can provide as well as relevant current research articles published in a variety of journals in psychology and business that not only bring these concepts to life but engage the reader with the material.

There are many important features of this textbook. A key element to encourage learning is through repetition of important research methodology concepts. Concepts are not only discussed in a theoretical manner but also reinforced through practical examples and current literature. Current research articles in business and psychology journals supplement the complex concepts taught to reinforce and engage students in learning. Throughout various chapters, tools and tips are provided in text boxes from current practitioners in the field. We also discuss the relationship between the selection of necessary research design elements and selection of the appropriate statistical calculations (i.e., the "When do you run a t test and when do you run a one-way ANOVA?" question). Lastly, research methodology concepts are translated into practice to facilitate the process of bridging the science-practice gap.

This textbook can be used for any business or psychology course that integrates applied research methodology with its discipline-specific content, such as Industrial/Organizational Psychology, Community Psychology, School Psychology, Program Evaluation, Organizational Behavior, Marketing, and Human Resource Management. Research methods is unlike other courses in that it can be considered a *horizontal* in terms of subject matter since most (if not all) disciplines in business and the social sciences conduct research as part of an ongoing effort to answer critical questions and seek validation for better understanding a wide scope of behavioral phenomena across relevant field settings.

ACKNOWLEDGMENTS

Back in 2006, a wise professor told us that with research design there is "pain" with every decision we make. Throughout our PhD program, he was always pushing us to think differently and approach any research design by carefully calculating how to design the study. Little did we know, approximately two years later we would venture down the path of writing our own textbook on this very subject. It is with much appreciation and gratitude that we thank Dr. William Metlay, Hofstra University, for his wisdom and guidance to push us beyond what we thought was possible.

In 2010, the Society for Industrial/Organizational Psychology (SIOP) annual conference was held in Atlanta. We were walking through the vendor area and stopped at the SAGE Publications booth to talk about an idea we had about a research methodology textbook. We were given the advice to "submit a proposal," so over the course of the next year we began working on our proposal. After exchanging a lot of back and forth ideas, we met with SAGE representatives again in 2011 at the SIOP annual conference in Chicago to discuss feedback from anonymous reviewers. To our surprise, we had received overwhelmingly positive feedback on our proposal. We were ecstatic and began to further solidify our plans to create this book. We want to acknowledge the SAGE Publications staff that helped us throughout the process, Sarita Sarak, Reid Hester, Beth Hammond, Olivia Weber-Stenis, and Chris Cardone.

We also want to thank the applied practitioners that we were able to persuade to contribute a Practitioner Spotlight. We know it wasn't easy to take time out of their busy schedules to help us. Their expertise with current organizational issues is tremendously valuable. Thank you to Justin O'Neal, Chris Rosett, Sarina Tomel, and Rania Vasilatos for your contributions. We hope that students and practitioners reading the Practitioner Spotlight features will benefit from their experiences incorporating research methodology components into practice.

We would also like to acknowledge our families for their encouragement to follow our dreams, even when it meant spending hundreds of hours sequestered away writing and editing. Kevin would like to thank his better half, Rob Tursi-Masick, for his patience and understanding throughout this process. We would also like to thank our families, parents Sam and Johanna Picardi and Nancy and Donald Masick, Carrie's brother Michael, Kevin's brothers and sisters-in-law Donald, Sharlene, Brian, and Cathlyn, and nieces and nephews Benjamin, Nathaniel, Hailey, Annabelle, and Nicholas, who have always given us unconditional love and support, and our four-legged "kids," Kira, Carter, and Bailey, who remind us when we need to take a breather and enjoy life along the way.

About the Authors

Carrie A. Picardi (PhD, Hofstra University) is an industrial/organizational psychologist with more than 17 years of experience in field settings, in a variety of human resources positions and as an organizational research analyst and consultant. She is currently Assistant Professor of Management at the University of Bridgeport, Connecticut.

As a human resources practitioner, she led initiatives in the areas of selection, job analysis and design, training and development, compensation benchmarking, performance management, employee relations, management coaching, and team building.

As a research analyst, Carrie provided consulting support to clients on organizational development initiatives, with projects spanning needs such as talent management, employee engagement and retention, learning and development, management coaching, compensation strategy, and technology/systems decisions. In her current academic role, her focus is on course development and instruction in undergraduate and graduate-level courses in Organizational Behavior, Leadership Strategy, Business Ethics, Human Resource Management, Group Dynamics, and Consumer Behavior. Carrie continues to conduct research studies in the areas of performance management, organizational culture, and ethical decision making, and has presented her research at conferences and meetings globally.

Kevin D. Masick, PhD, is a current applied practitioner and adjunct professor. Currently, he is the Informatics Manager at the Krasnoff Quality Management Institute of the North Shore-LIJ Health System. He oversees an analytic team to provide guidance and direction on statistical analysis of health data, research project development, research methodology education, hypothesis development, and survey design to provide clinical staff and administrators with a foundation to objectively assess and improve the quality of care. In addition to his full-time employment, he has been an adjunct professor since 2007 in both business and psychology departments at Hofstra University, CUNY Baruch, Iona College, and University of Phoenix. He teaches courses in univariate and multivariate statistics, quantitative research methodology, and experimental research methodology at the graduate level and research methodology at the undergraduate level. He has a Bachelor of Arts in Psychology from State University of New York at Albany, a Master of Arts in Industrial/Organizational Psychology, and a PhD in Applied Organizational Psychology from Hofstra University.

PART I

Foundation of Research Methods

CHAPTER 1

Introduction to Research Methods

As a psychologist, the entire framework behind learning about psychology is being able to study human behavior. Not everyone will ultimately conduct research for a career, but in order to understand human behavior, we must have an appreciation for the research process and experimental design to better understand how to critically evaluate research results. By nature, we are all consumers of information, and understanding research design will help broaden your ability to interpret and critically analyze research no matter what your career choice is. As you begin to embark on your journey through a research methods course with the end goal of a career in academia, practice, or research, there are probably a lot of questions that come to mind. Every time a new research methodology class begins or someone consults with a new client to solve a problem, we always ask, Why do we conduct research or what does research methodology mean to you? The simple answer to this is "to learn things or solve a problem" or "to advance science and practice through control and innovation."

After completing a course in research methodology, you may be left with a feeling that all that was accomplished in the course was a laundry list of different concepts and topics with little connection or relevance to the real world or that this textbook will make an excellent paperweight. However, this couldn't be further from the truth, because in some capacity (whether scientifically controlled or simply through observation), research is conducted every day. In a scientifically controlled **experiment**, a researcher may desire to understand the impact that an **independent variable** has on a **dependent variable**. In other words, in an experiment, a researcher develops a **hypothesis or research question** and then implements an

experiment: A specific research design consisting of manipulating an independent variable and measuring a dependent variable

independent variable: A variable in research that is manipulated or changed

dependent variable: A variable in research that is measured

hypothesis: A scientific prediction that is suspected to occur in a study based on previous research findings

research question: A question developed based on a problem where limited knowledge or research exists

intervention (i.e., the independent variable) that is designed to have an effect on a specific outcome (i.e., the dependent variable). The complexity of an experiment is up to the discretion of the individual conducting the experiment.

RESEARCH PROCESS

Conducting research for the first time is a very time consuming iterative process to validate and replicate results. While we may all want to save the world with a grand idea, consider the resources and time you have to conduct and evaluate research. You may not be able to solve all the problems at work, but there is always a solution to a problem. Through proper planning and critical thinking, you can create a well thought out research study. The major advantage to having a thorough understanding of research design is that it is possible to know any potential issue that may arise prior to conducting an experiment. Therefore, researchers are aware of and can prevent many of the problems before they become issues. This is where proper planning and critical thinking before conducting research is imperative. These problems, as you will learn soon, are threats to the **validity** of the results. Think about it for a minute. How would you like to have the ability to know any potential problem you would encounter and how to fix it before it actually happens? You may be thinking that this is not possible, but we can assure you that this is possible. After reading this book and understanding research design and threats to validity, you will be able to improve the validity of conducting research at work or critically evaluating existing research results to better understand how to interpret research.

Throughout this book, we bring you through the complexities of research methodology with a focus on applying science with practice to foster your understanding of research methodology or enhancing your skills to evaluate existing research. In other words, we provide you with the steps, tools, and knowledge to develop a well thought out and high quality research design or evaluate an existing study. In addition to our expertise, we weave together examples from problems faced by current practitioners and how these examples relate to research design in order to bridge the gap between science and practice. These examples provide reinforcement of the research methodology concepts within this text- book and insight into what problems organizations may be currently facing. We provide you with a foundation of the importance and practicality that a solid research design has on delivering valid and reliable results.

validity: The accuracy of the results of a research study

reliability: The extent to which a measure in a study is consistent, dependable, precise, or stable

Research methodology would not be complete without an in-depth discussion of **reliability** and validity. Besides, reliability and validity are the crux of conducting quality research, and we believe in the importance of knowing these concepts in detail because the link between reliability and threats to validity with research design is not always clear. Therefore, we have intertwined threats to validity with various research designs as well as the trade-offs of validity threats. Essentially, validity and their associated threats are discussed in their own chapters and throughout this book to provide a clearer understanding of how these components operate and a direct link to how they impact research design.

This next statement is going to be a recurring theme that you may hear multiple times! No matter what the selected research design is, the only limitation between what you want to do and what you actually get to do is dependent upon your own creativity and ability to reduce validity threats, aside from concerns of ethics and constraints of time and reources. Creating a study is relatively simple, but defining how to do it thoroughly while maximizing validity and reliability is the challenge. Before venturing into the world of research, it is expected that there is a certain level of understanding about research. With that said, this chapter is aimed at providing a general overview of concepts and topics that you should be familiar with. Should some of these concepts be unfamiliar, definitions and examples are provided along the way to enhance and reinforce your understanding of the terminology.

RESEARCH AND EXPERIMENTS

We conduct research to learn about a topic or to seek answers to a question. In order to be able to answer these questions, we must conduct experiments, which fall into four broad categories:

1. Experimental Research Design (Chapter 7) – Involves the manipulation of an independent variable to determine the effect on a dependent variable where participants are randomly assigned.

2. Quasi-Experimental Research Design (Chapter 8) – Involves the manipulation of an independent variable to determine the effect on a dependent variable where participants are not randomly assigned.

3. Nonexperimental Research Design (Chapter 9) – Utilizes primary analysis, secondary analysis, or meta-analysis to describe data, examine relationships or covariation between variables, and compare groups.

4. Survey Research Design (Chapter 10) – Utilizes experimental, quasi-experimental, or nonexperimental designs to study a cause and effect relationship or examine relationships between variables through the use of a survey/questionnaire.

Each one of these categories has advantages and disadvantages, which are discussed in their own respective chapters. The purpose of conducting research/experiments and evaluating existing research is to better understand a phenomenon of interest. As we reflect on our education, teaching experience, and applied experience, the one statement that is always a topic of discussion revolves around predicting behavior.

Have you ever been told or heard that the best predictor of future behavior is past behavior? This statement is the result of conducting research! Many researchers have explored this very phenomenon in an effort to be able to predict future behavior. When examining past research on predicting behavior, Tolman (1946) was interested in predicting behaviors for incarcerated individuals being given probation. Approximately 60 years later, the topic of

> **meta-analysis:** A nonexperimental research technique utilizing statistics to compare and contrast various articles on a particular topic

predicting behavior is still being researched today! Helzer and Dunning (2012) were interested in examining future aspiration versus past achievement. To aggregate multiple research studies on a similar topic, Ouellette and Wood (1998) conducted a **meta-analysis** to examine a variety of past studies to determine what factors may influence this past behavior–future behavior relationship. The purpose of a meta-analysis is to review multiple studies on a given topic to statistically analyze a theme that emerges from these studies and recommend future areas of research.

The process of conducting or evaluating research is important because research is continually evolving and changing over time. A few applied organizational topics that could be researched using the past behavior–future behavior link are as follows:

1. A recruiter is interested in examining the extent to which biodata on an application form predicts future behavior (Mael, 1994; Yan, Wu, & Zhang, 2010).

2. Understanding how using personality variables can predict future job performance (Barrick, Mount, & Judge, 2001).

3. A retail organization wanting to know if asking customers about future behavior would impact the likelihood of repeating past behavior (Chandon, Smith, Morwitz, Spangenberg, & Sprott, 2011).

Each one of the above problems can be answered through one of the four main categories of research. The only limit to conducting research is your own creativity to design a study.

Throughout our lives, we will always encounter situations and problems that may not have a clear answer. This is where research can help! Research methodology is a science that is critical to know and understand, but the limited creativity and numerous concepts can be confusing and overwhelming. One of the main problems with learning about research methodology is that the light bulb rarely goes on or is so dimly lit that there is no real understanding of what was supposed to be learned and why. Therefore, we provide an in-depth discussion of research methodology with a focus on real-world application to bridge the gap between science and practice while intertwining the nuances of research design and the impacts on validity to provide you with the tools to conduct and evaluate research.

HOW WE LEARN

As human beings, we desire to learn new ways of doing something or understanding why we learn things in an effort to explain a phenomenon of interest. This inquisitive nature may lead to the question, How do we learn things? Now you get the idea! Research methodology is about acquiring new knowledge or advance existing knowledge to solve a practical problem. When determining an effective solution to a problem, there are two different ways of arriving at a conclusion. Induction and deduction are two types of

Box 1.1	Induction and Deduction

Induction – Using common sense as a way of learning. For example, what does it mean to know what common sense is to someone, and how do we know it is common sense? Zhao (2009) conducted a study examining the use of common sense for management decision making.

Deduction – Utilizing logical reasoning and/or current knowledge as a way of learning. For example, students attend school to learn about and master the material required to complete a degree. The challenge is when a student uses what they learned in school to apply on the job because the transition from textbook to practice may be difficult (Le Maistre & Pare, 2004).

reasoning a researcher/practitioner can use to approach a problem.

induction: Using common sense as a way of learning

deduction: Using logical reasoning or current knowledge as a way of learning

Through these methods of learning, researchers can begin to understand and explain behavior in a meaningful way that may lead to specific questions. These questions then lead a researcher to create a solution as to how to answer these questions. Maybe it is just us, but have you ever wanted to know why someone engages in one behavior and someone else engages in a different type of behavior? Through conducting research, we can begin to learn about behaviors and provide a framework to understand the implications of these behaviors to predict how someone may react in a given situation.

As part of inductive reasoning, a researcher/practitioner reviews the existing literature to better understand what previous researchers have done to explore the phenomenon of interest. Upon reviewing the relevant literature, the researcher/practitioner begins to develop a specific question that can be addressed through research. Then the experiment is conducted, and results are analyzed to determine if the current experiment supports the original question of interest. As part of deductive reasoning, a researcher/practitioner can take the results of an experiment or an observation then come up with a tentative explanation as to why these results occurred and refer to the literature or theory to assist in explaining this observation. Regardless of the type of reasoning used to arrive at a result, the results and findings can lead to the development of different theories that provide the scientific and practitioner community with ways to address a phenomenon of interest.

BASIC VERSUS APPLIED RESEARCH

Prior to beginning the discussion on different research designs, within the realm of research, there are many different types of research designs, categories of research, and multiple ways to solve a problem. It is important to take a step back and examine different categories of research. The first phase of thinking about research is to understand what category of research you are conducting. There are two main categories that research can fall into: **basic research** and **applied research**. Basic research applies when questions are developed that aid in understanding the fundamental process of behavior or why something is done. The goal is not necessarily to create new knowledge but rather provide an understanding of existing knowledge, theories, or behaviors. Once a researcher has enough knowledge to understand a phenomenon of interest, then basic research may in turn drive applied research experiments. Applied research is conducted to solve problems that are dealt with on an everyday basis. More specifically, applied research is utilized to predict a phenomenon of interest and how someone would behave in a given situation.

> **basic research:** Type of research where questions are developed to understand the fundamental process of a phenomenon
>
> **applied research:** Type of research conducted to solve a problem that occurs on an everyday basis

Box 1.2   Practitioner Spotlight: Basic Versus Applied Research

A recent conversation with a fellow colleague led to the discussion of a potential problem within an organization by implementing a solution through utilizing basic and applied research. While this particular practitioner did not think in terms of basic versus applied research, we pulled out the nuances between the two and thought this would be a good example to highlight the differences between research categories.

The surrounding problem within this particular organization was a result of high turnover in one particular department. The organization utilized a two-step approach to solve the problem. One approach we deem as basic research because the purpose was to provide a more thorough understanding of why the turnover existed. The other approach was applied research because the organization wanted to solve the problem of turnover and determine an intervention that would result in decreasing turnover.

- Basic Research – The first approach was through the use of basic research. To better understand why there was a high degree of turnover in this department, the organization development team utilized focus groups to further understand the existing behavior in an attempt to better understand why the turnover was high. The overall purpose of this focus group was to conduct a gap analysis between employees to determine any training opportunities that may exist. After completing the focus groups, it was determined that there was a disconnect between management and employees. This disconnect was a result of a lack of knowledge and skill that employees were required to have in order to be successful in their current position. This qualifies as basic research because the intention was to understand the why there was a high degree of turnover rather than try to fix the problem.

- Applied Research – The second approach to this turnover problem was through utilizing the results of the focus group to develop a four day leadership training program aimed at providing theoretical knowledge and practical application to efficiently and effectively lead a department. The program began with a thorough assessment of the leader and the team through various tools that evaluate the current leader. The remaining days of the training program involved a hands-on approach to solve practical problems through integrating theoretical concepts with application. The purpose of this leadership training program was to enhance the skill level of management and reduce turnover. This is an applied research project because the intention was to provide the management team with the knowledge and skills on how to be successful in a given situation in the future.

SCIENTIFIC METHOD

With an understanding of the two main categories research falls into, the next step is to begin the process of how to conduct research. Researchers have long relied on a concept known as the scientific method to execute an idea. The scientific method is a common means to conduct research. It is a cyclical methodology of conducting research that is comprised of the following seven steps:

1. Identify the problem
2. Utilize research to understand the problem
3. Create a hypothesis or research question
4. Design a methodology for conducting the research
5. Collect the data and analyze results
6. Interpret findings and draw conclusions
7. Report findings or revisit the hypothesis/research question starting at step 3

The first step in beginning the process of conducting research involves thinking of a potential problem that you want to provide an answer to. After a problem of interest is identified, the next step is to examine the literature in detail to ensure you have a clear and thorough understanding of the research and how variables are defined. At this step of the research process, you may only have an idea, which then becomes a starting point for further exploration. Keep in mind that the question or hypothesis may change while reviewing previous literature, which is a normal process of refining your initial idea.

When conducting and analyzing your own research, you may find yourself venturing down a different path than what you originally started with. This is part of the process of determining an appropriate research design. Once the experiment is conducted, it is also important to remember that despite our best efforts to develop a hypothesis, the results may or may not be statistically significant findings. While the goal is to find statistically significant results, not finding significant results is also as important as finding significant results. There will always be something to learn from a study, whether it is learning from mistakes in the current experiment to construct a better quality research design or learning about a different approach to a problem. For purposes of this textbook, we review the scientific method up to step 3 with the remaining Chapters 7 to 10 focusing on step 4 and the data collection of step 5. Chapter 11 discusses briefly the analysis of data in step 5 and step 6, Chapters 12 and 13 bridge the gap between science and practice and introduce tradeoffs to research design, and Chapter 14 discusses reporting your findings.

CHAPTER SUMMARY

- Conducting and evaluating research is a complex iterative process that focuses on designing a study that is both reliable and valid.

- Research can fall into four main categories: experimental design, quasi-experimental design, nonexperimental design, and survey research.

- As a means to learn about a phenomenon, induction and deduction are two ways that can be used. Induction is when you use common sense as a way of learning, and deduction is when you use logical reasoning or current knowledge as a way of learning.

- When conducting research, basic and applied research are the two main categories. The purpose of basic research is to provide an understanding of existing knowledge, and applied research is used to predict a phenomenon of interest or how someone would behave in a given situation.

- The scientific methodology is an overarching cyclical framework that utilizes a series of seven steps to conduct research.

DISCUSSION QUESTIONS

- How would you utilize the concepts of induction and deduction to develop two similar study designs that measure the same dependent variable?

- Compare and contrast basic and applied research and how both can be utilized in organizational settings.

- Develop a research design that follows the seven steps of the scientific method that you could implement in an applied setting.

CHAPTER KEY TERMS

Deduction
Experiment
Experimental Design
Hypothesis
Induction

Meta-Analysis
Nonexperimental Design
Quasi-Experimental Design
Reliability
Research, Applied

Research, Basic
Research Question
Survey Research Design
Validity

CHAPTER 2

Variables, Measures, and Hypotheses

The world of research is a complicated one. Whether you are learning to become a researcher or being a consumer of information, you will have to critically conduct or evaluate research. Think back to the time when you were first learning to drive and the process you went through to get your permit to drive. Oh . . . the excitement of turning 16 (again) and then to be given this enormous book to read on driving. What was the meaning behind all those symbols and how were we supposed to remember *all* that information? Would using this book to study really have an impact on passing the permit test, or would it make a good paper weight? The time comes when you have to take that dreaded permit test. After your nerves subside and you realize you passed the permit test, the next step was to get in a car and apply what you learned. To make matters more challenging, the path to getting your license requires a road test where you apply what you learned. In looking back on this experience, there were a lot of components that are similar to research methodology!

To relate this experience to research, you have to break apart the example and think in terms of research design. When examining research, there are **hypotheses, variables**, and measurements. The first step of any problem is to understand what question or hypothesis you want to address with the research. In the above example, a potential hypothesis would be, "Does reading a book on driving improve your chances of passing the test?" In order to answer this question, we need to determine what the variables are. In this case, one variable is the book on driving. This would be equivalent to the **independent variable,** or a variable that you can manipulate, because you can either read the book or not read the book. Your measurement, or **dependent variable** in this case, would be the test because the score you receive will determine whether or not you pass the test. You could then conduct an experiment to see if there is a difference between people who read the book on driving compared to people who do not read the book to determine if there is a difference in passing the test.

> **hypotheses:** A scientific prediction that is suspected to occur in a study based on previous research findings
>
> **variables:** Construct, measure, or object that can be studied
>
> **independent variable:** A variable in research that is manipulated or changed
>
> **dependent variable:** A variable in research that is measured

While the above example may be a simplistic view of conducting research, we can assure you that not all research studies are straightforward. Consider the following example from a current practitioner from an international consumer packaged goods organization. This practitioner works in an assessment center designed to compare internal incumbents for succession decisions into future roles. The role of the practitioner is to integrate a battery of assessments to gauge an incumbent's ability of success in a given role on the basis of specific technical abilities, career experiences, and behavioral competencies to gauge overall aptitude, performance, personality, and resilience. The challenge for this practitioner is successfully identifying the assessments required to assess these incumbents and how to rank between two to ten internal candidates from greatest to least fit based on risks associated with each plausible successor. The standardization of this assessment allows the practitioner the ability to behaviorally and experientially compare equivalent criteria required for success in the role. From a research methodology perspective, there are multiple hypotheses, variables, and different designs for conducting the assessment. To be able to critically evaluate this scenario, you have to be able to break this scenario apart into various components of research design.

VARIABLES

So far, we have mentioned the term *variables* multiple times, and by now, you should know what variables are. A variable is any construct, measure, or object that can be studied and varies across individuals. While this definition may appear vague, realistically anything that can be studied or examined has the potential to be a variable in a research experiment. The first step of any research is to determine what variables are of interest. In the driving example, these variables could be the book on driving and the test you need to take. These variables are often defined based on what previous research has examined or based on past experience. To complicate matters, there are many different types of variables, but the most common types of variables in research are independent, dependent, and **control variables**. In addition to these variables, there are other types of variables with different names depending on the type of research design or statistical analysis used. Keep in mind that any variable can fall into any one of these types with the only limitation being your own creativity with defining your variables.

> **control variables:** A variable in research that is designed to remain constant

Table 2.1 Variables Found in Research

Variable	Definition
Independent	A variable in research that is manipulated. This variable is expected to be the cause of the effect on the dependent variable within an experimental or quasi-experimental study.
Dependent	A variable in research that is measured. This variable is expected to be the effect that the independent variable has an impact on within an experimental or quasi-experimental study.

Variable	Definition
Predictor	Similar to an independent variable. This variable is expected to have an effect on the criterion variable within a research study that is aimed at predicting an outcome such as a regression study.
Criterion	Similar to a dependent variable. This variable is expected to be the presumed effect from the predictor variable within a research study aimed at using a predictor to explain a criterion such as a regression study.
Control	A variable that is held constant within a research study.
Confounding/ Extraneous	A variable that may be known or unknown that interacts or may explain the relationship between the independent and dependent variables. Usually, this variable is not included in the research study because it is not considered or overlooked during the design phase.
Covariate	A variable that is known to interact with the relationship between the independent and dependent variables and is included in the research study.
Dichotomous	A variable that only has two possible outcomes and is often denoted as a 1 and 0.
Continuous	A variable that is generally quantitative in nature. These variables often utilize an interval or ratio scale of measurement.
Categorical	A variable that is generally qualitative in nature. These variables often utilize a nominal or ordinal scale of measurement.
Quasi-Independent	A variable that cannot be manipulated by the researcher for a specific reason but is used in a research study as an independent variable. An example of this would be gender because it is not possible to change a participant's gender.
The below variables are associated with advanced statistical analysis (i.e., path analysis, structural equation modeling, factor analysis, etc.).	
Latent	A variable that cannot be directly observed or measured. This variable is believed to be a higher order construct that is made up of manifest variables, which can be directly measured. An example of this would be personality because the overall construct of personality consists of many different variables.
Manifest	A variable that can be directly observed and measured. This variable can be directly measured to assess the presence of a latent variable that cannot be directly observed. An example of this would be using measures of conscientiousness, neuroticism, openness, extraversion, and agreeableness as measures to assess a latent variable of personality.
Exogenous	A variable that is found outside of an identified model. In the example of a model that states the following path Motivation → Training Program → Performance, Motivation would be considered an exogenous variable because it is outside the training program being studied.
Endogenous	A variable that is found inside or is considered part of an identified model. In the example of a model that states the following path Motivation → Training Program → Performance, Training Program would be considered an endogenous variable because it is inside of what is being studied.

(Continued)

(Continued)

Variable	Definition
Mediating	A variable that must be present in order for a relationship to exist because without this variable there is no relationship. An example of this would be money. You may have a desire to purchase a new car, but without money you can never purchase a car.
Moderating	A variable that strengthens or weakens a relationship. The variable only has an impact on the relationship, but the relationship would still exist without a moderating variable. An example of this would be money. You may have the desire to purchase a new car, but the amount of money you have will determine whether or not you can purchase a luxury car.

Box 2.1 *Time* Disguised

Oftentimes it can be overwhelming when creating a research design and determining how and when to use variables. Let's look at an example of a time spent in training and the impact that this training has on an employee's performance. When conducting a research study, this time variable could be an independent, dependent, or control variable. The main difference between the uses of these different variables is the type of question that can be asked and answered.

1. A research design could be set up with time as an independent variable. A researcher could create two training programs where one training program is 30 minutes and another condition where the training program is 60 minutes. In this design, a researcher may want to determine if specified times attending training is related to an improvement in performance with the ultimate goal to determine the optimal training time required in order to maximize the employee's performance.

2. A research design could be set up with time as a dependent variable. A researcher could measure the amount of time that an employee spends in training. In this design, the researcher may want to determine how much time an employee spends in training with an overall goal of knowing how long it would take for an employee to learn the material in the training program to improve performance.

3. A research design could be set up with time as a control variable. A researcher could mandate that all training programs created have to be 30 minutes. In this design, a researcher may be trying to prove that employees can attend a training program with a fixed amount of time. The purpose of keeping time as a control variable in this example would be to determine if there are other factors beyond time that may interact with the learning of the material in the training program.

The overall development of a hypothesis using time as three different variables may be slightly different, but conducting a research design with time as an independent, dependent, or control variable would be drastically different. Therefore, prior to constructing the design of the experiment, it is important to determine the overall purpose of the experiment. This also includes identifying the variables of interest.

SCALES OF MEASUREMENT

If you have thought about an organizational problem and a variable you want to examine, then this is the first step! Think about the discussion on *time* or measuring performance. How would you measure these variables? This is important because the type of measurement you use will dictate the type of statistical analysis that can be conducted (Remember this when reading Chapter 11!). Not knowing the scale of measurement for a variable may lead to an error when analyzing the results. There are four main types of scales of measurement that can be broken up into two broad categories:

1. Qualitative Scales of Measurement
   a. Nominal
   b. Ordinal
2. Quantitative Scales of Measurement
   a. Interval
   b. Ratio

Each scale has its own unique properties, and as the scales of measurement proceed up the hierarchy, the next scale contains the properties of the scales below them as well as its own unique properties. It is possible to convert a ratio or interval scale into a nominal or ordinal scale, but it is not possible to convert a nominal or ordinal scale into a ratio or interval scale. However, it is not recommended to move down the hierarchy by changing a ratio scale to a nominal scale because there is a loss of the analysis and interpretation that can be conducted. These scales of measurements are critical when designing survey research, which is discussed in Chapter 8, and also when conducting statistical analyses, which is discussed in Chapter 11.

NOMINAL SCALE

Starting with the first type of scale, a nominal scale is used for naming purposes. Variables on a **nominal scale** serve the function of being able to provide the researcher with the ability to quantify a variable with a number, but the number only provides a categorical response. A categorical response is a way for a researcher to assign a number as a place holder for a word. This way a researcher has the ability to collect data on categorical responses to questions and has the ability to statistically analyze the results.

An example of a nominal variable would be gender because a number can be assigned to a female or male (i.e., 1 for females and 2 for males). By doing so, a researcher can generate the percentage of females and males in a given study. Another example of a nominal variable in an organization could be the title of the employee. An employee could be a supervisor, manager, assistant director, director, assistant vice president, vice president, etc. Each of these titles could be assigned a

> **nominal scale:** A qualitative scale of measurement used to provide a categorical response to a variable

numerical value to allow the researcher to aggregate the results by different titles. The conclusion from this type of analysis could be that approximately 15% of employees are supervisors, 10% are managers, etc. In essence, demographics using a nominal scale would allow a researcher to describe the sample and compare it to the population through percentages.

ORDINAL SCALE

An **ordinal scale** is the next scale on the hierarchy after a nominal scale. This scale is used for rank ordering categorical responses with the purpose to enable a researcher to order responses from the lowest level to the highest level on a continuum. However, it is imperative to know that the distance between each level on the continuum is unknown. The purpose of this scale would be to determine if one value is greater than or less than another value. With an ordinal scale, it would be impossible to determine how much greater or less than one response is to another response.

An example of an ordinal scale would be to determine who came in 1st, 2nd, 3rd, etc. in a race. In this example, the researcher would only know which individual came in 1st, 2nd, or 3rd, but the researcher would not know how much time elapsed between the individual in 1st place versus the individual in 2nd place. Another example would be if a recruiter was asked to indicate the number of telephone calls made to applicants on a daily basis and was provided the following response categories: none, one to five, six to ten, or ten or more. The important distinction is that the distance between none and one to five is not the same as ten or more. You just know that someone making more than ten calls is larger than someone making one to five calls. These response categories are ordered in a way to determine a rank in which calls are made or place an individual comes in, and each difference in response is not equal.

> **ordinal scale:** A qualitative scale of measurement used to rank order categorical responses

INTERVAL SCALE

An **interval scale** is next on the hierarchy after the ordinal scale and is used to provide a rating with equal intervals between points. The most common and well-known type of interval scale is a multipoint Likert-type scale. When utilizing an interval scale, it is important to remember that the interval scale does not have a true 0. The purpose of an interval scale is to provide a way for the researcher to have points on a scale that are equally spaced without being able to make direct comparisons between intervals. What this means is that if you have a 1 to 5 scale rating satisfaction, the points between each scale is equal. However, a rating of a 4 does not mean someone is twice as satisfied as someone rating a 2.

An example of an interval scale would be a 1- to 7-point Likert-type scale with 1 being "completely dissatisfied" and 7 being "completely satisfied." This would allow a participant to rate the extent to which they are dissatisfied or

> **interval scale:** A quantitative scale of measurement that has equal numeric intervals between values that does not have a true 0

satisfied with each point being an equal interval from the next point. Therefore, it is possible to compute an average value and interpret the meaning of it. For example, if an average of 6.34 is computed on a 7-point Likert-type satisfaction scale, then it is possible to state that the results of the study may indicate that participants are satisfied.

RATIO SCALE

The last and final scale of measurement is the **ratio scale**. A ratio scale has all the properties of the other scales. The only difference between an interval scale and ratio scale is the presence of a true 0. The ratio scale contains equal intervals between points, but the added value of a true 0 means there can be a direct comparison with each interval, such that comparisons between the distances of each point on a ratio scale can be quantifiable. An example of a ratio scale would be age in

ratio scale: A quantitative scale of measurement that has equal numeric intervals between values that does have a true 0

| **Box 2.2** | **The Meaning of True 0** |

A common issue for practitioners and students is to be able to differentiate an interval scale from a ratio scale and what does this true 0 actually mean. A general rule of thumb is that if a researcher is not able to say with 100% certainty that one value on a scale is twice (or 3 times, etc.) as much as another value, then the scale will not be a ratio scale or that a score of 0 indicates a complete absence of something.

To illustrate the differences between a ratio scale and interval scale, it is worthwhile to discuss the different ways to measure temperature. Temperature can be measured by the following scales: Fahrenheit, Celsius, and Kelvin. For Fahrenheit and Celsius, these scales are interval scales because a temperature of 0 degrees is not the lowest possible value that would represent a true absence of temperature. Temperature values can be negative, and it is not possible for someone to say that 100 degrees Fahrenheit or Celsius is twice as hot as 50 degrees Fahrenheit or Celsius. Therefore, temperature in Fahrenheit and Celsius are interval scales because each degree on the scale is equally distanced from the next. On the other hand, the Kelvin scale is a ratio scale because 0 Kelvin indicates a complete absence of temperature, and it is possible to say that 200 Kelvin is twice as much as 100 Kelvin.

Now what does this mean for organizations? Do we use ratio scales or interval scales more often? The answer to this question is that it depends on what you are doing or what you want to do. When you are researching a topic on behavior, performance, or satisfaction, you have to ask yourself if it is possible that a score of 0 indicates a complete absence of behavior, performance, or satisfaction, or does a score of 10 mean that the value is twice as much as a score of 5? One may argue that a low rating on satisfaction may not indicate that there is a complete lack of satisfaction. However, if your department is based on sales performance and you have a score of 0, then this means that there were no sales conducted in that department.

years because someone who 30 years old is twice as old as someone who is 15 years old. Another example would be the variable of time to complete a task. A researcher would be able to determine the amount of time it takes one participant to complete a task versus another participant. If it takes one participant 3 minutes to complete a task and another participant 21 minutes, then the researcher could conclude that the second participant took 7 times as long as the first participant to complete the task.

It is crucial when designing a study to understand the scale of measurement that a variable is on because this will determine the type of statistical analysis that can be conducted. Now with all this talk of variables and scales of measurement, how does this relate with what you will encounter at work or in research? Research is conducted every day, often without thinking about it.

As an example, consider a research study that measures performance. There are multiple options for measuring performance using the scales of measurement. The key is to determine how we want to analyze this data. We could measure performance as follows:

1. Asking yes or no questions related to performance (i.e., nominal scale)

2. Rank ordering the level of performance by asking if there was an increase or decrease (i.e., ordinal scale)

3. Providing a 5- or 7-point Likert-type scale on performance (i.e., interval scale)

4. Rating performance as a percentage from 0 to 100 with 0 being a complete absence of performance (i.e., ratio scale)

The major difference between analyzing these scales of measurements is based on the type of statistics that could be conducted. Chapter 11 provides a discussion on data interpretation and analysis.

HYPOTHESES AND RESEARCH QUESTIONS

Once variables have been finalized, then the process begins to develop a hypothesis/research question that can be empirically tested. Keep in mind that the idea you have to conduct research on may not be unique and others may have thought of or researched it! This is why it is critical to not only be able to conduct research but also review and evaluate existing literature to determine what has been done because there is no reason to reinvent the wheel.

research question: A problem addressed in research that may have limited scientific support. May lead to a hypothesis.

hypothesis: A proposed explanation for the results of a study

After reviewing the existing literature, themes begin to emerge in relation to the existing problems as well as potential solutions to the problem. A thorough review of the literature provides you with an understanding of what has been done and allows you to further refine your **research question** or **hypothesis**. Additionally, by becoming familiar with the literature, you will have a better understanding of variables that have been tested and defined and how other researchers have conducted the experiment.

Prior to delving deep into the specifics of research design, it is imperative to take a step back and start with the question because this is where the scientific method begins. Crafting a question or idea into an executable study is half the battle. In research, there are two main types of questions: a hypothesis and a research question. The main difference between a research question and a hypothesis is the amount of literature support that has been conducted. A hypothesis is based on previous literature findings with the purpose to advance science or prove an alternative solution to a problem. A research question is developed when there is limited research in a specific area that may lead to the development of a hypothesis. The purpose of a research question is to explore innovative ways to address a problem that may not have been accomplished before.

The analysis of a hypothesis or research question can result in three outcomes:

1. Supported

2. Not Supported

3. Partially Supported

If the hypothesis is supported, then consider publishing the research to share the knowledge with other practitioners and academics. However, if a hypothesis is not supported, then revisit the concept to understand why. Remember . . . not finding statistical significance is equally as important as finding statistical significance. In other words, there is much to be learned when a study does not turn out as expected. This could be due to the research design, variables used, threats to validity, etc. Lastly, it is possible that you are conducting or evaluating a study with multiple hypotheses where not all hypotheses are supported. In this case, the results of the study may partially support the hypothesis.

With these outcomes, don't get discouraged if you don't get the results you want! It has happened and likely will continue to happen. This is all part of the process with conducting research. Even in a well-developed and controlled study, the results of a study may not support the hypothesis! The ultimate goal of conducting research is to advance science and discover innovative techniques to solve a problem. Keep in mind that whenever a researcher publishes in a journal, there is always someone out there trying to disprove or replicate the results.

To be able to create a well-written hypothesis, it is advised to write a hypothesis that states that an independent variable has an effect on a dependent variable. In referring to the example discussed earlier with going for a road test, the following could be two different hypotheses that are designed to evaluate the same information:

- There will be a main effect for the driving book on the results of the permit test.

- Students who read the driving book will be more likely to pass the permit test compared to students who do not read the driving book.

While this example may appear straightforward, when you add the complexity of the second example with a practitioner from an international consumer packaged goods company selecting incumbent successors for an international role, hypotheses become more complex. There are multiple hypotheses that can be created from that scenario, but two examples of hypotheses for the assessment center predicting cognitive ability could be as follows:

- There will be a main effect for cognitive ability test on person-environment fit.

- Incumbents with high performance on a cognitive ability test in the assessment center will have a greater fit for a general manager role compared to incumbents with a low performance on a cognitive ability test.

> **null hypothesis:** Opposite of alternative hypothesis. A statement that a study is trying to disprove. States that there is no relationship or effect within the population.
>
> **alternative hypothesis:** Opposite of null hypothesis. A statement that a study is trying to prove. States that there is a relationship or effect within the population.

The bottom line is that any research study can be broken down into the variables that are being examined. Commonly, when creating a hypothesis, the independent and dependent variables are stated within the hypothesis. Hypotheses can be written multiple ways. In the examples provided above, the first hypothesis states that there is an effect and the second hypothesis states a direction of the relationship. By explicitly stating the hypotheses in terms of the independent and dependent variables, determining how to analyze this data will be clearer and easier.

To complicate matters, there are many different types of hypotheses. Each hypothesis is designed with the overall purpose of predicting what the expected results from a study would be. To begin to break down the differences in hypotheses, it is important to recognize the two categories: a **null hypothesis** and an **alternative hypothesis**. The null hypothesis is what a researcher is always trying to disprove because it is defined as there is no difference between groups or a relationship/effect does not exist in the population of interest. In other words, a null hypothesis is predicting that there is no relationship that exists in the population. A null hypothesis is signified as H_0. The null hypothesis for the assessment center example would be that there is no difference or relationship between the cognitive ability tests to assess person-environment fit for incumbents.

On the other hand, the alternative hypothesis is contradictory to the null hypothesis because with this the researcher is trying to prove that a relationship/effect exists in the population. The alternative hypothesis can be signified as H_a or H_1. An alternative

Table 2.2   The Nuances Between Questions

	Hypothesis	Research Question
Definition	A statement that has a specific prediction that is believed to occur as a result of conducting a study	A question developed based on a problem or phenomenon that a researcher desires to answer in a study
Use	Developed from previous research findings and is used to explain a relationship between variables that can be tested empirically	When little to limited knowledge is known, these questions are used to explore relationships between variables that may ultimately lead to a hypothesis
Goal	Provide further literature support or contradict previous findings that have been empirically tested	Explore a phenomenon in an innovative way that has not been done before

hypothesis for the assessment center example would be that there is a difference or effect between the cognitive ability tests to assess person-environment fit for incumbents.

The process of writing a hypothesis begins with identifying a problem and reviewing the existing literature. This review allows the researcher to better understand the phenomenon of interest and refine the initial question into an executable hypothesis. As mentioned, the purpose of an alternative hypothesis is to specifically state the relationship/effect that the variables in a study would have because any ambiguity with the prediction could result in potential threats to validity. The decision of which hypothesis to use is left to the researcher, but no one type of hypothesis is better than the other. The following are three types of hypotheses that could be created:

1. Theory-Driven vs. Data-Driven Hypotheses

2. Directional vs. Nondirectional Hypotheses

3. Descriptive vs. Causal Hypotheses

THEORY-DRIVEN VERSUS DATA-DRIVEN HYPOTHESES

A **theory-driven hypothesis** is crafted through utilizing existing theory to propose a relationship or effect on the variables of interest. In other words, a researcher engages in deductive reasoning to infer a specific prediction about a phenomenon that would happen in a study on the basis of a theory. For example, De Lange, De Witte, and Notelaers (2008) conducted a time lagged study using a Belgium panel to test a theory-driven hypothesis utilizing the job demands-resources model. The purpose of this study was to administer a survey 16 months later to examine the relationship between job resources, work engagement, and turnover across time focused on participants who stayed with an organization, obtained a promotion, or were external job movers. They propose multiple hypotheses within the study that focus on different aspects of predicting the relationship between the three groups. To develop a theory-driven hypothesis, they refer to the broaden-and-build principles of positive emotions (Fredrickson, 2001) to state that a theory-driven hypothesis as follows: "We expect normal causal effects of job resources in predicting work engagement across time for the group of stayers" (De Lange et al., 2001, p. 205).

A **data-driven hypothesis**, on the other hand, is based on previous findings from studies that have been conducted. With this hypothesis, a researcher engages in inductive reasoning through utilizing the results of previous studies to create a specific prediction about the current study of interest. For example, a **meta-analysis** does not involve the collection of data but rather it utilizes the results of previous research to draw conclusions. Van Iddekinge, Roth, Rymark, and Odle-Dusseau (2012) conducted a meta-analysis on the use of integrity tests for selection purposes to predict job performance, training performance, counterproductive work behavior, and turnover. There are

theory-driven hypothesis: A statement using deductive reasoning to predict a phenomenon on the basis of theory

data-driven hypothesis: A statement using inductive reasoning to predict a phenomenon on the basis of previous results

meta-analysis: A nonexperimental research technique utilizing statistics to compare and contrast various articles on a particular topic

multiple hypotheses included in the study. To develop a data-driven hypothesis, they examined prior results on integrity tests to develop the following hypothesis: "Criterion-related validity estimates for integrity tests will be larger in concurrent designs than predictive designs" (p. 502).

With the aforementioned discussion on these types of hypotheses proposing relationships between variables, the main differentiation between a theory-driven and data-driven hypothesis is how the hypothesis was created. In the first example, De Lange et al. (2008) relied on a theory to develop their hypothesis, whereas Van Iddekinge et al. (2012) utilized results found in previous studies to drive the development of their hypothesis.

DIRECTIONAL VERSUS NONDIRECTIONAL HYPOTHESES

The second type of hypotheses is developed based on focusing on the directionality of the relationship between variables in your study. This relationship between variables in the studies may indicate a specific direction of the effect or there may be no direction specified. These hypotheses are referred to as **directional hypothesis** or **nondirectional hypothesis** and may also be known as a one-tailed or two-tailed hypothesis, respectively. With directional or one-tailed hypotheses, previous results or theory may have specified a direction that a variable will have after the experiment is executed. The researcher can then utilize these results to develop a directional hypothesis.

Suazo and Stone-Romero (2011) administered a survey to employees for the purpose of investigating psychological contract breach (Breach) on supervisor-rated behaviors of performance and organizational citizenship behavior with perceived organizational support as a moderator. They propose a variety of hypotheses that also address a theory-driven hypothesis in addition to directional hypotheses. One of their hypotheses states, "Breach will be negatively related to supervisor ratings of in-role behaviors" (p. 368). This particular hypothesis is directional because they are proposing a negative relationship between the variables.

directional hypothesis: Also known as one-tailed hypotheses. A statement of the relationship between variables focused on implying the direction of the relationship.

nondirectional hypothesis: Also known as two-tailed hypotheses. A statement of the relationship between variables where the direction of the relationship is not known.

On the other hand, in nondirectional or two-tailed hypotheses, the researcher knows that a relationship exists, but due to competing theories or contradictory findings in the literature, a specific direction may not be clearly understood. Saunders (2012) conducted a study on the differences in responses for employee attitudes based on whether a mail-based survey (MBS) or a web-based survey (WBS) was used. The overall goal was to determine if one distribution method resulted in differences compared to the other. To test this hypothesis, Saunders (2012) proposes, "To what extent do employee's response rates now differ between WBS and MBS?" (p. 58). This is a nondirectional hypothesis because there is no specific direction of the differences between WBS and MBS. It is believed that there is a difference, but the exact difference at that time was not known.

DESCRIPTIVE VERSUS CAUSAL HYPOTHESES

The last type of hypothesis builds upon the previous types by specifying the relationship between the variables by determining if this relationship is a **descriptive hypothesis** or **causal hypothesis**. You may have noticed that the aforementioned hypotheses were not purely theory-driven, data-driven, or directional because components of theory may drive a direction or components of data may drive a direction. This component is critical because when examining different types of hypotheses, in particular a descriptive or causal hypothesis, the type of experiment that can be conducted may already be dictated by the hypothesis.

When utilizing a descriptive hypothesis, the researcher is making a specific prediction (based on theory or previous results) that will illustrate the relationship (directional or nondirectional) between the variables of interest. One caveat of this hypothesis is that the purpose is to describe the behavior of interest and not to explain a cause and effect relationship. The resulting design may be **nonexperimental design**, such as a **correlational design**, used to understand relationships between variables. Pierce and Maurer (2009) conducted a correlational study using a survey to examine the relationship between employee development with social exchange theory and organizational citizenship behavior with perceived organization support (POS) as a moderator. The descriptive hypothesis is, "The relationship between perceived benefit to the organization and development activity will be moderated by POS. The relationship will be stronger when POS is high" (p. 141). This hypothesis is descriptive on the basis that a relationship between variables is proposed rather than a specific cause and effect relationship and it is also directional based on saying the relationship will be stronger.

On the other hand, a causal hypothesis is one where the researcher is predicting a specific cause and effect relationship that will occur between variables. The type of design that may be conducted is an **experimental design** or **quasi-experimental design**. Cojuharenco, Patient, and Bashshur (2011) conducted three different studies using two surveys and one experimental design to incorporate organizational justice theory components to determine the relationship between temporal perspective and employee concerns about being treated unfairly at work. Study two consisted of an experimental design and proposed a variety

descriptive hypothesis: A statement driven by theory, data, or direction that specifies a relationship between variables

causal hypothesis: A statement driven by theory, data, or direction that specifies a cause and effect relationship between variables

nonexperimental design: Utilizes primary analysis, secondary analysis, or meta-analysis to describe data, examine relationships or covariation between variables, and comparing groups

correlational design: A nonexperimental design that examines relationships between variables that are not manipulated

experimental design: Utilizes random assignment and purposely introduces a manipulation to observe an effect

quasi-experimental design: Utilizes other design features to account for lack of random assignment to study the impact of a cause and effect relationship

of hypotheses. One particular causal hypothesis states, "Inducing future (versus past) temporal orientation will relate positively to the proportion of distributively unjust events reported" (p. 22). This particular hypothesis is causal in the sense that a cause and effect relationship (i.e., future temporal orientation will impact unjust events) is proposed. In addition to this relationship, they also specify a direction, which is indicated by saying this relationship will be positive.

HYPOTHESIS SUMMARY

Based on the discussion of different types of hypotheses, you will notice that there is a relationship between each one of them. Regardless of the type of hypothesis you want to create or what you are evaluating in research, it is imperative to develop a hypothesis that can be tested. Once a hypothesis/research question is finalized, the next step is to begin to preliminarily think about what research design you are going to use. The next phase is to evaluate existing research or create your own research design to intertwine all these concepts (i.e., inductive and deductive reasoning, applied and basic research, scales of measurement, ethics, legal issues, variables, and hypotheses) to understand how they impact the design and evaluation of research.

At this point, you may be anxious to pick up a research article to evaluate or start the process of conducting your own research. Before you do this, let's take a final step back and revisit the variables, scales of measurement, and the hypothesis/research question. All of these components may shed light and provide hints as to how to set up the experiment. The types of variables used can potentially indicate the research design because if an independent variable is present, then the design could be experimental or quasi-experimental. The scale of measurement provides a clue as to whether the results are to be analyzed qualitatively through a nominal or ordinal scale or quantitatively through an interval or ratio scale. Lastly, a hypothesis that is descriptive or causal also provides information as to whether a research design is going to provide a description of behavior through a correlational design or a cause and effect relationship through an experimental or quasi-experimental design. The bottom line is, when thinking about research design, the discussion should begin as early as the review of the literature and continue through every phase of the design.

CHAPTER SUMMARY

- Variables are the crux of conducting experiments and are any construct, measure, or object that can be studied and varied across individuals. There are many different types of variables that are found within experiments, but the most common are independent, dependent, and control variables. The type of variable varies depending on the statistical analysis or research design used for the experiment.

- Scales of measurement are used to classify how variables are measured and dictate the statistical analysis that can be conducted. There are four different types of scales of measurement: nominal, ordinal, interval, and ratio. Nominal and ordinal are qualitative variables, and interval and ratio are quantitative variables.

- When conducting research, there are two types of questions that can be answered: hypotheses and research questions. A hypothesis is a scientific prediction that is suspected to occur in a study based on previous research findings. A research question is developed based on a problem where limited knowledge or research exists and may ultimately lead to a hypothesis.

- Null or alternative hypotheses are the two different categories of hypotheses. A researcher proposes an alternative hypothesis because the null hypothesis indicates no relationship or effect exists. Alternative hypotheses can be directional/nondirectional, theory/data driven, or descriptive/causal.

DISCUSSION QUESTIONS

- Similar to Box 2.1, *"Time* Disguised," discuss how you could create one variable in your organization that could be an independent, dependent, and control variable.

- How do the different scales of measurement impact the measurement of a variable in a study?

- Develop a hypothesis and research question that can be addressed in an organization setting.

- Create multiple hypotheses on a similar topic that can qualify as a theory-driven, data-driven, directional, nondirectional, descriptive, and causal hypothesis.

CHAPTER KEY TERMS

Correlational Design	Hypothesis, Nondirectional	Ratio Scale
Experimental Design	Hypothesis, Null	Research Question
Hypothesis	Hypothesis, Theory-Driven	Variable
Hypothesis, Alternative	Interval Scale	Variable, Confounding
Hypothesis, Causal	Nominal Scale	Variable, Control
Hypothesis, Data-Driven	Nonexperimental Design	Variable, Dependent
Hypothesis, Descriptive	Ordinal Scale	Variable, Independent
Hypothesis, Directional	Quasi-Experimental Design	

CHAPTER 3

Ethical and Legal Considerations in the Research Process

As you develop your research idea, whether you are planning to examine a construct of interest by conducting a controlled lab-setting study, a field-setting study, or even by using archival data records, it is important to fully understand and remain aware of the ethical and legal requirements that impact each stage of the research process. There are specific guidelines that affect how the study is designed; how participants for the sample are obtained, treated, and protected; how data are collected and presented; and lastly, but perhaps most critical for field settings, how decisions are made based on the findings.

In this chapter, we discuss ethics in research, a topic that has received an increasing amount of awareness and focus in recent years across many applied settings. As researchers, we are held accountable for ensuring research studies are designed and conducted safely and ethically for our participants, and we are also obligated to follow ethical guidelines for the analysis and reporting of study findings. To explain and clarify what this really means in practice, we differentiate the difference between ethics and the law because a study that is legally compliant may still not be ethical. We describe the origins of today's focus on research ethics through a historic timeline of critical events and experiments which resulted in a body of standardized definitions and protocol. Lastly, we examine the importance of understanding and adhering to ethical and legal standards that are relevant to the manner in which a research study is designed and conducted.

WHAT IS ETHICS?

First things first—we need to define ethics and ethical standards. Ethics is a subject that encompasses human behavior and the motives and decisions that impact one's actions. In other words, ethics explores (1) how individuals act; (2) individual, group, and societal judgments about these actions (good or bad, right or wrong); and (3) rules for categorizing these actions. From a foundational and objective perspective, ethical behaviors and actions should result in more good than harm and should have positive consequences for as many individuals as possible, also referred to as *the greater good*.

The difficulty with understanding the difference between what is ethical and what is unethical lies in the fact that *ethics*, like other constructs such as performance, personality, and intelligence, can be interpreted in many ways, depending on one's culture, upbringing, environment influences, experiences, and outcomes. Simply put, the same behavior you may consider unethical may be considered ethical by someone else. This is a highly subjective and debatable area! So, what does this mean for the research community—how can we ensure that studies conducted are upholding ethical standards?

AREN'T ETHICS AND THE LAW THE SAME?

Local, state, and federal laws provide certain levels of protection to a population, and this also applies to samples from a population serving as research subjects in a study. Researchers must be cognizant of the laws that apply to the area in which they are conducting research to provide those areas of protection to their subjects and avoid legal violations. However, laws vary quite a bit across cities, states, and countries. This variation adds a layer of complexity to a researcher's long list of design and methodology considerations and requirements. Additionally, there are many practices that, while perfectly legal, are not ethical. As we mentioned earlier, what is deemed *ethical* can be interpreted quite differently among individuals! Not only do researchers need to abide by the law, they also must defer to a common core of ethical standards and practices agreed upon and abided by the research community and enforced by the institution in which they work, whether that institution is a Fortune 500 company, a university, public school system, hospital, or any other applied setting where research occurs. We will conclude this chapter with an overview of key legal requirements for working with data in several real-world applied settings.

> **ethics:** examines how individuals act; the individual, group, and societal judgments about these actions (good or bad, right or wrong); and rules for categorizing these actions

THE ETHICAL EVOLUTION OF RESEARCH

To fully understand the evolution of this area and the reason for such focused attention among today's researchers, we do need to step back in time and examine key historical events that prompted unethical research experiments that violated the physical and psychological health and well-being of their human subjects, including such practices as forced participation, deception, lack of confidentiality and privacy, and withholding of necessary treatments.

Nuremberg Trials

During the Nazi regime in the 1930s and 1940s, a great deal of exploitive and torturous experimentation was conducted on concentration camp prisoners: much of it carried out by reputable German doctors and researchers. As a result of the discovery and investigation of these atrocities, the Nuremberg Trials took place. One of the outcomes of these trials was the development of The Nuremberg Code. The Nuremberg Code (1949), recommended by an international court in the late 1940s and adopted by the United Nations General Assembly, is comprised of ten principles for researchers to follow:

Principle 1:

The voluntary consent of the human subject is absolutely essential.

This means that the person involved should have legal capacity to give consent; should be so situated as to be able to exercise free power of choice, without the intervention of any element of force, fraud, deceit, duress, overreaching, or other ulterior form of constraint or coercion; and should have sufficient knowledge and comprehension of the elements of the subject matter involved as to enable him to make an understanding and enlightened decision. This latter element requires that, before the acceptance of an affirmative decision by the experimental subject, there should be made known to him the nature, duration, and purpose of the experiment; the method and means by which it is to be conducted; all inconveniences and hazards reasonably to be expected; and the effects upon his health or person, which may possibly come from his participation in the experiment.

The duty and responsibility for ascertaining the quality of the consent rests upon each individual who initiates, directs, or engages in the experiment. It is a personal duty and responsibility which may not be delegated to another with impunity.

Principle 2:

The experiment should be such as to yield fruitful results for the good of society, unprocurable by other methods or means of study, and not random and unnecessary in nature.

Principle 3:

The experiment should be so designed and based on the results of animal experimentation and a knowledge of the natural history of the disease or other problem under study that the anticipated results will justify the performance of the experiment.

Principle 4:

The experiment should be so conducted as to avoid all unnecessary physical and mental suffering and injury.

Principle 5:

No experiment should be conducted where there is an a priori reason to believe that death or disabling injury will occur; except, perhaps, in those experiments where the experimental physicians also serve as subjects.

Principle 6:

The degree of risk to be taken should never exceed that determined by the humanitarian importance of the problem to be solved by the experiment.

Principle 7:

Proper preparations should be made and adequate facilities provided to protect the experimental subject against even remote possibilities of injury, disability, or death.

Principle 8:

The experiment should be conducted only by scientifically qualified persons. The highest degree of skill and care should be required through all stages of the experiment of those who conduct or engage in the experiment.

Principle 9:

During the course of the experiment, the human subject should be at liberty to bring the experiment to an end if he has reached the physical or mental state where continuation of the experiment seemed to him to be impossible.

Principle 10:

During the course of the experiment, the scientist in charge must be prepared to terminate the experiment at any stage if he has probable cause to believe in the exercise of the good faith, superior skill, and careful judgment required of him that a continuation of the experiment is likely to result in injury, disability, or death to the experimental subject.

Trials of War Criminals Before the Nuremberg Military Tribunals Under Control Council Law No. 10, Vol. 2 (pp. 181–182). Washington, DC: U.S. Government Printing Office, 1949. Retrieved from http://www.hhs.gov/ohrp/archive/nurcode.html

Milgram's Obedience Study (1963)

Stanley Milgram's famous (or infamous) experiment examining obedience to a perceived authority figure is one of the most ethically debated studies. Milgram (1963) was interested in research on blind obedience, a shocking phenomenon demonstrated through Nazi command in World War II, and he specifically studied the psychological connection between blind obedience and harmful or dangerous behavior. Milgram conducted experiments in which subjects were instructed to test *learners* on particular tasks and to administer electric shocks when the learners made a mistake. Milgram instructed the subjects to increase the voltage of the electric shocks as the learners made more mistakes. In reality, the learners were working with Milgram as confederates, and no electric shocks were actually administered. Milgram found that the subjects were willing to comply with his instructions throughout the experiment and no one refused or dropped out, despite hearing perceived screams of pain coming from the learners in another room as *shocks* were administered. Milgram inferred from this finding that individuals would be willing to obey a perceived authority figure's request blindly, even if the request involved physical harm to others. While Milgram was successful in supporting his hypothesis with these findings, the ethical issues clearly depicted in this study involve deception of subjects as well as designing a study that may result in psychological harm or trauma to subjects who, though compelled to follow orders, believed they were inflicting harm on others.

> **confederate:** an individual working with a researcher, pretending to be a participant in the study and acting in a specified role necessary to the procedure

Zimbardo's Stanford Prison Study (1971)

Another controversial study that involved role play was conducted by a social psychologist, Philip Zimbardo (1971). Zimbardo was interested in examining behaviors of subjects during a 2-week prison simulation experiment conducted at Stanford University. He recruited 24 male college students who were randomly assigned to one of two roles: prison guard or inmate. The inmate subjects were put through a complete simulation from a mock arrest, frisk, and fingerprinting to a bodily search and delousing; were issued prison clothing; and locked in cells. The guard subjects wore uniforms, were issued billy clubs, and had complete control over the inmate subjects. All of the guards demonstrated abuse of power, some more severe than others. Inmate subjects became depressed and despondent, and some demonstrated seriously disturbing psychological changes in just a few days. The study was discontinued after just 6 days. Even though this study was merely a role play simulation exercise and it was stopped when excessive danger and harm to subjects were apparent, it is still a valuable example of a study with a rather unethical design: a *too real* simulation environment in which subjects became absorbed in their respective roles and harm was inevitable.

The Tuskegee Experiments (1932)

The Tuskegee syphilis research study began in 1932 and continued for 40 years until this experimentation became public knowledge in 1972 (Heller, 1972). Several hundred African American men diagnosed with syphilis and living in poverty in Alabama were studied. Even though the medication used to treat syphilis was available during the time of the study, the subjects were not provided with treatment. This study caused a significant increase in public mistrust in medical research and doctors, particularly among African Americans, once it became public knowledge. It also brought to light a critical issue concerning the manipulation of treatment in an experiment that uses field subjects who may actually need the treatment, a consideration that requires researchers today to rethink experimental treatment and control conditions and may necessitate the inclusion of quasi and nonexperimental design elements.

THE NEXT STEP: ETHICAL STANDARDS TO ENSURE HISTORY WILL NOT REPEAT ITSELF

At this point you may be asking yourself, "What resulted in the discovery of these unethical experiments?" The good news is that many standards and protocols were put in place across all research communities, from schools and universities to business settings and health care settings, to ensure researchers are following the same definitions of research ethics as well as a research protocol that includes some key elements of *checks and balances* and providing information about a study's purpose and methodology that we will discuss next.

The Belmont Report

The Belmont Report, published by the U.S. Public Health Service's National Commission for the Protection of Human Subjects of Biomedical and Behavioral Research (1979), is an important document for researchers because it contains principles and guidelines for the research community to follow across many disciplines and field settings. The Belmont Report contains three ethical principles as well as guidelines for the protection of human subjects in research studies.

Ethical Principles

1. Respect for Persons

This principle states that research subjects should be treated as *autonomous agents*, which means that each individual subject is physically and mentally capable of making decisions and choices regarding entering and participating in a study and that participation in a study is voluntary. Any subjects that are determined to have diminished autonomy, including children, prisoners, the developmentally disabled, and individuals with psychological/emotional disorders, are entitled to receive special protection.

2. Beneficence

This principle states that researchers should not cause harm to their subjects and that researchers should strive for positive outcomes for the subjects as well as for themselves, the research community, and society. The primary goal should always be maximizing benefits of the research while minimizing the risk of both probability and degree of harm.

3. Justice

This principle states that researchers should not conduct exploitive research, that subjects not be deprived of necessary treatments, and that there should be an equitable distribution of risks and benefits across all subjects.

Box 3.1 | **Privacy Matters: What Is the Difference Between Anonymity and Confidentiality?**

Privacy issues and our need for controlling access to information about ourselves is a concern for all of us, especially in today's society of electronic information access and the digitization of our identities on the Internet. Our privacy concerns are particularly heightened when we are instructed to provide information about ourselves and our behaviors through research studies, surveys/questionnaires, and for record-keeping purposes (for example, school records, medical history, employment files). A researcher should be cognizant of this concern and be prepared to alleviate participants' worries with a sound study design that clearly protects participants' identities and information.

A research study is anonymous when the identity of the participants is not known by anyone who is reading or involved in the research, including the researcher. All data are collected in a manner in which no participant's name, demographic information, individual codes, or any other personal identifier appears on any research study item, including hard copy forms of data, electronic and web-based forms of data, and audio and video recordings, they have provided to the researcher.

A research study is confidential when the researcher knows the identity of the participants but does not disclose that information to anyone and ensures no identifiers exist anywhere in the research report itself for readers to *figure out* which participants provided which pieces of data. If identifying information is provided during data collection, the researcher should remove this information and replace it with an identification code and secure the file containing the participants' information and their corresponding codes. Additionally, a researcher is responsible for safeguarding all archives of raw data (typically under a lock and key file system for hard copy records or secure data encryption for electronic files), including forms, journals, notes, and recordings that may identify the participants to others.

These two terms, anonymous and confidential, are often misunderstood and used interchangeably. It is a researcher's responsibility to accurately explain to participants if they will be identifiable through the data they provide and to what extent.

Informed Consent

To put these principles into action, the U.S. Public Health Service (PHS) requires that researchers conducting studies that it funds show evidence of informed consent among its subjects. The main purpose of informed consent is to provide potential research subjects with adequate information regarding a study, including what to expect and its risks and benefits, in order to make an informed decision regarding whether or not to participate. The PHS does not require informed consent for surveys or questionnaires or for educational tests. Typically, subjects read a written informed consent document and sign a hard copy or provide an electronic signature for the researchers' records. Researchers obtain consent from parents or guardians when using minors as subjects. In most circumstances, informed consent includes the following components:

1. An explanation of the purpose of the research, its expected duration, and a brief explanation of the procedures to be followed

2. An explanation of any foreseeable risks or potential instances of discomfort to the subjects

3. An explanation of benefits to the subjects that are anticipated as a result of the research

4. An explanation of appropriate alternative procedures that may be beneficial to the subjects

5. A description of the manner in which the confidentiality of the subjects will be maintained

6. For studies involving more than minimal risk, an explanation of any compensation or medical treatments that may be available to the subjects

7. A statement including contact information for answers to questions regarding the research study and/or subjects' rights

8. A statement that participation in the study is voluntary, that subjects may refuse to participate without threat of coercion or may leave the study at any time, and that no punishment or penalty would result from a subject deciding to discontinue participation and leave the study

9. A statement informing subjects that the researcher will provide them with a debriefing of the study upon conclusion of their participation

While informed consent is an additional step in the research protocol, it is an important safeguard against deception or harm. In some instances, researchers take issue with providing subjects with *too much* information that may influence subjects' decisions and behaviors during the study. However, in many instances, researchers not only respect this protocol for ethical reasons but also support its inclusion because it can protect the researcher from liability for any discomfort or harm that subjects may experience during the study.

The Institutional Review Board (IRB)

The U.S. Public Health Service also requires that institutions receiving PHS funding to use to conduct studies involving human subjects establish an Institutional Review Board, or IRB. Institutions may include businesses and corporations, universities and colleges, government agencies, and health care institutions and hospitals. An institution's IRB is structured to review research study proposals and make decisions regarding their approval, rejection, or need for modification. An IRB examines a study's procedural elements, such as subject selection and assignment to conditions, informed consent, and methodology, and may review the scientific rigor, quality, and value of potential benefits of the research before allowing researchers to use funds, time, and other resources to proceed. An IRB is accountable to its institution for identifying any aspects of a research study proposal that appear to involve unnecessary risk or harm, risk without sufficient benefits, harm or deception, and requiring justification or alteration on the part of the researchers involved. If subjects in a research study experience unexpected negative effects, or if a treatment condition is producing significantly better or worse effects than the other conditions, it may be deemed necessary to discontinue the study, and it is the responsibility of the researchers involved to keep their institution's IRB apprised of such a development.

Box 3.2   Deception and Debriefing

While we have discussed several examples of excessive, inappropriate, and potentially harmful deception tactics used by researchers in past studies, it is important to note that certain types of deceptive practices may be acceptable in a research design. For example, a study may require that the researcher conceal his or her identity as the researcher in order to reduce the potential for participants to alter their behaviors or responses in a certain way (i.e., impression management and social desirability bias). The most critical considerations include necessity, type and degree of deception, and risk of harm to participants. A researcher must provide compelling justification to an IRB regarding the need for and nature of the deception involved in a research study proposal. Even with adequate justification, an IRB could still reject the inclusion of deception and recommend an alternative approach in the proposed study methodology. One common approach is the inclusion of a debriefing session after the study has concluded. In a debriefing session, the researcher explains the study's purpose and procedures in detail to the participants. More detail is often provided during debriefing than in the informed consent. In addition, participants are interviewed by the researcher to learn about their experiences in the study and discover problems they may have encountered or questions they have. There are two main goals of the debriefing process. The first goal is to ensure the participants have no negative feelings about the study and their participation; in other words, to leave feeling informed and good about the study and the role they played. The second goal is to identify problems and ambiguities in the study design from feedback the participants provide in order to correct weaknesses for further data collection or replication.

ETHICS IN REPORTING RESEARCH FINDINGS

Just as researchers have an obligation to their participants to follow ethical protocol in designing and conducting studies, researchers are also held accountable for their conduct in reporting study findings to their peers and colleagues, their clients, and the population that may be impacted by their research. Researchers must report not only the study findings that support any of their hypotheses but also the instances in which support for hypotheses was not obtained following statistical analysis of the data. Additionally, it is imperative that researchers provide information regarding a study's weaknesses, flaws, and limitations so that other researchers can address these issues through improved design and methodology in future studies.

A researcher should carefully examine the results of their study for potential errors in reporting their findings. While researchers are often under a great deal of pressure from funding entities, special interest groups, clients, and colleagues to provide significant and notable findings, the omission of data, inaccurate reporting of data findings, and misrepresentation of findings in conclusions made are considered practices that constitute serious research reporting misconduct. Researchers are expected to provide a detailed description of their methodology and analyses as well as all data findings and supporting information in their reporting, including lack of support for hypotheses and results that may contradict findings from well-supported findings obtained from previous studies. Additionally, researchers are obligated to not create (i.e., fabrication), modify, or distort (i.e., falsification) data in any way, perhaps in an effort to improve statistical power or yield significance, remove outliers, or align with data findings from previous research studies. Lastly, researchers should ensure that any inferences or conclusions made are consistent with the findings they obtained by making sure they do not include irrelevant information and by making clear connections

fabrication: the creation of data that were not collected through the actual research study

falsification: the distortion of data that were collected in a research study in order to appear a certain way

between the hypotheses originally developed and the results obtained, whether or not the hypotheses were supported. These practices enable a researcher to provide a clear and accurate report of the study, thus maintaining integrity and scientific rigor.

No research study is perfect in its design and execution, and a researcher should be prepared to address any issues in the discussion section of the research report. This not only provides readers with an accurate depiction of the study's positive and negative attributes, it also equips other researchers with critical knowledge about methodology flaws and limitations to (a) not replicate in the same manner and (b) consider addressing in a follow-up study to remediate the issues and improve upon the scientific rigor of the study. This level of commitment and integrity from all researchers will enable growth and progression of credible research findings that inform and provide societal value.

Ethics and ethical compliance continue to be an area of paramount importance to researchers and require adherence and ongoing attention to developments and trends (e.g., data obtained and studies conducted via the Internet, the emergence of global ethics codes). For researchers in applied settings, we must also focus on the laws and legal guidelines respective to our fields of expertise as well as the structure, parameters, and policies of the settings in which we work. Many organizations have developed their own sets of ethical standards and codes of conduct relative to their industry, products and services, and outreach to various populations. As researchers, it is our responsibility to balance the requirements and expectations from all perspectives to ensure respect and fairness to all of our societal stakeholders as we design, conduct, and report on our research.

Legal Spotlight: Handling Real-World Data and Ensuring Compliance in Field Settings

Depending on the field setting you work in, data records may be maintained on a variety of different individuals and groups for different reasons. As applied researchers, we often collect or access data such as an individual's age, race, marital status, income, measures of performance, physical and mental condition, health history, criminal activity including arrests and convictions, and family background. Of course, the ethical codes and guidelines we have discussed equip researchers with the protocol for appropriately using and maintaining this type of sensitive personal data. However, in many field settings, laws have been established to legally protect the individuals for whom data are collected, reported, and archived. The primary focus across these laws is to ensure privacy and prohibit discrimination, though there are other needs that the laws address and specifics within the legal parameters that vary according to the individuals being protected. In the final section of this chapter, we will discuss three applied settings and their primary legal compliance requirements: business settings, educational settings, and health care settings.

Business Settings

Employers are required to comply with several pieces of legislation when employee data are the focus. The protection of employee rights is mandated largely by Title VII of the Civil Rights Act of 1964, the Americans with Disabilities Act (ADA), and the Age Discrimination in Employment Act (ADEA). Title VII of the Civil Rights Act of 1964 prohibits discrimination on any employment decisions including hiring, promotion, compensation, training and development opportunities, and termination based on race, color, religion, sex, and national origin. The ADA prohibits employment-related discrimination based on physical or mental impairment that affects major life activities and requires employers to make reasonable accommodations to enable disabled individuals to perform a job for which they are otherwise qualified. The ADEA prohibits employment-related discrimination against individuals age 40 and older.

These and other important pieces of legislation, such as the Lily Ledbetter Fair Pay Act of 2009, are enforced by the U.S. Equal Employment Opportunity Commission (EEOC). The EEOC is primarily responsible for the auditing of employers' workforce decisions, practices, and recordkeeping as well as investigating and following the protocol for formal complaints of employer discrimination.

(U.S. Equal Employment Opportunity Commission, http://www.eeoc.gov/laws/index.cfm)

Educational Settings

Educators and educational administrators are required to comply with the Family Educational Rights and Privacy Act (FERPA) when student data are the focus for research and reporting. FERPA is a federal law that protects the privacy of student education records. The law applies to all schools that receive funding through U.S. Department of Education programs. FERPA gives parents certain rights for the access and review of their children's education records. The student becomes eligible to have these rights when he or she reaches the age of 18 or attends a school beyond the high school level. FERPA rights and protocol are currently stated as follows:

Parents or eligible students have the right to inspect and review the student's education records maintained by the school. Schools are not required to provide copies of records unless, for reasons such as great distance, it is impossible for parents or eligible students to review the records. Schools may charge a fee for copies.

Parents or eligible students have the right to request that a school correct records which they believe to be inaccurate or misleading. If the school decides not to amend the record, the parent or eligible student then has the right to a formal hearing. After the hearing, if the school still decides not to amend the record, the parent or eligible student has the right to place a statement with the record setting forth his or her view about the contested information.

Generally, schools must have written permission from the parent or eligible student in order to release any information from a student's education record. However, FERPA allows schools to disclose those records, without consent, to the following parties or under the following conditions:

- School officials with legitimate educational interest;
- Other schools to which a student is transferring;

- Specified officials for audit or evaluation purposes;
- Appropriate parties in connection with financial aid to a student;
- Organizations conducting certain studies for or on behalf of the school;
- Accrediting organizations;
- To comply with a judicial order or lawfully issued subpoena;
- Appropriate officials in cases of health and safety emergencies; and
- State and local authorities, within a juvenile justice system, pursuant to specific State law.

Schools may disclose, without consent, "directory" information such as a student's name, address, telephone number, date and place of birth, honors and awards, and dates of attendance. However, schools must tell parents and eligible students about directory information and allow parents and eligible students a reasonable amount of time to request that the school not disclose directory information about them. Schools must notify parents and eligible students annually of their rights under FERPA. The actual means of notification (special letter, inclusion in a PTA bulletin, student handbook, or newspaper article) is left to the discretion of each school.

(U.S. Department of Education, http://www2.ed.gov/policy/gen/guid/fpco/ferpa/index .html)

Health Care Settings

Health care providers and administrators are required to comply with the Health Insurance Portability and Accountability Act of 1996 (HIPAA) when patient and client data in health care settings (doctors' offices, hospitals, clinics, counseling centers) are the focus. Again, the priority with HIPAA compliance is to ensure patient and client information privacy. To achieve this objective, the Secretary of the U.S. Department of Health and Human Services (HHS) developed regulations protecting the privacy and security of certain health information. There are two main components to the HIPAA legislation: the Privacy Rule and the Security Rule. HIPAA requirements and protocol are currently stated as follows:

The *Privacy Rule* establishes, for the first time, a set of national standards for the protection of certain health information. The U.S. Department of Health and Human Services ("HHS") issued the Privacy Rule to implement the requirement of the Health Insurance Portability and Accountability Act of 1996 ("HIPAA"). The Privacy Rule standards address the use and disclosure of individuals' health information—called "protected health information" by organizations subject to the Privacy Rule — called "covered entities," as well as standards for individuals' privacy rights to understand and control how their health information is used. A major goal of the Privacy Rule is to assure that individuals' health information is properly protected while allowing the flow of health information needed to provide and promote high quality health care and to protect the public's health and well being. The Rule strikes a balance that permits important uses of information, while protecting the privacy of people who seek care and healing. Given that the health care marketplace is diverse, the Rule is designed to be flexible and comprehensive to cover the variety of uses and disclosures that need to be addressed.

The Privacy Rule protects all *"individually identifiable health information"* held or transmitted by a covered entity or its business associate, in any form or media, whether electronic, paper, or oral. The Privacy Rule calls this information "protected health information (PHI)."

"Individually identifiable health information" is information, including demographic data, that relates to:

the individual's past, present or future physical or mental health or condition,

the provision of health care to the individual, or

the past, present, or future payment for the provision of health care to the individual,

and that identifies the individual or for which there is a reasonable basis to believe it can be used to identify the individual. Individually identifiable health information includes many common identifiers (e.g., name, address, birth date, Social Security Number).

The *Security Rule* is designed to protect the privacy of individuals' health information while allowing covered entities to adopt new technologies to improve the quality and efficiency of patient care. It establishes a national set of security standards for protecting certain health information that is held or transferred in electronic form. The Security Rule operationalizes the protections contained in the Privacy Rule by addressing the technical and nontechnical safeguards that organizations called "covered entities" must put in place to secure individuals' "electronic protected health information" (e-PHI).

Within HHS, the Office for Civil Rights (OCR) has responsibility for enforcing the Privacy and Security Rules with voluntary compliance activities and civil money penalties.

(U.S. Department of Health and Human Services, http://www.hhs.gov/ocr/privacy/index .html)

FURTHER READING: LINKS TO ETHICAL STANDARDS AND CODES OF CONDUCT

National Institutes of Health – The Belmont Report

http://ohsr.od.nih.gov/guidelines/belmont.html

American Psychological Association - Ethical Principles of Psychologists and Code of Conduct http://www.apa.org/ethics/code/index.aspx?item = 2

Academy of Management - Code of Ethics

http://www.aomonline.org/aom.asp?id = 14&page_id = 235

Society for Human Resource Management (SHRM) - Code of Ethics

http://www.shrm.org/about/Pages/code-of-ethics.aspx

National Association of Social Workers (NASW) - Code of Ethics

http://www.naswdc.org/pubs/code/code.asp

U.S. Department of Health and Human Services - The Nuremberg Code

http://www.hhs.gov/ohrp/archive/nurcode.html

CHAPTER SUMMARY

- It is important to understand and remain aware of the ethical and legal requirements that impact each stage of the research process. As researchers, we are held accountable for ensuring research studies are designed and conducted safely and ethically for our participants, and we are also obligated to follow ethical guidelines for the analysis and reporting of study findings.

- Ethics is a subject that encompasses human behavior and the motives and decisions that impact one's actions. In other words, ethics explores (1) how individuals act; (2) individual, group, and societal judgments about these actions (good or bad, right or wrong); and (3) rules for categorizing these actions. From a foundational and objective perspective, ethical behaviors and actions should result in more good than harm and should have positive consequences for as many individuals as possible, also referred to as *the greater good*. However, ethics can be interpreted in many ways, depending on one's culture, upbringing, environment and influences, and experiences and outcomes. The same behavior you may consider unethical may be considered ethical by someone else.

- Legal considerations are as important as ethical considerations in research. There are many practices that may not be ethical but are not in any legal violation. Researchers must ensure ethical compliance by following the protocol outlined in the necessary codes of ethics and conduct as well as legal compliance in accordance with federal and state legislation relevant to the field setting throughout the process.

- Over the past century, historical events such as World War II prompted unethical research experiments that violated the physical and psychological well-being of the subjects involved and included such practices as forced participation, deception, lack of confidentiality and privacy, and withholding of necessary treatments. Public reaction to these violations resulted in the development of the Nuremberg Code and the Belmont Report that are comprised of ethical codes, guidelines, and protocol for researchers to follow. The increased focus on eliminating unethical research practices also resulted in the establishment of Institutional Review Boards (IRB) for the review and approval of research proposals. An IRB is responsible for identifying any aspects of a research study proposal that appear to involve unnecessary risk or harm, risk without sufficient benefits, harm or deception, and requiring justification or modification of the research design and methodology before allowing researchers to proceed.

- Researchers are also held accountable for their conduct in reporting study findings to their peers and colleagues, their clients, and the population that may be impacted by their research. Researchers must report not only the study findings that support any of their hypotheses but also the instances in which support for hypotheses was not obtained following statistical analysis of the data. The omission of data, inaccurate reporting of findings, and misrepresentation of findings in a study's results are considered practices that constitute serious research reporting misconduct. Researchers must also provide information regarding a study's weaknesses, flaws, and limitations so that other researchers can address these issues through improved design and methodology in future studies.

DISCUSSION QUESTIONS

- What is the difference between ethical and legal compliance? Why may simply adhering to legal requirements throughout the research process be inadequate in terms of maintaining ethical standards?

- What was the main influence that prompted the development of the Nuremberg Code? How does the Belmont Report align with the principles as stated in the Nuremberg Code?

- How do confidentiality and anonymity differ from each other? How can a researcher ensure confidentiality and anonymity of participants in terms of specific processes?

- What are three examples of misconduct in the reporting of research results? What can researchers do to ensure the results they are reporting are clear and accurate?

- Consider the following scenario:

  You are a consultant retained by an organization to develop a training program for managers. During your assignment, you gathered much information via interviews, surveys, personnel records, and observation. This information is intended for use to develop specific training targeted to areas where development is most needed. Midway through the project, the president of the organization met with you to discuss progress and then requested that you rank the managers in terms of their leadership competence. Additionally, you were asked to identify those managers on the low end who should be terminated. The goal, as it was explained to you, is to terminate 10% of the lowest rated managers. When you expressed concern about the change in scope of your assignment, especially for ethical reasons, the president replied that all information collected by you is *owned* by the company and, therefore, should not be your concern.

  What are the ethical and/or legal violations here? What should you do and why?

CHAPTER KEY TERMS

ADA	Debriefing	HIPAA
ADEA	Deception	Informed Consent
Anonymity	Discrimination	Institutional Review Board
Autonomous Agents	Ethics	Nuremberg Code
Belmont Report	Fabrication	Privacy
Beneficence	Falsification	Title VII of the Civil Rights
Confidentiality	FERPA	Act of 1964

CHAPTER 4

Reliability

Achieving consistency in research is as complicated as it is in everyday life. We may often have the expectation that most things we plan for on a daily basis are actually going to happen. Whether you are in the working world or a college student, you are faced with the daily task of getting from where you live to either work or college. Regardless if you get to your expected destination by train, car, bicycle, or whatever mode of transportation you take, you have the expectation that it will consistently get you where you need to be. What would you do if every time you get in your car, you are faced with never knowing if the car will start or not? What would you do if sometimes the train does not arrive at the time it is supposed to or if it stops running during the commute? We all have the expectation that there is a level of consistency with everything we do.

With that being said, research is no different. We expect some level of consistency when conducting research. The process of consistency in research is referred to as reliability. Prior to beginning a discussion on reliability, it is logical to ask, "What is **reliability**?" Reliability has a variety of different definitions such as the extent to which a measure is dependable or consistent (Gatewood & Field, 2001), the consistency of a measure across subsequent tests or over time, the stability of results on a measure, the preciseness of a measure, systematic or consist scores (Schwab, 2005), consistency (Shadish, Cook, & Campbell, 2002), or the degree to which the results can be replicated under similar conditions (McBride, 2010). Regardless of the definition, the common theme among the various definitions is that when a measure is reliable, then the results are consistent, dependable, precise, or stable. Reliability is based on probability with a reliability coefficient ranging from 0 to 1. A reliability coefficient of 1 would mean that there is 100% reliability in the measure, and a reliability coefficient of 0 would mean that there is 0% reliability in the measure.

In addition to reliability, another important concept is discussed in Chapters 5 and 6, which is **validity**. Validity is related to the accuracy of the results or process in a study. Not only are we concerned about how consistent or reliable the measures used in an experiment are, but we also need to ensure that these results are accurate or valid.

> **reliability:** The extent to which a measure or process is consistent, dependable, precise or stable
>
> **validity:** The extent to which a measure or process is accurate

The problem with measuring variables within an organization is that human behavior or any process relying on human interaction is not always 100% predictable. There will always be some variation within the measurement of any variable.

Regardless of this variability, reliability is important for two reasons:

1. Reliability is a necessary, but not sufficient condition for validity.

2. Reliability is the upper limit to validity.

The first statement implies that having a reliable measure does not mean that it will always be valid. For example, you may have a scale that consistently measures an individual's weight. However, if the scale is set back five pounds without anyone knowing, then the weight is not valid. The second statement implies that the validity coefficient will never be higher than the reliability coefficient. This means that if the reliability coefficient that is calculated from your measure is 0.6, then the validity coefficient cannot be higher than 0.6. This is critical because when studying human behavior, no one test is perfect.

RELIABILITY THEORIES

As previously mentioned, reliability is concerned with the consistency of a measure with the goal of reducing errors in measurement. Almost every measure of human behavior has some degree of error associated with the tool. Reliability errors are referred to as **random errors** and **systematic errors**, but the terms *random errors* and *nonrandom errors* may be used respectively.

While the purpose of this book is to provide a researcher with the tools to conduct well- developed applied research or evaluate existing research, we must still refer to some critical theoretical concepts. Two such theories for errors in measurement are as follows:

1. classical test theory or true score theory

2. generalizability theory

The purpose of **classical test theory** or **true score theory** is based on an assumption that measurement error exists. This theory is derived from the thought that a raw score (X) of a measure is comprised of a true component (T) and a random error (E) component, such that the formula for a raw score is $X = T + E$. The true component portion of the formula represents the score that the participant received on a measure. The random error component represents the amount that the participant's score was influenced by other factors unrelated to the construct at the time the measurement was observed. The combination of the true component and random

random error: A type of error in measurement where any factor or variable randomly has an impact of the measured variable

systematic error: A type of error in measurement where any factor or variable that is not random has an impact on the measured variable

classical test theory: Also referred to as True Score Theory. A measurement error theory derived from the thought has a raw score consists on a true and random component.

true score theory: Also referred to as classical test theory. A measurement error theory derived from the thought that a raw score consists of a true and random component.

error component is equal to the raw score or the actual score that was obtained from the measure used. This relationship implies that every measure used in an experiment has a portion of the result that truly represents the intended construct and that there is also some degree of error associated with the measurement. Based on this formula, it can be derived that when random error is reduced, then the true component is increased. In other words, removing the error that does not

> **generalizability theory:** A measurement error theory extending the principles of classical test theory with the exception of not assuming a raw score is combined of a true and random error component but rather the distinction is between the reliability and validity of a measure

occur by chance, but is associated with a measure, causes the end result to be a more reliable measure.

In addition to true score theory, a similar theory exists and is referred to as **generalizability theory**. This theory was first introduced by Cronbach, Gleser, Nanda, and Rajaratnam (1972) and has been said to extend the principles in classical test theory with the exception of not assuming a raw score is combined of a true score and random error component. The thought process behind this theory is that the distinction made between reliability and validity could be overcome through developing a set of observations that can be generalized from the sample collected to the population it was sampled from. In other words, the measures developed that utilize generalizability theory are referred to as dependable and generalizable rather than creating a distinction between validity and reliability. This line between validity and reliability is removed because measures are defined through maximizing construct validity. This means that before a measure is used in an experiment, it is properly operationalized or defined, and therefore, the measure will represent the intended construct. For a further discussion on generalizability theory, refer to Cronbach et al. (1972).

The bottom line to the discussion of these two theories is that there is always going to be some degree in measurement error. Whether this error is associated as both a true component and random error component or if the measurement is well developed to incorporate both validity and reliability is not the focus of this chapter. Measurement error does exist, and there are many theories on how to reduce this error. More importantly, there are many types of reliability that are critical to the developing of not only measures of constructs but also to the design of a research study. Knowing that measurement error exists, the next phase of research design is to determine what type of reliability is the most efficient with regards to research methodology. Similar to research design and variables, no one design or variable is better than the other. Each one has its own advantages and disadvantages, and they are all used with specific purposes.

GOALS OF RELIABILITY

When looking at reliability, there are five main goals, purposes, or types of reliability.

Test-Retest Reliability – Researchers may want to know if results are consistent when the same instrument is administered multiple times. For example, practitioners may want to assess job performance ratings over time to determine if the measures are consistent with the passage of time (Salgado, Moscoso, & Lado, 2003; Viswesvaran, Ones, & Schmidt, 1996).

Interrater Reliability or **Intrarater Reliability** – A researcher may desire to ensure that multiple items on a given survey or questionnaire produce a similar participant response to all the items on the survey or questionnaire: for example, a measure of job performance based on the same person rating performance versus different people rating performance (Viswesvaran et al., 1996).

Parallel Forms Reliability or **Equivalent Forms Reliability** – If multiple tests are developed to measure the same construct or variable, then these subsequent tests should measure similar items. For example, standardized tests, such as the graduate record exam (GRE), scholastic assessment test (SAT), or graduate management admission test (GMAT), etc. all have multiple versions that are designed to measure the same constructs. Bing, Stewart, and Davison (2009) examined the multiple forms of the Personnel Test for Industry-Numerical Test and an Employee Aptitude Survey Numerical Ability Test examining results based on using a calculator versus not using a calculator. To test this comparison, they utilized Forms A and B, which are two different, but identical tests for assessing ability and found support for both tests reliably assessing the same constructs.

Split Half Reliability – A test may be divided into multiple parts and compared to ensure they are measuring the same constructs. For example, Damitz, Manzey, Kleinmann, and Severin (2003) conducted a study examining the validity of using an assessment center to select pilots. The assessment center consisted of data on nine cognitive ability tests, four different assessment exercises measuring nine behavioral dimensions, and nine behaviorally anchored peer ratings on training performance. Split half reliability was calculated by using the peer ratings because each group of peers rated the same student. Therefore, they were randomly divided into two groups to calculate a mean rating for each group and then used a Spearman-Brown correction to estimate reliability.

Internal Consistency/Coefficient Alpha – Items that measure similar constructs that appear throughout a test should be related to each other. For example, Cheng, Huang, Li, and Hsu (2011) conducted a self-administered questionnaire to Taiwanese workers to examine the extent to which burnout had an impact on employment insecurity and workplace justice. In total, there were six items on employment insecurity and nine items on workplace justice. The purpose was to determine if these items measure the variables they were developed for.

Test-Retest Reliability

The first type of reliability is intuitive from the name of it. Test-retest reliability is when a researcher provides a participant with the same test at two different points in time. The purpose of this type of reliability is to show that scores are consistent on multiple administrations of the same test over time. When a test is found to have test-retest reliability, it is expected that a participant's scores on multiple administrations would be similar.

Salgado et al. (2003) examined the test-retest reliability with measures of job performance. Since supervisory ratings are frequently used for validation purposes within selection research (Barrick, Mount, & Judge, 2001), Salgado et al. (2003) conducted a study assessing the reliability of supervisory ratings on several dimensions of job performance and overall job performance. They found support that the test-retest reliability of overall job performance was 0.79 and other measures of performance ranged from 0.40 to 0.67: thus, providing support that there is test-retest reliability on ratings of performance.

Similarly, Sturman, Cheramie, and Cashen (2005) conducted a meta-analysis using 22 studies on the test-retest reliability of job performance ratings over time. They found test-retest reliability coefficients over time for low complexity jobs to be 0.83 and 0.50 for high complexity jobs. Despite these findings, they state that it is impossible to estimate the true stability of job performance because time is an important factor with impacting the job performance ratings.

The main issue with test-retest reliability as Sturman et al. (2005) point out is that the difference in measures between the first and second administration could impact the reliability due to the following factors:

1. Time interval between test administrations

2. The test or other factors associated with the participant

With respect to the time interval, a researcher measured job dissatisfaction through negative affectivity and hypothesized that this measure is stable over time. As a result, the researcher measured the negative affectivity 1 year later. In this case, the time lapse between both administrations of the same test may influence the reliability of the measurement. The result was that the true value of this measure a year later may have been underestimated. The error in measurement was associated to transient factors, such as the participant's mood, emotion, or feeling at the time. These measures could be different a week or day later and

test-retest reliability: The consistency to which the test scores are similar when participants are given the same test more than once

interrater reliability: The consistency to which the test scores are similar when participants are given the same test more than once

intrarater reliability: The extent to which measurement ratings are consistent among the same raters

parallel forms reliability: Also referred to as equivalent forms reliability. The extent to which two tests are developed to measure the same construct of interest.

equivalent forms reliability: Or also referred to as parallel forms reliability. The extent to which two tests are developed to measure the same construct of interest.

split half reliability: Measures the internal consistency of items on a test when different items assessing the same construct throughout the test are compared

internal consistency: Also referred to as coefficient alpha. Measures the consistency of the same items on a test that measure the same construct.

coefficient alpha: Also referred to as internal consistency reliability. Measures the consistency of the same items on a test that measure the same construct.

are not actual measures that impact the negative affectivity the researcher intended to measure (Schmidt & Hunter, 1996).

In addition to the time interval between administrations, a possibility exists that the scores from the first administration can influence the results of the second administration. This means that the participant taking a test the second time may learn from his or her mistakes during the first administration or review the items being asked after the test is completed. This would be a greater possibility when the time between administrations of the same test is a short time interval. For example, a researcher administers a vocabulary test once and then a month later the same test is administered. In this case, the test-retest reliability may be overestimated due to the lack of controlling for specific factors, such as personality factors, with each administration of the test (Schmidt & Hunter, 1996).

Interrater/Intrarater Reliability

The second type of reliability is interrater and intrarater reliability. The concept behind this reliability is that either the same (interrater) or different (intrarater) raters assess an individual rating on a specific variable. The challenge is that each rater, regardless if they are the same or not, must consistently assess the same behavior in the same consistent manner.

Interrater reliability is defined as measuring the consistency of ratings across different raters. In a quasi-experiment, Lievens and Sanchez (2007) examined the impact that a frame-of-reference training would have on the interrater reliability of competency ratings completed by human resources consultants in either a training group or a control group. The purpose of the program was to have consultants determine the competencies that were required for a specific job. They found that the consultants that received the training resulted in an interrater reliability coefficient of 0.65 compared to the 0.44 coefficient found for the control group not receiving the training.

Intrarater reliability, on the other hand, is when a researcher examines the consistency of one particular individual's ratings at multiple points in time. Within the realm of applied research, intrarater reliability is assessed in conjunction with job analysis research (Dierdorff & Wilson, 2003). The purpose of intrarater reliability is to determine the sustainability of an individual's ratings at two different points in time. Dierdorff and Wilson (2003) conducted a meta-analysis of 46 studies to explore the reliability of job analysis data. They found in cases of measuring task data, intrarater reliability results were higher than interrater reliability results and in cases of measuring general work ability, interrater reliability results were higher than intrarater reliability.

Similarly, Viswesvaran et al. (1996) conducted a meta-analysis on overall job performance to compare and contrast the impact of interrater and intrarater reliability. In the meta-analysis, Viswesvaran et al. (1996) utilized 10 measures of job performance to assess the differences in reliability using both peer and supervisory performance ratings. They found that interrater reliability measures of overall job performance were lower than that of intrarater reliability and that supervisory ratings have higher interrater reliability than peer ratings.

Parallel or Equivalent Forms Reliability

The next type of reliability is parallel or equivalent forms reliability. By definition, this type of reliability is where a researcher creates two different but similar tests that measure the same construct. One of the more well-known tests that are parallel or equivalent forms is standardized tests. The process to developing a standardized test is extremely arduous and requires an extreme precision to ensure the psychometric properties of the items are similar. In practice, it is possible to create parallel or equivalent forms of a test, but it may not be widely used due to the process of developing multiple tests.

The idea behind parallel or equivalent forms reliability is to have two conceptually identical tests that utilize separate questions to measure the same construct of interest. The number of items used to measure a particular construct of interest can be unlimited. Therefore, it is not possible for a test or measure to include every possible item to measure the constructs of interest. This has an important implication on reliability because creating a test to measure human behavior with a reliability coefficient of 1.0 is unlikely. On the other hand, having multiple items to measure the same construct could be a benefit for using parallel or equivalent forms reliability to create multiple similar but different tests. The challenge you face when multiple tests are created to measure the same construct is that the items on both versions of the same test may not actually measure the same construct.

From an applied perspective, Chan, Schmitt, Deshon, Clause, and Delbridge (1997) were interested in the relationships that factors such as race, test-taking motivations, and performance had on a cognitive ability test. To do this, a parallel form cognitive ability test battery was created that was used in an actual employment testing project. They found that the correlation between the first test and the parallel test was 0.84 (p < 0.05). This indicates that the two forms of the cognitive ability test were adequate in regards to parallel form reliability.

Similarly, Bing et al. (2009) conducted a study that utilized multiple forms (Form A and B) of a Personal Test for Industry-Numerical Test and an Employee Aptitude Survey Numerical Ability Test that involved the comparison of results for participants using a calculator compared to participants not using a calculator. Multiple comparisons were conducted to examine the reliability of these different conditions, and they found support that the results of both the calculator and noncalculator condition were similar on both forms of the test.

Split Half Reliability

The next type of reliability is split half reliability. The purpose of the split half reliability is to divide the test or measure into two halves and test the internal consistency of the items used. Split half reliability is similar but different to the parallel or equivalent forms reliability with a couple exceptions. Parallel or equivalent forms reliability requires two versions of a test. With split half reliability, a researcher only conducts one administration of the test or measure and splits the test in half (i.e., even vs. odd questions or the first half vs. the second half). This is different from parallel or equivalent forms because multiple versions of a test are not necessary.

One common criticism of this technique is determining where to split the test because of how the items are divided within the test or measure. A few techniques to split the test or

---

| **Box 4.1** | In-Basket Test Reliability |

When looking to select the most appropriate employee for a position, it is important to properly evaluate their ability to succeed because the cost to replace an employee can be extremely costly. In the day and age of cutting budgets to conserve money, an employer must be able to consistently (reliability) and accurately (validity) select one qualified candidate from a pool of applicants. One methodology to select employees is through the use of an assessment center. Within an assessment center, an applicant is given a variety of test batteries that may include simulations, tests, exercises, etc. in which they are designed to perform in a simulated work environment (Berry, 2002).

One such test battery in an assessment center is an in-basket exercise. The purpose of this is to provide an applicant with the ability to manage a variety of issues that could be accumulated in a day such as letters, memos, telephone messages, reports, or other items that may come up throughout the course of a day (Berry, 2002). In an effort to assess the reliability of the in-basket test, Schippmann, Prien, and Katz (1990) reviewed the existing literature on various components of the reliability of an in-basket test. In terms of reliability, the psychometric properties of an in-basket test reliability was examined through interrater reliability, parallel forms reliability, and split-half reliability.

While none of these three reliability techniques proved superior in assessing the reliability of the in-basket test, a lot of useful information was learned. In terms of interrater reliability, it was found that the range of reliability coefficients for this technique suggests that some other variable may create the rating patterns that may be a function of rater training. Parallel form reliability differences in coefficients may potentially be a result of being confounded with performance on the test. Lastly, for split-half reliabilities of odd and even numbers, Schippmann et al. (1990) suggest that there may be a need in further developing the test content or a more systematic and objective approach to scoring the test may yield more encouraging reliability coefficients. In summary, the in-basket test for reliability and validity provides only modest support for the usefulness.

measure include using odd and even numbered items, randomly selecting the items, or using the first half and second half of the test. The most commonly used method of split-half reliability within research is through odd and even items (Aamodt, 2007). As an example, Damitz et al. (2003) examined the validity of an assessment center used to select pilots. As a part of the assessment center, each group of peers had rated the same students and therefore, they randomly divided the group into two equal-sized subgroups. This grouping allowed for calculation of split half reliability utilizing the Spearman-Brown correction.

Internal Consistency/Coefficient Alpha

The last reliability technique is internal consistency reliability and is also referred to as coefficient alpha or Cronbach's alpha. This is most common and widely used reliability technique for purposes of reporting the reliability of a test or measure in experiments in applied settings (Edwards, Scott, & Raju, 2003) and is also by far the most commonly reported measure of reliability (Hogan, Benjamin, & Brezinski, 2000; Rogers, Schmitt, & Mullins, 2002). It is similar to split half reliability because this technique also measures the internal consistency or correlation between the items on a test. The main difference between split half and internal consistency/coefficient alpha is the entire test is used to estimate the correlation between the items without splitting the test or measure in half. The correlation utilized to calculate internal consistency is similar to the correlation used with inter/intrarater reliability.

Internal consistency is calculated by examining the pairwise correlations between the items on the measure. Cronbach (1951) outlined that a coefficient alpha of greater than or equal to 0.7 is generally acceptable. Despite the widespread use of Cronbach's alpha, there are a couple of caveats to its use. First, alpha is strongly influenced by the number of items on a measure, so the calculated alpha could be higher by increasing the number of items. The other problem with alpha is when it is too high, because a very high Cronbach alpha could indicate redundancy in the items.

In addition to examining parallel or equivalent forms reliability, Bing et al. (2009) also assessed internal consistency reliability for the 30 measures on mathematical reasoning and the 75 items on computational skill. Coefficient alpha for the measures were above 0.7, which by Cronbach's (1951) standards is acceptable. This means that the 30 measures included within the test for mathematical reasoning and the 75 items on computational skill reliably assessed their respective constructs.

In another study, Dirani and Kuchinke (2011) conducted a survey using a convenient sample of Lebanese banks to assess the validity and reliability of two measures of organizational commitment and job satisfaction. The survey consisted of 38 items comprised of three sections. Job satisfaction consisted of 20 items, nine items consisted of organizational commitment, and nine items assessed demographic questions. The results from the current study replicated previous reliability results with a coefficient alpha of greater than 0.84, thus indicating that the measures used to assess job satisfaction and organizational commitment were reliable.

RELIABILITY SUMMARY

While all types of reliability are important, internal consistency/coefficient alpha is the most widely used in applied settings (Edwards et al., 2003). The main reason why this type of reliability is the most widely used is because it only requires one administration of a test to determine the relationship between the items on the test. Other types of reliabilities need multiple versions of a test, many different raters, or multiple administrations of a test to generate a reliability coefficient. In applied settings, a researcher may not have the time, resources, or availability to conduct multiple administrations of a test.

As we know, a measure can be reliable and not valid, but it cannot be valid and not reliable. Additionally, reliability is a necessary, but not sufficient, condition for validity. Therefore, it is important to take a look at the reliability coefficient from the perspective of validity to better understand the relationship between reliability and validity and ensure the measure is both reliable and valid. Keep in mind that regardless of the type of reliability, the goal is to have a reliability coefficient close to 1, which would indicate a high degree of consistency and a low degree of measurement error with the measure. Simply having a high reliability coefficient in your study does not necessarily equate to the assumption that the measure on your test is valid. The reason is because there may be potential threats to validity that can provide an explanation to a high reliability coefficient.

When discussing the different reliability methods, the main conclusion drawn between the results of the different types of reliability is the explanation of the results found within the research. For example, when evaluating research that states the best predictor of future performance is past behavior, you, as a consumer of information, have to know that this result is true and that there is no other explanation that can justify this result. Whenever a measure of human behavior exists, there is some level of measurement error that occurs. While the reliability coefficient ranges from 0 to 1, with 1 being perfectly reliable, we know that no measure of human behavior is capable of achieving perfect reliability. There is bound to be some error associated with any measurement. Even classical test theory posits that the raw score of a measure is comprised of a true component and a random error component.

Therefore, the goal of being a consumer of information is to know and understand the various aspects of reliability techniques as well as understand the relationship between reliability and validity. Whenever a possibility exists that the relationship within an experiment can be explained by alternative explanations this means that there is a threat to the validity of the experiment and the reliability of the results. **Validity** is discussed in detail in Chapters 5 and 6. An alternative explanation for a result means that some other variable can explain the relationship between the cause and effect relationship.

> **validity:** The accuracy of the results of a research study

CHAPTER SUMMARY

- Reliability is the consistency of a measure with a coefficient between 0 and 1 and is important for two reasons: (1) Reliability is a necessary, but not sufficient, condition for validity and (2) reliability is the upper limit to validity. This implies that a reliable measure may not always be valid and a validity coefficient can never be higher than the reliability coefficient.

- When developing tests to measure a construct, it may not be perfect, and there could be a degree of error associated with the test, but techniques can be utilized to improve the reliability of a test. Error in measurement can be categorized as random or systematic (nonrandom) errors.

- All tests or measures have some degree of error associated with the measurement, and there are two theories aimed at understanding these errors in measurement. Classical test theory or true score theory is based on an assumption that every raw score observation is comprised of two components, which are a true measurement and an error measurement. Generalizability theory extends the principles of classical test theory/true score theory by the premise of developing a set of observations that can be generalized from the sample collected to the population it was sampled from.

- There are five main goals of reliability and they relate to the different types of reliability, which are as follows: test-retest, interrater/intrarater, parallel or equivalent forms, split half, and internal consistency/coefficient alpha reliability. These different types of reliability are aimed at ensuring that a test consistently measures a construct of interest.

DISCUSSION QUESTIONS

- What are some ways that a researcher or practitioner can reduce systematic errors within a study design?
- How does classical test theory/true score theory or generalizability theory apply to research design?
- Given internal consistency reliability is the most commonly reported reliability technique, how might you use split half, parallel forms, intra/inter or test-retest reliability to demonstrate the consistency of your measures?

CHAPTER KEY TERMS

Classical Test Theory
Generalizability Theory
Random Error
Reliability
Reliability, Coefficient Alpha
Reliability, Equivalent Forms

Reliability, Internal
    Consistency
Reliability, Interrater
Reliability, Intrarater
Reliability, Parallel Forms
Reliability, Split Half

Reliability, Test-Retest
Systematic Error
True Score Theory
Validity

CHAPTER 5

Statistical Conclusion and Internal Validity

To begin our discussion of validity, we would like to share a story about a practitioner's experience at a job interview. Imagine this: You just landed an interview for your dream job right after graduating. You anxiously prepare yourself for all the difficult questions they could potentially ask you. You have done your due diligence with preparing yourself to do well on this interview and work at your dream company. You have reviewed your resume, and you know there is no question they can ask you that you couldn't provide a well thought out answer based on experience or what you learned in school.

The day comes, and you sit down with your future manager. The interview begins with a review of your past employment history and the typical behavior based questions, which you had prepared for. As far as you're aware the interview is going well, and you begin to develop a rapport with the manager. Then your future manager asks you this question, "Approximately how many television sets were sold in the United States within the past year?" A sudden sense of panic comes over you, and you begin to wonder how relevant this question was to being able to do the job. This is the question of **validity.** You may be thinking, What does purchasing television sets have to do with your ability to be a successful management consultant? You may even begin to ask what the purpose of this question is. The bottom line with that question is not actually how many television sets were sold but rather the thought process behind how you arrive at the answer. This particular question was being used to assess critical thinking skills and your ability to creatively solve a problem.

> **validity:** The extent to which a measure or process is accurate

Whenever the accuracy of a problem or question is brought up, then you are referring to the concept of validity. In addition to the accuracy of the problem or question, there may be other factors that may influence your response to the question. These other factors are what we refer to as threats to validity because they may get in the way of your response.

By now you should have an understanding that validity, or the accuracy of the results, is important in studies for a variety of reasons. As mentioned in previous chapters and potentially in every chapter beyond, the term *validity* will come up in one way or another. The reason is because validity is a critical component to any research study and needs to be considered within all aspects of the process to designing and evaluating a study. Validity, by definition, is the accuracy of the results. When questioning the validity of the results, a researcher can question the validity of the measures used in the study, the response scale used to rate the responses, the statistical procedures used, how the measures were operationalized, the sample used in the study, etc.

Ultimately, there are many different opportunities that allow a study to have invalid results. The purpose of this chapter is to provide the necessary framework to understand the intricacies of the different types of validities and ways to reduce their associated threats. There is one caveat: No matter what type of research design is conducted or what research you may be evaluating, it is impossible to eliminate every possible threat to validity. The trade-off is to determine what threats to validity you are willing to deal with and what threats you need to reduce. Remember that every decision made in regards to the design of a research study will create an additional problem.

Similarly, you may be wondering how the concept of reliability from Chapter 4 is related to validity. A common challenge when trying to understand reliability and validity is being able to differentiate between the two concepts both conceptually and from an applied perspective. Validity is referred to as the accuracy of the results and reliability is defined as the consistency of the results. In order for results to be accurate, they have to be consistent, but a measure can be consistent and not accurate. This concept may be slightly confusing, but the important point is to think back to the purpose of accurate and consistent results.

Box 5.1   Validity and Reliability Demystified

The concepts of validity and reliability are highly complex and can be easily confused for one another. It is critical that you understand the nuances between the practical application of both concepts. Consider an example of questioning the validity and reliability of an automated teller machine (ATM) where a customer wants to withdraw $20 from the ATM.

Reliability: The concept of reliability is related to the consistency of the result, or did the ATM consistently do what it is supposed to do, which would be to provide the customer with money. If the ATM always gives money when requested, then the ATM is deemed reliable. However, if the ATM sometimes gives money and sometimes does not, then this would not be reliable.

Validity: The concept of validity is related to the accuracy of the result, or did the customer receive the $20 that was requested. If the ATM always gives the customer $20 when the customer asks for $20, then the ATM would have produced a valid result. If the ATM sometimes gives the customer $40 when only asked to give $20, then this would be an invalid result.

It is important when examining reliability and validity to think of them as two separate terms and think about what the purpose of the measure would be. In the second example using validity, if you request $20 and the ATM sometimes gives $40 and other times gives $20, then this is an example of the ATM being reliable but not valid.

Box 5.2	**Practitioner Spotlight: Standardized Practices?**

Consider an example from a practitioner working for a large technology organization in the eastern United States. In this particular example, there was a research project that involved monitoring and interpreting analytics within the organization to determine the top performing departments. The purpose of the analytics was to track department specific information in regards to performance, satisfaction scores, budget information, products sold, and other customer focused measures. This information was provided to each department on a monthly basis while tracking previous month's performance. This allows for a comparison between departments as well as the practitioner's ability to monitor performance of their department over time. Monthly meetings were held to discuss changes in trends and create action plans to address potential issues. At one such meeting there was a question in regards to an upward trend of products being sold, and one department manager concluded that their department had significantly improved the number of products being sold.

The practitioner was concerned about the interpretation of the results and further probed into how these values were calculated. After the meeting ended, the practitioner spoke to a few of the other department managers and asked how they calculated the number of products being sold. It turned out that this large organization had different computer systems for tracking information. The end result is that each department was calculating these values slightly differently. Despite the fact that the department managers were consistently or reliably capturing the same information on a monthly basis, there was no standardized practice put in place to indicate the proper procedures to obtain this information. Since there was no standardized methodology to operationally define the number of products sold between departments, this indicates that there is an impact on the validity of the results. In other words, it is possible that while the results of the department performance were reliable, the validity of these results was questionable.

The complexity of this example highlights the many other variables that can explain the relationship of increasing the number of products sold. The variability could be due to the staff, the computer system, the particular products sold within the department, how each individual person was defining a sale, etc. The bottom line is that, as researchers and consumers of information, we must question everything when provided results. It is highly critical to review the methodology for how information was gathered because this may uncover some flaws in the logic.

Now getting back to validity, it is comprised of four main categories: **statistical conclusion** and **internal**, **external**, and **construct validity**. There are other types of validity that are mentioned within the four main categories, but these are the main four that are commonly recognized within research. This chapter provides a foundation for validity at a conceptual understanding of statistical conclusion and internal validity, which both focus on the covariation of the cause and effect relationship. Chapter 6 provides a foundation for external and construct validity, which both focus on generalizations.

statistical conclusion validity: Covariation of the cause and effect relationship through the appropriateness of the statistical procedure used for the analysis

internal validity: Covariation of the cause and effect relationship

external validity: Generalizability of the cause and effect relationship across changes in the participants, settings, treatments, or the outcomes

construct validity: Generalizability that the variables used in a study represent the variable they intend to measure

Furthermore, Chapters 7 to 10 provide an application of validity to different research designs and Chapters 11 to 14 discuss the impact of research in the real world. When conducting or evaluating research, there are a few important points you want to know:

1. The result found in the research was due to the independent variable and not some other variable (i.e., internal validity).

2. The variables utilized in the study are defined well enough to be truly representative of the variables (i.e., construct validity).

3. The results of this particular research can also be found in other situations (i.e., external validity).

4. The appropriate statistical analysis was used to analyze the results (i.e., statistical conclusion validity).

Each of these issues you want to evaluate are all related to the different types of validity with research. The four main types of validity can be grouped into two main categories. Statistical conclusion and internal validity both focus on the covariation between the relationship of the cause and effect relationship found within research. External and construct validity both focus on the generalization of the results found within the research and are discussed in Chapter 6.

STATISTICAL CONCLUSION VALIDITY

The first type of validity examining the covariation of the cause and effect relationship is statistical conclusion validity. By definition, statistical conclusion validity is defined as the covariation of the cause and effect relationship through the appropriateness of the statistical procedure used to analyze the results. The purpose of understanding statistical conclusion validity is based on two components:

1. Whether or not the cause and effect covary

2. The strength to which they covary

To examine this cause and effect relationship, statistical analyses are conducted to determine if the cause and effect covary and to also assess the strength of this relationship. Although statistical conclusion validity is highly statistical in nature, advanced statistical discussions are reserved for statistical textbooks. Interested readers should consult a statistical textbook for further review on the assumptions of various statistical analyses, such as Field (2006) for univariate statistics and Meyers, Gamst, and Guarino (2006) for multivariate statistics.

Throughout the process of analyzing the results, a possibility exists that a researcher can make a mistake. These mistakes are known as **Type I** and **Type II errors**. With a Type I error, it is concluded that the cause and effect relationship covaries when it actually does not. With a Type II error, it is concluded that the cause and effect relationship does not covary when it actually does. In an effort to reduce the chances of making an error, it is important to understand the various threats associated with statistical conclusion validity. Box 5.3 presents the nine threats associated with statistical conclusion validity.

When examining the threats for statistical conclusion validity, they can be grouped in three different categories as follows:

> **Type I error:** An error in decision making where it is stated that the cause and effect covaries when there is no relationship
>
> **Type II error:** An error in decision making where it is stated that the cause and effect does not covary when there is a relationship

1. Design of the methodology

2. Measurement of the variables

3. Components of the statistical analysis

Design of the Methodology

The first category of the design of the methodology is related to the composition of the sample and the experimental setting. Any variation within the setting of the study as well as the composition of the sample could potentially make the process of identifying a statistically significant effect more challenging. The first two threats, restriction of range and heterogeneity of units, are in reference to threats of statistical conclusion validity from the design of the methodology.

Restriction of Range

When there is restriction of range, this means that when a sample is generated with a small range of participants, it may result in a weakened effect. When we say a small range of participants, we are referring to collecting data from a small subset of the population. It may be common in educational and organizational settings to have range restriction occur. An example of restriction of range in an educational setting is utilizing a standardized test, such as the Law School Aptitude Test (LSAT) or the Graduate Record Exam (GRE), to admit potential students. The data available from the school is only based on students that are admitted to that school, thus resulting in restriction of range (Hunter, Schmidt, & Le, 2006; Schmidt, Oh, & Le, 2006). From an organizational perspective, Berry, Sackett, and Landers (2007) conducted a meta-analysis of 63 studies to examine the correlation between interviews and cognitive ability tests. They found support that range restriction is believed to occur in the interview-cognitive ability relationship as well as the relationship between personality and general mental ability in job and training performance (Schmidt, Shaffer, & Oh, 2008)

| **Box 5.3** | Statistical Conclusion Validity Threats |

1. Restriction of range – generating a sample with a small range of participants may weaken the results.
2. Heterogeneity of units – most parametric statistics require that the sample is normally distributed, which means that the participants in the sample are homogenous. When a sample is heterogeneous, the possibility exists that this increased variability may impact the ability to detect a significant relationship.
3. Extraneous variance in experimental setting – when conducting studies, the possibility exists that there is some variability within the experimental design. This variability may make it more challenging to be able to detect a statistical significant relationship.
4. Unreliability of measures – every measure taken has to some degree measurement error. When measures are unreliable, then the validity of the results is decreased.
5. Unreliability of treatment implementation – any variation in the way a study is conducted from participant to participant may impact the reliability of the treatment that is implemented.
6. Low statistical power – the study does not have an adequate power to be able to detect a cause and effect relationship.
7. Fishing and error rate – every study should be conducted with a specific purpose. Additional unplanned analyses that are conducted may result in an inflation of statistical significance.
8. Inaccurate effect size estimation – some statistical procedures may inherently over or under estimate the size of the effect within the study.
9. Violated assumptions of tests – every statistical analysis procedure has specific assumptions associated with each test that must be met in order to conduct the analysis. Researchers that violate these assumptions may lead to an inaccurate result.

Each one of the aforementioned studies (Berry et al., 2007; Hunter et al., 2006; Schmidt et al., 2006; Schmidt et al., 2008) discuss potential corrections techniques for both direct and indirect range restriction. Direct range restriction is said to occur when applicants for a position are selected based on test scores top down. On the other hand, indirect range restriction occurs if applicants are selected for a position based on some other variable correlated with the test. It is believed that indirect range restriction is a more common event than direct range restriction (Schmidt et al., 2008). Regardless of the technique used for correction of range restriction, it is important to consider the implications on validity because not correcting for range restriction may result in underestimating the validity coefficient (Schmidt et al., 2006).

Heterogeneity of Units

In addition to restriction of range, a researcher needs to be concerned with the heterogeneity of the sample or the differences between the participants in a study. Variation within the collected data, such as the differences between individual responses, may lead to a statistically significant effect that may not exist. Statistical analyses are used to examine the variability within the groups. If the heterogeneity between participants is correlated with the cause and effect relationship, then the possibility exists that the error also increases. Thus, the probability increases of making a Type I error or stating a statistically significant relationship exists when one does not exist.

For example, Oswald, Saad, and Sackett (2000) utilized a simulation study with two large databases with diverse job samples examining relationships between personality and ability. These relationships were gathered from a military setting using Project A and the General Aptitude Test Battery (GATB) databases that contain a diverse set of job samples and a wide variability of subgroups. The overall purpose of the study was to examine subgroup variance ratios using a traditional F test. They found enough heterogeneity within the error variances used in the current study that they urged applied psychologies to explore the data set and consider an alternative statistical test for heterogeneity.

Extraneous Variance in Experimental Setting

The last threat associated with the research design or participants in the sample is the extraneous variance in the experimental setting. Since not all studies can be perfectly conducted, the possibility exists that there is some variation within the research design. This variability may make it challenging to detect a statistically significant relationship because the error associated with making the decision is increased.

This variation can be referred to as systematic or random variance. With random variance, the variability is considered random and is typically unable to be controlled, so it is not a major concern. On the other hand, systematic variance is problematic because this is variance that can be controlled. The classic example in applied settings is the Hawthorne Effect; whereby, the study originated the Hawthorne Plant of Western Electric. The premise was that illumination levels would have an effect on worker performance. The end result was suggested that it was not the lighting levels that increased performance but rather the fact that the manager was observing employee behavior (Aamodt, 2007). In this case, it is possible that the manager being present during the study was an extraneous variance in the experimental setting that was not taken into consideration and potentially caused the effect. While not all extraneous variances can be controlled for, it is critically important to measure the source of variance to handle during the statistical analysis.

Measurement of the Variables

The second category of threats are related to the measurement of the variables. If there is any variation with the variables within the study, then this poses a potential issue with determining statistical significance. Whenever a study is conducted, it must be done with extreme precision and standardization. However, knowing that no study can be perfectly controlled, it is possible that there may be variability in the measures of the study or through the implementation of the procedures.

Unreliability of Measures

When a researcher determines a conclusion based on the results of the study, it is critical to ensure that the measures used to evaluate that variable are reliable (refer to Chapter 4 for a further review of reliability). Any variation in this measurement may result in drawing an incorrect conclusion. Taylor, Pajo, Cheung, and Stringfield (2004) examined the process of a telephone reference checking procedure on employee selection. These types of assessments for employee selection are typically not structured, so the measures assessed may vary from rater to rater. Of equal importance is that often times recruiters may ask questions that are not typically related to the job resulting in a variation in the measured construct.

There are many opportunities a researcher has to increase the reliability of the measures such as increasing the amount of measurements that are taken during a study; enhancing the quality of the measures that are being used; or in some advanced statistical analysis, using a technique utilizing latent variable modeling. A latent variable is a variable that a researcher cannot directly measure. Therefore, through modeling, a researcher would be able to extract out the error variance associated with the measured variables, which would increase the reliability of the measured variable (Shadish, Cook, & Campbell, 2002).

Unreliability of Treatment Implementation

Any potential variation in data collection from location to location or participant to participant poses an issue with concluding an accurate statistical significance. Unless a study is conducted in a highly controlled laboratory, then there may always be some form of variation within the data collection process. As previously mentioned, random error is generally not as large of an issue as systematic error. It is recommended that a standardized protocol for administering the treatment and collecting the data is well thought out prior to beginning a study. Through increasing standardization when possible, a decrease in the unreliability of the implementation of the treatment may occur.

As previously mentioned, Taylor et al. (2004) examined the use of a structured telephone reference procedure for improving the validity of the reference. It was determined from the information gathered from the unstructured telephone reference procedure that there was no systematic way to score the data and integrate it with other assessment data. Therefore, it is recommended that a structured procedure for conducting telephone references should be implemented to improve the validity of the assessment and reduce the unreliability of treatment implementation.

Components of the Statistical Analysis

The last category of threats to statistical conclusion validity is related to the statistical procedures used to analyze the data. No matter what statistical analysis is conducted, there are specific assumptions prior to conducting each analysis that must be met. It is also imperative that the statistical analysis of the data is taken into consideration prior to conducting the study. This thought process enables the researcher with the opportunity to address potential issues prior to beginning the study.

Low Statistical Power

Low power is a common issue with studies and can result from not conducting an appropriate power analysis. When a researcher does not utilize a power analysis prior to conducting a study, the opportunity exists for not having an adequate level of power to be able to detect a statistically significant effect. One of the potential consequences of low power is usually due to a small sample size (Mone, Mueller, & Mauland, 1996). The purpose of the power analysis is to determine the appropriate sample size required to find statistical significance. Typically, a power of 0.8 or above is recommended when conducting research.

It is always recommended to conduct a power analysis to determine the appropriate sample size needed for a specified level of power. If a study suffers from low power, then the researcher has the ability to increase the sample size, which would also increase the level of power. One caveat about increasing sample size to increase power is that there is a point of diminishing return with increasing the sample size. When a researcher increases the sample size to increase the power to detect an effect, the effect may be an artifact of the large sample. This would be a Type I error because the researcher is stating a statistically significant effect exists when it really does not. Other ways to increase power would be to improve the reliability of the measurement of the variables or increase the standardization of the protocol used to administer the treatment and collect the data.

In a review of 210 articles, Mone et al. (1996) found that one in three studies achieved an adequate level of power. In a follow-up study, 179 lead authors were surveyed on their use of power analyses when conducting research. It was found that 108 of these lead authors never used a power analysis. To reduce the chances of making a Type II error, a power analysis can be conducted to determine the appropriate sample size required for a research study (Sun, Pan, & Wang, 2011). Readers interested in a review of power analysis are encouraged to review the guidelines set forth by Cohen (1988).

Fishing and Error Rate

After a study is completed, a researcher may feel inclined to further analyze the data from what was originally decided to examine. Additional unplanned analyses of results is known as fishing and must be avoided. When a research fishes through a dataset to find statistically significant effects, this results in an inflated error rate. These additional analyses also apply to researchers investigating and analyzing previously collected datasets (Denton, 1985) or conducting multiple tests comparing many groups (Field, 2009).

Any time a study is designed, the purpose of the analysis is solely based on the developed hypothesis. An alpha level may have been set at 0.05 in the beginning, but additional analyses may lead to an increased alpha, which would result in a greater risk of making a Type I error. A researcher may have the option of conducting a post hoc corrective procedure like the Bonferonni correction to produce a corrected alpha to ensure all future statistical tests will not exceed the set alpha level of 0.05. (The scope of this textbook is on research methodology and not advanced statistical procedures. Therefore, interested readers are advised to consult Field [2009] for univariate statistics and Meyers et al. [2006] for multivariate statistics for a further review of statistical correction procedures.)

Box 5.4   The Effect of Conducting Multiple Tests

Field (2009) provides an excellent example for the impact on conducting multiple tests and the relationship with alpha. Even with alpha set at 0.05, when multiple tests are conducted, the chance of making a Type I error increases. Under the assumption that each test is independent, the probability of making a Type I error can be multiplied. Therefore, conducting three tests with an alpha set at 0.05 for each test means that there is a 95% chance of not making a Type I error. When you conduct this test on different groups three times, this means you can multiply $0.95 \times 0.95 \times 0.95 = 0.857$. This means there is an 85.7% chance of not making a Type I error. To calculate the alpha from these three tests, you can subtract 1 from 0.857, which equals 0.143. This implies that by conducting three of the same tests, the alpha level increases from 0.05 to 0.143, which is a level that exceeds the level of significance that is typically accepted to indicate statistical significance. This increase in error rate is known as familywise error rate.

Inaccurate Effect Size Estimation

When conducting statistical procedures, a possibility exists that some statistical analyses may lead to an over/underestimation of the size of the effect within the study. This could potentially be due to low power resulting from an inappropriate sample size (Sun et al., 2011). The purpose of an effect size is to examine the strength of the relationship between the cause and effect variables. For a further review of the importance of effect size, readers are suggested to consult Cohen (1988). As an example, the presence of outliers within a data set can have a dramatic influence on reducing the effect size estimation (Wilcox, 1995). When estimating an effect size, it is important to examine the data that have been collected for evidence of outliers as they often result in this type of inaccurate estimation. As a means to improve effect size estimation as a result of outlier data, Zijlstra, Van der Ark, and Sijtsma (2011) evaluate six different procedures used for outlier detection.

Violated Assumptions of Tests

With statistical analysis, there is a list of assumptions that must be met in order to conduct a statistical procedure. It is critical that researchers become familiarized and aware of these assumptions to be able to handle any potential issue that may arise. If a researcher violates an assumption to a statistical procedure, then that particular procedure should not be utilized.

Wilcox (1998) outlined that modern robust statistics, which are defined as statistical analyses that can maintain the Type I error rate as well as the power of the test, exist that can resolve many issues of violated assumptions of parametric tests. However, for real-world data, these assumptions are rarely met. The result may be an inaccurate p value, effect size, or confidence interval that could impact the interpretation of the data (Erceg-Hurn & Mirosevich, 2008). As a test, Finch and Davenport (2009) simulated four standard multivariate analysis of variance or MANOVA test statistics using a Monte Carlo simulation. They found that with small samples power was low for all analysis and Type I error rates were inflated when assumptions to statistical analyses were violated. To anticipate potential issues prior to conducting a study, the researcher is encouraged to review the statistical procedure and assumptions in detail to know what potential issues may be encountered.

Statistical Conclusion Validity Summary

Statistical conclusion validity is concerned with the issue of covariation with the cause and effect relationship and that the appropriate statistics were utilized to detect the cause and effect relationship. To reduce the threats to statistical conclusion validity, a researcher needs to become familiar with the statistical procedures and assumptions of the procedures that are warranted for the analysis of the study. Statistical conclusion validity can be influenced by sample size (Mone et al., 1996; Sun et al., 2011), effect size (Wilcox, 1995; Zijlstra et al., 2011), power analysis (Mone et al., 1996; Sun et al., 2011), and violated statistical test assumptions (Erceg-Hurn & Mirosevich, 2008; Finch & Davenport, 2009; Wilcox, 1998). Through this understanding, the researcher is able to properly conclude the appropriateness of the cause and effect relationship and reduce Type I and Type II errors: thus, enhancing the accuracy of the results concluded in the study.

INTERNAL VALIDITY

Similar to statistical conclusion validity, internal validity is also concerned with the covariation of the cause and effect relationship. The main difference between the two is that statistical conclusion validity is related to the statistical covariation and internal validity is related to stating that the covariation was a result of the causal relationship. In other words, internal validity is concerned with ensuring that the cause and effect relationship is due to the manipulation of the cause (i.e., **independent variable**) and no other variable (i.e., **extraneous** or **confounding variable**) can explain the relationship.

Internal validity has the most threats associated with it and typically is the most challenging when conducting and evaluating research. In fact, Brutus, Gill, and Duniewicz (2010) conduct a study in which they reviewed 2,402 articles between 1995 and 2008. They found that 41.1% of articles reported at least one threat to internal validity with the most common threat of not being able to infer causation. This is highly problematic because there are many opportunities where the cause and effect relationship can be explained by another factor. Despite the fact that there are many different threats to internal validity, these threats are the easiest to reduce through the use of random assignment. The thought process is that utilizing random assignment would equally distribute the threats to internal validity across conditions, which make these threats less plausible. However, Corrigan and Salzer (2003) suggest that the use of random assignment may introduce nuisance threats by removing treatment preference from the participant. Participants choose to be in a study, and when their choice of treatment preference is replaced with randomization, this can significantly impact behavior in a study. In an applied setting, organizations may not likely see the benefits of random assignment or not allow random assignment, so alternative resolutions must be made to reduce these threats.

> **independent variable:** A variable in research that is manipulated or changed
>
> **extraneous variable:** Similar to confounding variable. A variable that may influence the relationship between the independent and dependent variable.
>
> **confounding variable:** Similar to extraneous variable. A variable that may influence the relationship between the independent and dependent variable.

With that being said, Box 5.5 lists the threats associated with internal validity. All of these threats are associated with the individual participants within the study. When conducting a study, there are many opportunities for issues to arise with the participants during the course of the study. By becoming familiar with these threats and ways to reduce the possibility of other variables, being able to explain the cause and effect relationship will enhance the accuracy of the results.

Selection

The first threat is an important one and has to do with selecting participants to be part of the study. A selection threat indicates that there is a systematic difference between individual participants prior to the study taking place. In other words, every participant brings individual differences to every study. Therefore, a possibility exists that these differences could potentially be the reason why a cause and effect relationship was found.

Vevea, Clements, and Hedges (1993) conducted a study on the General Aptitude Test Battery (GATB) to answer the question if selection bias existed as critics suggest. The GATB is an assessment tool designed to measure nine cognitive, perceptual, and psychomotor skills that are thought to predict job performance. Critics believe that not all cases were included in the database, and therefore, a possibility exists that selection bias has occurred. Vevea et al. (1993) did find in some components of the GATB that selection bias did occur in the database.

This leads to another problem with selection bias. Rosenthal (1979) referred to selection bias as the *file drawer effect*: acknowledging there are many studies that are conducted in research that are not published that show nonsignificant results. This is critical because you cannot know exactly how many studies are conducted on your topic of interest because many of these studies are typically not reported or published in journals.

Box 5.5   **Internal Validity Threats**

1. Selection – participants differ from each other at the start of the experiment.

2. Ambiguous temporal precedence – cause must precede an effect, but it may not be known whether the cause preceded the effect.

3. History – an event that may occur during the beginning, middle, or end of the experiment could have produced the effect in the absence of a treatment.

4. Attrition – loss of participants from the beginning to end of the experiment.

5. Maturation – natural changes over the course of time occur regardless of the presence of a treatment.

6. Regression to the mean – participants selected to participate based on extreme high (low) scores on a measure will likely decrease (increase) to the average score on the measure.

7. Testing – test scores on a posttest may be influenced by pretest scores.

8. Instrumentation – an instrument used to measure a variable may change over the course of time even in the absence of the treatment.

Ambiguous Temporal Precedence

When conducting an experiment, they are designed for the purpose of manipulating a variable to determine the effect that this manipulated variable has on the measured variable. In the event that the cause does not precede the effort or if it is unknown whether the cause precedes the effect, then this is referred to as ambiguous temporal precedence. Ambiguous temporal precedence is typically not an issue with experimental design features because the manipulation or intervention is controlled to take place prior to the measurement or intended effect (Edwards & Bagozzi, 2000). Survey research, nonexperimental research, and correlational research do not have the rigor of experimental features to guarantee the cause precedes the effect, and therefore, ambiguous temporal precedence could result in an alternative explanation for the effect.

As an example, Pawar (2009) conducted a study to integrate workplace spirituality with four organizational behavior concepts, which were transformational leadership, organizational citizenship behavior, organizational support, and procedural justice. All four of these concepts have been shown to be interrelated and can take the role of antecedents or outcomes. This creates the possibility that either of these concepts can precede workplace spirituality. Additionally, based on the literature, the four organizational behavior concepts emerged around the 1980s, which precedes the workplace spirituality concept that emerged in the 1990s. Pawar (2009) indicates that these four concepts are precursors to workplace spirituality based on time of emergence and not suggesting that they are the cause of workplace spirituality. The discussion of which came first, the four organizational behavior concepts or workplace spirituality, is not the issue. What is most important is that Pawar (2008) highlights the complexity of concepts emerging in the literature and whether or not they are precursors to another concept.

History

A history threat is when any potential event that occurs from the start to completion of the experiment could explain the relationship between the cause and effect. This threat can be potentially challenging to deal with in field settings because it is possible that any event external to the study could explain the cause and effect relationship. However, plausibility of a history threat can be reduced when the researcher carefully considers as many extraneous variables as possible.

In a study utilizing data collected from Danish health care employees, Randall, Nielsen, and Tvedt (2009) examined employee well-being and satisfaction after an intervention had occurred. This intervention affected all participants in the study; whereby, the intervention reorganized work groups into teams, and data was collected before and after the intervention. While the results of the study showed that there is some relationship between outcome measures and intervention processes, the results may have been driven more by the behavior of the manager and possibly the history of the time compared to the actual intervention. This is important because while the results of the study were positive, the researchers also recognized that their findings may have been impacted by a history effect of not measuring the manager behavior or history of the team. Similarly, the manager observing employee behavior resulting in the Hawthorne Effect at Western Electric could have been a result of history effects by not accounting for this behavior.

Attrition

Attrition may also be referred to as mortality, experimental mortality, or differential attrition. Regardless of what this threat is called, it occurs when participants fail to complete all components of the experiment or the participant drops out of the study. When attrition occurs, the remaining participants in the experiment may be different than the ones that drop out, which creates a bias in the experiment. In other words, attrition not only impacts the internal validity of the study but differential attrition can impact the external validity of the results as well (Cook & Campbell, 1979). Additionally, this is one threat that cannot be controlled for by random assignment but can be less plausible when implementing a control group.

Attrition is more problematic with longitudinal experiments, but any research design may result in participants deciding not to complete the entire experiment. Sitzmann and Ely (2010) conducted a longitudinal study that examined whether or not self-regulatory processes would mediate the effects of prompting self-regulation on reducing attrition of online learning. A total of 479 adults were recruited for a training intervention that involved free Microsoft Excel training that consisted of a 4-hour online course divided into four modules. In terms of attrition, 161 participants started the course but withdrew before completing the first module, 173 participants completed at least one module, and 145 participants completed all modules. Self-regulation was found to be the strongest form of the intervention that resulted in an attrition rate that was 17% lower for participants continuously prompted with self-regulation compared to the control. Despite these findings, one of the limitations to the study is that 161 participants withdrew prior to completing the first module, so it is possible that the results of the study may be due to differential attrition.

Maturation

As time passes, changes in behavior are expected to occur. These natural changes that occur during the course of the experiment have the potential to explain the causal relationship found within the study. This suggests that the cause and effect relationship may have occurred naturally even in the absence of the intervention. For example, Terrion (2006) conducted a study examining the impact that a 2001 management training program consisting of 13 different modules would have on improving management skills, improving productivity, and changing corporate culture. Despite the fact that six positive themes emerged from the results, Terrion (2006) recognizes that as a result of time passing since the completion of the first module, the change in behavior of these administrators may have been a result of maturation rather than the 13 modules on management training.

Regression to the Mean

Regression to the mean may also be referred to as regression artifacts or regression. This is said to occur when participants are selected for their high (low) scores on a given measure because it is expected that on subsequent measures a participant will regress toward the mean value on the measure. This is problematic for quasi-experimental designs (see Chapter 8 for quasi-experimental designs) that may select participants based on specific criteria or any design where a pre- and posttest are involved.

As an example, Grant (2008) conducted three different field experiments that task significance had on job performance with the first and third field experiment focusing on fundraising callers soliciting donations for a university and the second field experiment focusing on life guards protecting swimmers at a recreation center. While the results of all three field experiments showed that task significance had an impact on job performance in two different industries, regression to the mean with these experiments could possibly explain this relationship. Grant (2008) recognizes that employees in the task significance and control conditions started with lower levels of performance compared to employees in the personal benefit condition prior to the manipulation of the intervention. Therefore, by virtue of regression to the mean, it is possible that job performance levels may converge over time. However, this is unlikely to be the case since task significance was replicated over three field experiments with different samples, but small sample sizes between the three experiments make it worth mentioning regression to the mean as a potential threat to internal validity.

Testing

Throughout the discussion of experimental research designs (Chapter 7), quasi-experimental research designs (Chapter 8), nonexperimental research designs (Chapter 9), and survey research designs (Chapter 10), the utility of a pretest and posttest may enhance the validity of the results. However, a possibility exists that the scores on the pretest may influence the participants' responses on the posttest. Thus, a testing effect becomes a possible threat to the validity of the research design whenever a pretest and posttest is utilized.

Oostrom, Bos-Broekema, Serlie, Born, and Van der Molen (2012) examined pretest and posttest reactions on differences between in-basket exercises through comparing paper-and-pencil to computerized versions. Applicants were administered a pretest measuring reactions to the test and then administered the posttest measuring the same reactions to the test. They found that general beliefs in tests had an impact on pretest reactions and that test performance had an influence on posttest reactions. Therefore, it is possible that when pretests and posttest are the same then posttest scores can be influenced by pretest measures.

Instrumentation

Instrumentation is when there is a change in the instrument used to measure the variable over time that may occur even in the absence of a treatment. This threat differs from testing because testing implies a change in the participant from one measure to the next and instrumentation implies a change in the instrument used to collect the measure. Throughout employment selection, drug testing is becoming a common method utilized for preemployment within the United States (Ozminkowski, Mark, Cangianelli, & Walsh, 2001). As a result, there are multiple tests that can be utilized for drug testing.

The urinalysis test is the most common method of drug testing and was found to result in a false-positive, which means that participants were identified as testing positive for drugs when they did not, a rate of between 0% to 66% (Harris & Heft, 1993). With that said, Kravitz and Brock (1997) conducted three experiments examining the use of drug-testing scenarios and found that the drug-testing programs were significantly affected by false-positive rates. The use of various drug testing initiatives for employment selections creates the need to ensure that instrumentation minimizes the false-positive rate.

Internal Validity Summary

Internal validity threats are the most common threats that are found in research with that most articles reported at least one threat to internal validity (Brutus et al., 2010). However, internal validity threats within research are not limited to one threat because multiple threats to internal validity can be present within the same study. What this means is that several internal validity threats may occur simultaneously that can create multiple problems for research studies. There are multiple methods for reducing threats to validity with random assignment being the most effective. The use of random assignment does not guarantee that all threats to internal validity are reduced. In fact, random assignment may introduce new nuisance threats that may not have been thought of (Corrigan & Salzer, 2003). However, there are additional research design elements that can be added to a study to reduce threats to internal validity.

CONCLUSION OF STATISTICAL CONCLUSION AND INTERNAL VALIDITY

Throughout the discussion of statistical conclusion validity and internal validity, it is apparent that both types of validity deal with the covariation of the cause and effect relationship. The difference between statistical conclusion validity and internal validity is how this covariation is examined. In general, statistical conclusion validity deals with the concerns that the statistics used in the analysis of the results were appropriate to ensure that the cause and effect relationship covaries accurately, whereas internal validity is concerned with the appropriateness that the covariation of the cause and effect relationship was directly due to the way the variables were being manipulated or measured. In conclusion, when statistics are not used appropriately or there are differences between participants prior to the start of an experiment, then a possibility exists that the cause and effect relationship can be explained by other variables. The overall goal of learning about these threats to the covariation of the relationship between the cause and effect variables is to ensure that proper precautions can be made to enhance the validity of this covariation.

CHAPTER SUMMARY

- Validity and reliability are two concepts that are integral to improving the results of the experiment by ensuring the findings are both consistent and reliable. For results to be accurate, they must be consistent, but results can be consistent and not accurate. There are four main categories of validity: statistical conclusion and internal, external, and construct validity.

- Statistical conclusion validity is related to the covariation of the cause and effect relationship and the appropriateness of the statistical procedures used to analyze the results of an experiment. There are three different categories of threats associated with statistical conclusion validity, and they are through the design of the methodology, measurement of the variables, and components of the statistical analysis.

- Internal validity is related to the covariation of the cause and effect relationship that was due to the manipulation of the cause, and no other variable can explain the relationship. There are many threats related to alternative explanation for the cause and effect relationship. Many of these threats can be reduced through the use of random assignment.

DISCUSSION QUESTIONS

- Similar to Box 5.1, create your own example using everyday items to explain the relationship between validity and reliability.

- What tips and techniques would you provide a beginning researcher/practitioner with to develop a study that minimizes threats to statistical conclusion validity?

- Although internal validity threats can be reduced through the use of randomization, not all studies/interventions can use random assignment. What threats to internal validity are the most important to reduce and why?

CHAPTER KEY TERMS

Ambiguous Temporal
    Precedence
Attrition
Extraneous Variance in
    Experimental Setting
Fishing and Error Rate
Heterogeneity of Units
History
Inaccurate Effect Size
    Estimation
Instrumentation

Low Statistical Power
Maturation
Regression to the Mean
Reliability
Restriction of Range
Selection
Testing
Treatment Sensitive
    Factorial Structure
Unreliability
    of Measures

Unreliability of
    Treatment
    Implementation
Validity
Validity, Construct
Validity, External
Validity, Internal
Validity, Statistical
    Conclusion
Violated Assumptions
    of Tests

Construct and External Validity

The conversation of recruitment and selection comes up multiple times. Whether the conversation is between our students or professional colleagues, the end result is usually very similar. The purpose of earning a college degree is to expand your skillset and pursue your desired career path. The continuum of a career path begins at various points in your professional life. You could be a 22-year-old recent graduate from college or you could be a 43-year-old returning to college to begin a new career path. How do you convince a recruiter that the knowledge, skills, and abilities you acquired in college or your professional life will transfer to another industry or different career path?

This is a common issue for job seekers—to transfer the competencies or skills they have acquired in their life into translating their potential on a resume. Students in our classes have often questioned how their job as a lifeguard or server translates into a management professional position in corporate or how being in a retail management position for 20 years can translate into a position in the financial industry. The issue of translating competencies from one industry to another is the same as research generalizing the results from one study to another. These issues with generalizations are referred to as external validity because the goal is to demonstrate that the results in one study can be generalized to another study and competencies learned as a lifeguard can translate to a position in organizational development.

For example, a server at a restaurant learns a new skill of time management by being able to effectively balance multiple priorities to ensure that all meals are served appropriately. The definition of time management in a restaurant setting may differ from time management in a professional position, but the underlying skill or competency is most likely the same. The question of being able to take your time management skill from the restaurant industry to another industry is related to **external validity**. The question of how to appropriately define time management is related to **construct validity**.

These questions and others relate to the validity of the results. Determining if this time management dimension is relevant from a construct validity perspective as well as being representative for two different candidates is an important component to validity. External and construct validity are

> **external validity:** Generalizability of the cause and effect relationship across changes in the participants, settings, treatments, or the outcomes
>
> **construct validity:** Generalizability that the variables used in a study represent the variable they intend to measure

concerned with the generalization of the results of the experiment. In other words, is the relationship between measuring time management skills for a server in the restaurant industry to a professional position in the financial industry the same? When conducting an experiment, a goal for any researcher would be able to state that the results found in their study also applies to other situations.

Another goal would be to state that the constructs utilized in the experiment actually measure the intended construct or variable. In other words, does time management in the service industry mean the same as time management in the management consulting industry? If not, then it is important to provide a clear definition for how time management is actually defined and being measured. Whenever there is a question of stating the generalizability of the cause and effect relationship or the variables used in the study, then there may be a threat to external or construct validity, respectively.

EXTERNAL VALIDITY

As previously mentioned, external validity is concerned with the generalizability of the cause and effect relationship across changes in the participants, settings, treatments, or the outcomes. Any question related to this relationship or other variations in participants, settings, treatment, or outcomes for participants that may impact the cause and effect relationship is related to threats of external validity. Scandura and Williams (2000) conducted a review of over 700 empirical research studies in three top-tier management journals between 1985 to 1987 and 1995 to 1997. They found a shift in research toward field studies. While field studies offer realism, the main trade-off found was in relation to a low external validity.

Similarly, Brutus and Duniewicz (2012) reviewed 174 research articles published in *The Leadership Quarterly* from 1990 to 2007. They found that 41.1% of the articles were conducted as a field survey and 63.8% of articles had identified threats to external validity. Likewise, Brutus, Gill, and Duniewicz (2010) found that external validity was the third most commonly reported threat to the validity of the research with the most common limitation being the inability to generalize results across people such as age, gender, students, volunteers, etc. These issues of generalizability can be categorized into four areas. As a consumer of information or a researcher, throughout your evaluation of results, you may ask yourself four questions:

1. Would these results of this experiment be the same with a different sample?
2. Would the results of a laboratory experiment generalize to a field setting?
3. Would the results be the same if the intervention is combined with another intervention or if there is a modification to the existing intervention?
4. Would the results be the same if another variable was measured?

These questions are all related to the extent to which the results of the existing research would be the same if there was variability within the experiment. Pinpointing when each question may apply is a challenge because multiple threats to external validity may be present within each study. For example, a field experiment conducted in the military (Van Iddekinge, Putka, & Campbell, 2011) to examine performance could have threats related to the participants, setting, treatment, or outcome. The participants could be a threat because military professionals may react differently than civilians in that they are contractually obligated to stay at their job. The setting could also be a threat on the basis of the military operating differently than a nonmilitary organization. The treatment or intervention of the Work Preferences Survey (WPS) utilizing 72 items to measure six scales could be used to predict placement or selection as intended by the military. The outcome could be a threat if the WPS was used in conjunction with other measures of job performance to select participants.

With that being said, Shadish, Cook, and Campbell (2002) recognized four threats to external validity in relation to variations in the cause and effect relationship on the basis of different participants, settings, treatments, or outcomes.

1. Variation in participants – a cause and effect relationship with the participants in the experiment may not hold when different participants are included in the experiment.

2. Variation in settings – a cause and effect relationship in one setting may not hold in another setting.

3. Variation in treatments – a cause and effect relationship with one treatment may not hold if the treatment is varied or combined with other components of different treatment.

4. Variation in outcomes – an effect found in an experiment may not hold if other outcome observations are used.

Variation in Participants

At the conclusion of an experiment, a researcher may question if the results of the experiment with the selected sample would be true if another sample of participants were used. Being the third most reported limitation in research (Brutus et al., 2010), variation in participants could be based on age, gender, student versus nonstudent, etc. The purpose of variation in participants is to state that the results found in a field experiment of younger employees is generalizable to older employees. As an example, Grant (2008) conducted three field experiments on the relationship between task significance and job performance. Within these three field experiments, Grant (2008) recognized that the sample in the three experiments consisted primarily of younger employees and future research should focus on older, more experienced employees to determine if this relationship holds.

Variation in Settings

When planning a research design, it is possible that a researcher may want to state that the results of the experiment in one setting would also be similar to the results of an experiment conducted in another setting. One of the criticisms with variation in settings is that laboratory experiments are not generalizable to field settings. However, in a review of both laboratory and field studies, Anderson, Lindsay, and Bushman (1999) found that laboratory and field study results are similar. Subsequently, Mitchell (2012) further replicated results found by Anderson et al. (1999) that there is a relationship between laboratory and field studies.

The laboratory to field setting is not the only issue with variation in settings. Van Iddekinge et al. (2011) conducted an experiment utilizing participants in the military that involved collecting data on performance requirements to examine the validity of technical job knowledge, interpersonal job knowledge, ratings of job performance, and continuance intentions. Despite the promising results found from this study, the first limitation brought up was the fact that the study was conducted using the military. It is unknown if these results would be found within nonmilitary organizations because contracts within the military make it more difficult for military employees to leave their job.

These examples shed light on the wide range of variability within generalizing results to different settings. When evaluating research, it is important to know the setting in which the current research is conducted. Not all research will be generalizable to every setting, but future research that is conducted within different settings will enhance the validity of the results and allow for generalizing results across settings.

Variation in Treatments

After the conclusion of an experiment, a researcher may desire to alter or change the treatment during this experiment. If this is the case, then the researcher would want to be certain that the cause and effect relationship would hold over changes in a treatment that include varying levels of treatment, combining the treatment with different components of another treatment, or a treatment used in one setting having the same impact as another setting. Stone-Romero (2002) provides an example of a treatment (i.e., sensitivity training) working in one setting but not another. This treatment may be similar to the WPS intervention used to predict placement or advancement in the military (Van Iddekinge et al., 2011) and the same effect being found in a nonmilitary setting.

Variation in Outcomes

A possibility exists that a researcher may desire to measure additional variables after the conclusion of an experiment. When this occurs, the researcher still desires to find the same results when other outcomes are used. In other words, this means that the same outcome of job performance defined by Van Iddekinge et al. (2011) should be the same in another situation if job performance is combined with personality variables or any other variable that is added. The question of external validity would be if this same outcome was found in another situation. However, it is possible that when additional outcomes are used that the same cause and effect relationship may not be found.

For example, in the military study conducted by Van Iddekinge et al. (2011) utilizing the Work Preferences Survey (WPS), it should have the same results on job performance if personality variables (i.e., conscientiousness or emotional stability from the Big Five Factors) were added. Van Iddekinge et al. (2011) recognized a possibility that faking behaviors may occur, which could potentially have an impact on the outcome of a job incumbent versus a job applicant. Further, Morgeson et al. (2007) identified faking as a potential concern for personality tests used in selection for the reason that job incumbents are less likely to engage in faking compared to job applicants. This is important because the outcome of job performance has the potential to be different when combined with other measures.

External Validity Summary

In conclusion, external validity is defined as the extent to which the results hold across variation in participants (Grant, 2008), settings (Anderson et al., 1999; Mitchell, 2012; Van Iddekinge et al., 2011), treatments (Stone-Romero, 2002), and outcomes (Morgeson et al., 2007; Van Iddekinge et al., 2011) and strengthens the validity of various interventions. The threats to external validity are closely related to each other, as Van Iddeking et al. (2011) identify a possibility that the setting or outcome may be different if the study was taken out of the military context and used on job applicants in a nonmilitary setting. As researchers may shift away from controlled laboratory studies and toward field studies in human resource management (Scandura & Williams, 2000) and leadership research (Brutus & Duniewicz, 2012), the issue of realism increases, but the external validity of field studies decreases. To reduce threats to external validity, validation studies (i.e., Anderson et al., 1999; Mitchell, 2012) can be conducted or future research can be conducted to replicate previous research with variations in participants, settings, treatments, or outcomes.

CONSTRUCT VALIDITY

The last type of validity is construct validity, and it is related to the extent to which the variables in an experiment represent the constructs they are intended to measure. Brutus et al. (2010) ranks this as the second most commonly reported limitations in research with the most common issue of a *less than ideal* way of operationalizing constructs in the study. Similarly, Rogelberg and Brooks-Laber (2004) argue that one of the main challenges faced in research is not having good measures or blindly relying on measures that lack construct validity.

Within research and everyday life, operational definitions are paramount in ensuring that the constructs utilized in a study are defined in a specific and clear manner. Whenever there is an issue with how a particular variable is measured or manipulated, then this is an issue of construct validity. Shadish et al. (2002) identify construct validity as being important for three reasons:

1. Constructs connect the information used within experiments to theory

2. Constructs have specific labels that carry implications

3. Constructs are continually created and defended

Box 6.1 **Construct Validity From a Practitioner and Researcher Perspective**

When speaking with various practitioners on the importance of construct validity, a common theme emerged from our conversations. Most of the practitioners made reference to assessment centers. The assessment center has been used since World War II for the Office of Strategic Services (OSS) to select secret service agents (Murray & MacKinnon, 1946). An assessment center is a selection method in which candidates are put through a battery of tests to determine if they are a good fit for a position. Assessment centers are not only discussed from a practitioner point of view, but they are also prevalent in the literature.

In addition to conversations with current practitioners, Lance (2008) wrote a focal article on the construct validity problem of assessment centers stating that they do not appear to measure the constructs they are intended to measure. He suggests two contrasting explanations: (1) Assessment centers were not designed to optimally assess constructs and could be reengineered, and (2) researchers have been asking the wrong questions about construct validity. In the end, assessment centers do well at measuring behaviors on specific exercises, but performance is not consistent across exercises. In response to this focal article, Rupp, Thornton, and Gibbons (2008) offer four arguments in favor of assessment centers being construct valid for measuring performance, and evidence shows that researchers should shift toward supporting the validity evidence that assessment centers measure the intended performance constructs. Similarly, Arthur, Day, and Woehr (2008) disagree with Lance (2008) and believe that assessment centers are construct valid but fail to engage in appropriate tests. In conclusion, there are many differing views in regards to the construct validity of assessment centers as brought up by Lance (2008) and subsequently followed-up by multiple commentaries in the 2008 Volume 1 of *Industrial and Organizational Psychology.*

Following Lance's (2008) focal article on assessment centers, Bowler and Woehr (2009) examined assessment centers from a construct validity perspective in an attempt to shed some light on the construct validity differentiation with assessment centers that has been happening over the past 20 years. The overall goal of this particular study was to examine the construct validity of assessment centers using a confirmatory factor analysis and a generalizability theory-based variance partitioning approach. The end result was that various methods used to statistically analyze the construct validity of an assessment center are possible. Additionally, it is feasible for assessors to be able to differentiate between individual performance in an assessment center from a reliability and construct validity point of view. From a research perspective, it is possible to statistically differentiate between construct measures in an assessment center to ensure the validity of the measures (Bowler & Woehr, 2009). With that being said, construct validity is a critical component to operationalizing variables within the experiment.

The purpose of construct validity and operational definitions is to be able to explicitly state how the researcher intends to measure or manipulate the higher order construct. Imagine searching scholarly articles for how the construct of performance is defined. There would be a vast array of topics and definitions for how these variables are defined. Having construct valid measures ensures that everyone reading the article will interpret the construct in the same exact way the researcher intended to use it. Construct validity is comprised of many different threats that can be grouped into the following three main categories:

1. Definition of Variables

2. Researcher/Participant Issues

3. Implementation of Design

Box 6.2   Construct Validity Threats

1. Definition of Variables
   a. Inadequate explication of constructs – researcher does not adequately explain the construct that may lead to incorrect conclusions about the variable and the construct it is meant to measure.
   b. Mono-method bias – researchers using one method to measure the dependent variable.
   c. Construct confounding – variables are complex and confounding occurs when a researcher does not adequately explain all constructs.
   d. Confounding constructs with levels of constructs – variables that do not account all possible levels of a construct may confound the results by not allowing a researcher to generalize results to the entire construct.

2. Researcher/Participant Issues
   a. Reactive self-report changes – participants required to respond to measures may be influenced when researchers ask participants to self-report measures.
   b. Reactivity to the experimental situation – participants may engage in a behavior to anticipate what the researcher is trying to study.
   c. Experimenter expectancies – expectancies from the researcher may influence the responses of the participants.
   d. Novelty and disruption effects – participants may respond well to a novel idea or poor to one that interferes with their routine.
   e. Compensatory equalization – when researchers provide compensation to the participant group not receiving the treatment.
   f. Compensatory rivalry – participants that do not receive the treatment may be motivated to do as well as the treatment group.
   g. Resentful demoralization – participants not receiving the treatment may become resentful and change their responses to the outcome measures.

3. Implementation of Design
   a. Treatment sensitive factorial structure – change in structure of the measure may be a result of the treatment.
   b. Treatment diffusion – participants not within the treatment group may receive parts of the treatment.
   c. Mono-operation bias – one operationalization of the independent variable may underrepresent the construct of interest and measure irrelevant constructs.

Definition of Variables

The first category of threats revolves around the definition of variables. The primary focus of these threats is on how the actual variables are defined within the study. Through understanding how to properly define constructs, the researcher ensures that the variables measured or manipulated in an experiment are the actual variables that were intended to be used. We already know from Brutus et al. (2010) that the second most commonly reported limitation is by defining constructs in research in a *less than ideal* way. Therefore, it is critically important to ensure that the constructs within research are explicitly defined.

These three threats are plausible whenever a researcher does not adequately explain the variables that are being used in an experiment. From a defining variable point of view, researchers have often relied on the use of content analysis for the purpose of resolving the construct measurement problems within experiments (Duriau, Reger, & Pfarrer, 2007; Morris, 1994; Short, Brobert, Cogliser, & Brigham, 2010). Content analysis is a computerized technique for researchers to analyze text to classify constructs (Morris, 1994). This allows researchers the ability to assess the construct validity of the measures to determine the adequacy with which these measures are defined utilizing a variety of techniques (Short et al., 2010). These techniques would provide an alternative for assessing the adequacy with which the variables within a research study are valid.

Inadequate Explication of Constructs

A possibility exists when a researcher does not adequately define a construct being used in an experiment that could cause the researcher to conclude incorrect results. In regards to construct validity threats, a less than ideal operationalization of the construct is the most widely reported threat when conducting research (Brutus et al., 2010). In the realm of leadership research, when examining the leader-member exchange theory for assessing leaders and subordinates, it is important that the constructs used with these measures are properly defined. When constructs are not adequately defined, there is a chance that ratings on these measures are different.

As an example, in reviewing research on leader-member exchange theory, the actual way in which items are written can potentially influence responses. Leader-member exchange theory is based on examining the quality of the relationship between a leader and a subordinate. It is expected that ratings on these behaviors between both groups should likely converge to some extent. In fact, Schriesheim, Wu, and Cooper (2011) conducted two studies comprised of MBA students to examine if item wording and content is the cause of poor leader-member exchange convergence. They found that in the case of leaders and subordinates rating behaviors, the wording and content of the measures introduced biases that lead to poor convergence between leaders and subordinate rating. This highlights the importance of properly defining the constructs used within a study.

Mono-Method Bias

This threat to construct validity is related to how the constructs are measured and pertains to the dependent variable only. This is a contrast to mono-operation bias, which is discussed later, that pertains to the operationalization of the independent variable. When a researcher uses the same method to collect all the data, then this is referred to as a mono-method bias. Using multiple methods to collect data may be useful, but many different methods used to collect the same data may influence the results. Therefore, it is likely that this threat may occur in studies. In order to reduce the plausibility of this threat, a researcher can conduct multiple studies utilizing different methods of collecting data on the construct.

In reviewing the existing literature on assessment centers, it is important to note a discrepancy between the existing literature could be a result of mono-method bias. Assessment centers are used to evaluate potential candidates for a position through the use of a battery of tests. The method used to evaluate the effectiveness of assessment centers was a confirmatory factor analysis approach to a multitrait-multimethod matrix, which has resulted in an inconsistency with results. The models within their study show that relying on empirical criteria to determine model fit may be problematic. The true models may not be the best fit and the false models may be a better fit than the true model (Lance, Woehr, & Meade, 2007).

When taking this information into consideration, it is possible that you may conclude that a battery of tests used in an assessment center may not be the most valid representation of selecting a candidate for a position. This is a case of relying of mono-method bias because in a subsequent study, Bowler and Woehr (2009) utilized both the confirmatory factor analytic technique and a variance partitioning procedure to analyze the effectiveness of ratings in an assessment center. The overall results were that using multiple methods is the most effective way to assess the utility of assessment centers. Therefore, this highlights the potential that relying only on one method may paint an incorrect picture.

Construct Confounding

Defining variables is complex because the operationalized variable is rarely a pure representation of the actual construct that it is intended to measure. This results when the researcher does not adequately explain all constructs or portions of one construct are confounded in another. It can be argued that any construct could be challenged in regards to the fact that the construct of interest either underrepresents the construct of interest or it is contaminated by other factors that are irrelevant to the construct of interest (Cook & Campbell, 1979).

As an example, measuring satisfaction can be complex because it is possible that a measure of performance can be confounded with other variables. For example, satisfaction is often shown to be highly correlated with loyalty and positive word-of-mouth (Masick, Shapiro, & O'Neal, 2010). Therefore, you could argue that the high correlation between variables may mean that factors within satisfaction may also be measured by factors found in loyalty and positive word-of-mouth. This means that measures of satisfaction may be contaminated with loyalty and positive word-of-mouth due to the high correlation between them.

Confounding Constructs With Levels of Constructs

As has been discussed, variables are typically not simplistic. It takes a lot of research and precision to define variables appropriately. In addition to the confounding that may occur with other constructs or not adequately explaining the construct, a researcher also needs to be concerned with confounding constructs that are different levels of the construct of interest. This is possible when the researcher does not take into consideration different levels of a construct.

For example, Deloise and Kolb (2008) conducted a study using full-time office professions at a university to examine the effects that ethics training would have on attitudes and knowledge on ethical dilemmas faced by office professionals. Participants were randomly assigned to either a treatment group or a control group. Participants in the treatment groups received three, 2-hour ethics training workshops covering a variety of topics on ethics. Immediately after the training, the treatment group scored statistically significantly higher than the control group, but this statistically significant effect did not last for the 90 day measurement. While the article did not specifically mention confounding constructs with levels of constructs as a threat, ethics training is highly complex and could consist of multiple levels. Sekerka (2009) provides an overview of ethics training with best practices and application. Developing a training program on ethics is highly complex with multiple levels associated with the training. It is possible that Deloise and Kolb (2008) found promising results with one particular training, but in reality, this may only be one of many levels of ethics training.

Researcher/Participant Issues

In addition to the threats of defining the construct as previously mentioned, there are other potential threats to construct validity. These next several threats pertain to construct issues that are related to the researcher/participant. The reason these are construct validity threats is due to how participants or researchers experience these variables in an experiment. For constructs to be perceived appropriately in an experiment, it is important that these threats are reduced. These particular threats are prevalent in survey research where participants are asked questions on particular attitudes and behaviors.

Reactivity to Self-Report Changes

A common issue with research design is when participants engage in self-report. Experiments that require participants to fill out information based on their self-perceptions are almost always a threat to self-report. This is highly problematic for survey research designs (see Chapter 10 for further discussions on survey research designs) because a participant's attitude or behavior may change based on providing their own responses to a survey.

Self-report ratings can be problematic and result in an inflation of self-ratings as compared to non-self-ratings (Ng & Feldman, 2012). Ng and Feldman (2012) conducted a study comparing self-ratings and non-self-report ratings on employee creativity. Due to the changing nature of organizations, employers are looking to creative employees as a method to streamline business processes and improve productivity (Gotsi, Andriopoulos, Lewis, & Ingram, 2010). The issue in what measures best reflect true creativity. To compare and contrast measures of self-report versus non-self-report, Ng and Feldman (2012) explored this phenomenon and found that self-ratings are more inflated than non-self-ratings. Overall, to overcome the inflated self-ratings would be to utilize multiple sources to validate the self-ratings.

Reactivity to the Experimental Situation

In addition to the researchers having to worry about participants reacting to self-report, they also have to worry about participants' reactions to the experimental setting. It is possible that participants may try to anticipate what the researcher is examining and respond accordingly to provide the researcher with results they want to see. A classic example of this type of phenomenon is known as the Hawthorne Effect. In the 1930s, a series of studies known as the Hawthorne studies were published. The studies took place at the Hawthorne plant of the Western Electric Company in the Chicago area. The main purpose of these studies was to see if factors such as lighting conditions, work schedules, salary, temperature, or breaks had an impact on performance. The end result was not what was expected because the variation in working conditions did not have the intended effect on performance. That is, an employee's performance may have increased after making conditions worse, such as decreasing the lighting or performance decreased after making conditions better, such as increasing the lighting. Upon further exploration of these findings, researchers interviewed employees to debrief. The results of this debrief was that performance changed because the employees were receiving attention from their managers (Aamodt, 2007).

Experimenter Expectancies

This particular threat is opposite of what the reactivity to the experimental situation is. With this threat, the researcher may be conveying expectations about the particular experiment to participants. Therefore, participants may be inclined to provide responses that coincide with what the researcher believes. This is slightly contrasting the previous threat because this one has to do with researchers placing emphasis on the purpose of the experiment, whereas the previous threat is related to the participants attempting to determine what the purpose of the experiment is. Any study that a researcher conducts involving participant interaction could result in the researcher influencing the results. This expectation may be part of a self-fulfilling prophecy to achieve the results you expect to find. Vecchio (2007) discusses the influence of these self-fulfilling prophecies specifically in organizational settings.

For example, study one of three that Grant (2008) conducted examined a longitudinal experiment using callers at a fundraising organization to measure two job performance measures. In this particular study, he recognized that he has his own personal biases and that these biases may influence the results similar to the self-fulfilling prophecy. Therefore, as an alternative to reducing the threat of experimenter expectancies, Grant (2008) had two research assistants who were used to coordinate the interventions and keep time of the interventions over the course of two days.

Novelty and Disruption Effects

Overall, participants may respond differently to many different types of situations. With this threat, it is possible that participants may respond well to an innovative idea or poorly to one that disrupts their routine. If this occurs, then the response to the situation must be included as part of the operationalization of the construct. Whenever new ideas are introduced, it is possible that participants may become excited and enthusiastic about the new idea. Therefore, the success of the new innovation may have been influenced by the excitement and not the innovation. Similarly, when a new innovation disrupts the work flow, then negative reactions may occur, which could explain the relationship between the innovation and perceptions.

Compensatory Equalization

Sometimes within an experiment, the group not receiving the treatment may be given some compensatory goods or services to equalize the treatment and nontreatment group. The decision to offer compensation to the nontreatment group may occur when the nontreatment group learns about the treatment and therefore, desire to be in the treatment group. As an example, participants that do not receive the training program may desire to do so. In an effort to make both groups equal, the nontreatment group may receive some sort of compensation (i.e., a different training program). This may be problematic in determining a significant difference between the two groups, and the compensation must be included in the operationalization of the variables.

Box 6.3   Market Research

We encounter what could be considered to be novelty or disruption effects quite often. Consider the field of market research. Market research is a growing field that involves analyzing trends in television viewing behavior, product purchasing, or any other variable that can be used to understand attitudes, preferences, and behaviors that consumers may have on products. The mobile phone world has gone through a major change with the introduction of smartphones, and companies are competing to gain market share.

Seva, Gosiaco, Santos, and Pangilinan (2011) conducted an experiment on attributes related to the aesthetic perception of a mobile phone and found that the aesthetics of the mobile phone could elicit affect and perception of usability. In a separate study, Mugge and Schoormans (2012) examined product appearance and usability of the product using a washing machine and digital camera. In the first study with the washing machine, the black washing machine was determined to be more novel than the white washing machine. The digital camera follow-up was designed to determine if the level of expertise had an impact on usability. In this study, consumer expertise moderated the effect of novelty such that experts and novices have different expectations with regards to a product's usability. Overall, novelty in this case had a negative effect with apparent usability.

These two studies highlight the importance that variations in novelty or disruption effects can have an impact on usability of a product. Whether or not we are aware of these minute details, they can have an impact on how we respond to this information. In this case, novelty could have both a positive and negative impact on a product.

For example, Lievens and Sanchez (2007) conducted a quasi-experiment to examine the impact that frame-of-reference training had on competency model ratings assessed by consultants. Within this study, they randomly assigned consultants to a training or control group. The training group consisted of a full day of a training technique called STAR (situation-task-action-result) interviewing. To reduce any potential biases involved with the control group, this group received a different type of training. This training was used as a means of providing a service to the control group to equalize the treatment provided to the training group. Lievens and Sanchez (2007) also mention that the training for the control group was to prevent the next threat, which is resentful demoralization. Additionally, one study that Grant (2008) conducted examining the impact of task significance on job performance utilized both a treatment and control group. Similar to Lievens and Sanchez (2007), Grant (2008) included a condition comparable to the treatment group to ensure equalization across conditions.

Compensatory Rivalry and Resentful Demoralization

Compensatory rivalry may exist when participants in the control group may try to show that they can do as well as participants in the treatment group. Therefore, competition to outperform the treatment group despite not receiving any of the benefits of the treatment group may cause the researcher to not find statistically significant results. Resentful demoralization is the opposite of compensatory rivalry. In this situation, the participants that receive a less desirable condition or no treatment may become resentful of being placed in that group. Therefore, the result may be participants changing their responses to the outcome measure as a result of not being chosen to participate in the treatment group.

As an example, Grant (2008) conducted three field experiments that examined the impact of task significance on job performance. In all three experiments, there were two conditions that participants could be assigned to. Since it was not possible to isolate the two groups, Grant (2008) recognized that the limitation to the studies is that participants may have spoken to each other about the interventions. The result is that participants may have learned that they have received different manipulations of the independent variable and therefore, altered their behavior for how they were expected to behave or felt apprehension for not receiving the alternate treatment. Thus, the participants could have engaged in compensatory rivalry to perform at a level similar to the alternate treatment condition or resentful demoralization for not being assigned to the alternate treatment.

Implementation of Design

In addition to the researcher or participant issues of construct validity, the last remaining threats are different. These particular threats have to do with how the treatment is implemented in an experiment. Therefore, it is important as a researcher to think about how the experiment is going to be conducted and to ensure that all potential issues within the implementation of the treatment is well thought out. Often times, it is possible that a researcher may not be able to reduce these threats due to the desire to experimentally control the treatment. However, as long as those threats are discussed and understood, then the researcher can suggest that future researchers explore different facets of the construct and design.

Treatment Sensitive Factorial Structure

As discussed with internal validity, instrumentation may change as a result of an absence in treatment. It is also possible that a change in instrumentation can occur as a result of the treatment. In this case, a threat to treatment sensitive factorial structure occurs when the treatment may cause a difference in how participants react to a measure.

Organizations have sought to implement diversity training programs in an effort to curb discrimination issues. In a review of 178 articles investigating diversity training programs, Bezrukova, Jehn, and Spell (2012) found that diversity training can be effective, but there is still a long way to go to fill the gap. One particular example found was that diversity training focused on one demographic group may be problematic due to the possibility that the training highlights the differences between the groups and creates priming effects that could result in discrimination.

The result could be potentially due to this treatment sensitive factorial structure because employees being trained on diversity may have resulted in altered perceptions as a result of the training.

Treatment Diffusion

Despite our best efforts to improve the validity of a study by using a control group and a treatment group, when these groups cannot be completely segregated, there is a possibility that participants in the control group may receive part or all of the treatment. The idea behind treatment diffusion is that when dealing with human subjects, it may not be possible to keep participants from speaking with each other and consequently discussing the intervention.

As mentioned with compensatory rivalry and resentful demoralization, Grant (2008) conducted three field experiments exploring the impact that task significance would have on increasing job performance in different settings (fundraising callers, lifeguards, callers participating in training). Despite the promising results that task significance was shown to increase job performance, Grant (2008) states that it is not possible to rule out treatment diffusion. This is because there is a possibility that within each of the three different experiments that employees may have discussed the interventions and recognized they received different treatments. This conversation could have resulted in an alteration of their behavior.

This makes it challenging to be able to measure the extent to which job performance was impacted by task significance. Therefore, it is best to try to reduce this diffusion from treatment to nontreatment group in order to measure the effects that the task significance has. To accomplish this and if it is feasible, then it is suggested to isolate the participants from one condition to another. However, this may not be possible or practical, so it would be recommended to measure the treatment in both groups to determine the extent to which diffusion has occurred.

Mono-Operation Bias

The last threat to construct validity is mono-operation bias and is related to the operationalization of the independent variable. This is in contrast to mono-method bias that impacts the operationalization of the dependent variable. We know that constructs are extremely complex, and it is challenging to be able to define them appropriately. As Brutus et al. (2010) state, the most common threat to construct validity is when there is a less than ideal operationalization of constructs found within a study. A trend was found where there was an increase in researchers only using one method or source for defining the constructs in a study as opposed to multiple sources or methods (Scandura & Williams, 2000).

With respect to mono-operation bias, this means that the researchers use one intervention to implement in your study. Conducting research can be costly and time consuming, so implementing multiple operationalizations of the same intervention may not be feasible. Researchers may not have the resources necessary to perform multiple interventions. Researchers are not limited to assessing one measure per phenomenon. There are many different methodologies for assessing the effectiveness of an intervention or measuring a variable. Consider the example of job turnover intentions. There are multiple ways this measure can be assessed. Jiang, Liu, McKay, Lee, and Mitchell (2012) conducted a meta-analysis using 52 studies that assessed the relationship between job embeddedness and turnover outcomes. For the purposes of this meta-analysis, turnover was defined as turnover intentions, which included studies with intentions to leave, turnover, exit, quit, or stay (reverse scored). They also included a measure of actual turnover defined as voluntary turnover. On the other hand, DeTienne, Agle, Phillips, and Ingerson (2012) also measured turnover intention but defined it as "simply whether an employee has the objective of self-terminating his or her employment" (p. 380). While both studies use the term *turnover intentions* and found promising results, the definition varies between the two studies. It is common in research that studies use similar terminology but slight variations in the definition.

Construct Validity Summary

As mentioned in the beginning of the chapter, Rogelberg and Brooks-Laber (2004) argued that one of the challenges we face with research is not having a good measure or blindly relying on measures lacking construct validity. This is evident based on the fact that any construct in research can be challenged on the basis of underrepresenting or being contaminated by other factors (Cook & Campbell, 1979). This has led to researchers reporting that the second most commonly reported validity issue in research is construct validity with the most commonly reported threat being a less than ideal operationalization of a construct (Brutus et al., 2010).

Despite the inherent issues with measuring variables well, multiple methodologies exist for establishing construct validity. Two recommendations by Brutus et al. (2010) are "to include multiple operationalizations of the same construct" and to use valid and reliable measures to assess constructs (p. 924). As a means to assess construct validity, researchers have relied on confirmatory or exploratory factor analytic techniques (Scandura & Williams, 2000). Another common technique is the multitrait-multimethod, but Bowler and Woehr (2009) suggest stepping beyond this technique and using a generalizability theory-based variance partitioning approach. Arthur, Woehr, and Maldegen (2000) also found that the generalizability theory-based approach was consistent with the results found using correlational and confirmatory factor analysis techniques. In addition to these recommendations, an alternative methodology would be to utilize computerized content analysis software in order to ensure that the operationalization of the variables is appropriate. This can be achieved using a computer-aided text analysis resulting from inductive and deductive content analysis of the constructs (Short et al., 2010). Regardless of the methodology used to establish construct validity, you must be cognizant of the issues surrounding the operationalization of variables found in research and while conducting research.

OTHER VALIDITIES

Every experiment that is conducted cannot be completely free of threats to validity because all research has at least one threat present in the study (Brutus & Duniewicz, 2012; Brutus et al., 2010). As a researcher, the purpose of understanding all the threats to validity is to create a sound methodology so that you can maximize the accuracy of your interpretation of the results while minimizing threats to validity. As a consumer of information, the purpose of understanding all the threats to validity is to be more informed about the research you are evaluating.

Although the four types of validity (i.e., internal, external, statistical conclusion, and construct validity) were discussed in depth, it is critically important for completeness to discuss other types of validity. Face, content, and criterion-related validities are other types of validity that are similar but different to construct validity. As you know, construct validity deals explicitly with how the operationalization of the variables examined in an experiment truly represent the construct or variable they were designed to measure. Face, content, and criterion-related validity can be associated with how these variables are defined but for different reasons within the realm of evaluating a research design.

Face Validity

Face and content validity may often be confused as the same type of validity. However, from a conceptual perspective, these two types of validity serve different purposes. When asking the question, "Is a test or measure face valid?" this is not meant to be a reflection of the validity of the constructs in a research design but rather, at a quick glance, Does this test or measure appear to examine what it is intended to measure? Face validity by definition answers the question, "Does this test or measure appear to look like it is valid?" but the operationalization of the variables is not a concern. Smither, Reilly, Millsap, Pearlman, and Stoffey (1993) provide a set of measures that have been used and validated that assesses face validity.

In terms of the impact of face validity on participants, Oostrom, Bos-Broekema, Serlie, Born, and Van der Molen (2012) conducted a pretest and posttest study to measure face validity perceptions of a paper-and-pencil compared to computerized in-basket exercise. The results of the pretest face validity of the paper-and-pencil in-basket test were not different from pretest face validity results of the computerized in-basket test. This indicates that face validity perceptions are the same regardless of the type of tool.

In a separate study, Ployhart, Zieger, and McFarland (2003) manipulated face validity as a variable to understand the impact of cognitive ability tests and stereotype threats in a selection setting for a retail management position. Face validity was manipulated through an alteration of the test's appearance and changing the test name and item format. They found that face validity can have an impact on applicant perceptions. While face validity may not be considered one of the main categories of validity, it is critically important to take into consideration. There is a possibility that how applicants or participants view a test may have an effect on test performance (Oostrom et al., 2012; Ployhart et al., 2003).

Content Validity

Content validity may also be related to construct validity, and it is possible that researchers might confuse these two concepts. As you know, construct validity is defined as the extent to which the measures used in the study assess the construct of interest. Content validity is defined as if the items on the test or measure represent the content of the material that is being measured. It is important to contrast the differences between content and construct validity. When the term *construct validity* is discussed, the purpose is to ensure that the construct you are measuring is appropriately operationalized to assess the construct of interest. Therefore, construct validity is assessed based on the measures included within the study. With respect to content validity, the purpose is to ensure that the information contained within the measure is reflective in the content of the test. Therefore, content validity is assessed by subject matter experts that are able to differentiate between a theoretical definition and an empirical measurement (Nunnally & Bernsetin, 1994).

There is a debate within the utility of content validity as a means to assess the validity of a test. In a study linking O*Net job analysis to job requirement predictors, Jeanneret and Strong (2003) found that the relationship between the content of the job and content of the test can be high when the two are related. Contrary to this, Brown, Le, and Schmidt (2006) examined specific aptitude theory and training performance and found that there was no relationship between the content of the test and the content of the job.

Criterion-Related Validity

Similar to the previous discussion with face and content validity, criterion-related validity is also related to construct validity. Criterion-related validity is used to examine the extent to which the researcher examines how much the current test or measure is related to some specified criteria. In other words, a criterion measure could be job performance, and there could be multiple variables such as cognitive ability tests or personality measures that can be used to predict the criterion of job performance. To complicate matters, there are four different types of criterion-related validity: convergent, discriminant, concurrent, and predictive validity. A researcher can assess the criterion-related validity through examining measures that are determined to be either theoretically similar or different (convergent and discriminant validity, respectively) or benchmarking against the same or a different population (concurrent and predictive validity, respectively). The main difference between convergent and discriminant validity is related to the construct. Convergent involves conceptually similar

Box 6.4 The Varying Views of Content Validity

The discussion of the extent to which content validation is useful for establishing the validity of a test is widely debated. The purpose is not to discount the use of content validity but rather provide a review of differing opinions on the utility of content validity. In a focal article, Murphy (2009) discusses the use of a content validation approach to the validity of a test used to predict performance by comparing the content of tests with the content of the job. The argument is that the content validity of a test is important but does not impact the validity of the test. Interested readers are suggested to review the multiple responses for and against content validity that are provided in the December 2009 Volume 2 Issue 4 of the *Industrial and Organization Psychology* journal.

In a separate issue, Silzer and Jeanneret (2011) wrote a focal article on individual psychological assessment in the September 2011 Volume 4 Issue 3 of *Industrial and Organizational Psychology*. They discuss the use of individual psychological assessment as a value to human resources. Their discussion reflects upon the use of supporting research revolving around a criterion-related validity. Despite the importance of individual psychological assessment, assessors of behavior can be accurate but can make judgment errors with respect to observing behavior, and test batteries did better than an assessor. This brings to question the ability of a human assessor assessing the behavior of a potential job applicant. Tippins (2011) responds with a view on using content-oriented validity studies within individual psychological assessments. This suggests that a content-oriented validation approach to individual psychological assessment can demonstrate evidence that these assessments measure job-related competencies. Regardless of your individual view of content validity, it is a widely debated topic and is important to be able to differentiate between content validity and other forms of validity.

items to be related to each other. Discriminant involves conceptually different items to not be related to each other. The main difference between concurrent and predictive validity is the dimension of time. Concurrent involves collecting data at one point in time to predict how the same sample will perform. Predictive involves collecting data at one point in time to predict a different sample in the future.

Convergent and Discriminant Validity

With respect to convergent and discriminant validity, confirmatory factor analysis, correlational analysis, and multitrait-multimethod matrices are statistical techniques that can be utilized to assess convergent and discriminant validity of the test. The criticism of these techniques is the limited focus to only the variance associated with the measures. Another choice of convergent and discriminant validity is the use of generalizability theory to calculate a coefficient that is similar to the reliability coefficient discussed in classical test theory. This is not to state that one technique is more effective than the other because results utilizing generalizability analysis were found to be similar for multitrait-multimethod matrix, correlational analysis, and exploratory and confirmatory factor analysis (Arthur et al. 2000; Bowler & Woehr, 2009).

Both convergent and discriminant validity are discussed together because studies assessing them typically discuss both within the same study. When examining a study with convergent validity, the purpose is to ensure that multiple items contained within the test are designed to measure the same construct. The idea is that multiple items on a test are designed to theoretically measure the same construct and should be related to each other. The reason multiple items are created to measure psychological constructs is because single item measures are presumed to have low reliability. However, it is common practice to accept single item measures on self-reported facts (e.g., age, gender, education, etc.). Alternatively, it is not possible to estimate internal consistency reliability with the use of single item measures (Wanous, Reichers, & Hudy, 1997). Therefore, in order to ensure that multiple items on a test are designed to measure similar constructs, it is important to examine the convergent validity of the test.

In terms of discriminant validity, the purpose is that multiple items measuring theoretically different constructs are expected to not be related to each other. As an example, Bauer et al. (2001) conducted a study examining applicant reactions to a Selection Procedural Justice Scale (SPJS). The SPJS scale was considered to have discriminant validity to other unrelated measures such as age, gender, and test scores. They found support for discriminant validity with a weak or negligible relationship between SJPS with other unrelated measures.

One methodology for examining convergent and discriminant validity is through the use of confirmatory factor analysis. Porath, Spreitzer, Gibson, and Garnett (2012) conducted a set of three studies examining thriving at work. In the first study, the purpose was to establish the construct validity through assessing convergent and discriminant validity on 10 measures each of self-reported positive and negative affect because the theoretical framework of thriving is related to other established constructs. Through confirmatory factor analysis, Porath et al. (2012) found support that model fit improved as a result of modeling thriving as distinct from positive and negative affect compared to when an additional latent factor of positive and negative affect was created. In other words, this means that the positive and negative affect items specified to be related to thriving were in fact conceptually related to the construct of thriving.

To compare and contrast the use of either generalizability or confirmatory factor analysis for convergent and discriminant validity, Arthur et al. (2000) conducted a study on assessment centers to assess the convergent validity. They analyzed the results using both a generalizability analysis and a confirmatory factor analysis technique to compare the validity of the results. In addition to these techniques, they also conducted a correlational analysis of the intercorrelations between ratings for each dimension in the assessment center. Regardless of the statistical analysis technique used, all three techniques produced similar results supporting the convergent and discriminant validity of the measures used in the assessment center.

Concurrent Validity

Concurrent validity is a type of criterion-related validity with the goal of collecting data from a sample at one point in time to predict some criterion of interest. Essentially, the predictor and criterion data are collected from the same sample at the same time. This means that the same sample is used to collect a predictor measure such as cognitive aptitude or personality that is then linked to a criterion such as task performance.

As an example, Van Iddekinge et al. (2011) utilized a concurrent sample of military participants to determine the extent to which cognitive aptitude and personality predict task performance. They recognize the limitation that using current job incumbents to predict performance may be a concern on the basis that a concurrent sample using job incumbents to predict job performance may not be the same as using applicant samples. This is critical to consider when utilizing concurrent job incumbent samples for validating job performance measures because they have less motivation to fake on the measure versus job applicants (Morgeson et al., 2007; Van Hooft & Born, 2012).

In another example, Banki and Latham (2010) conducted a study investigating the validity coefficients of a situational interview (SI) and a situational judgment test (SJT) to predict job performance in a government-owned automobile company in Iran. The sample consisted of 101 current employees in the sales department. They found that both the SI and SJT were correlated with job performance.

Predictive Validity

This type of validity is similar to concurrent validity with the exception of the time interval that passes between the administration of the test and the measure of the criterion. When using predictive validity, a current sample is assessed on a criterion measure and then utilized in a future sample to examine the validity. What this means is that if an organization creates a test to measure performance, the process of predictive validity would be for one group to take the test and then file away the results. After time passes, the criterion measure of performance is collected on the same group. After the results of the test are analyzed and the criterion measure of performance is collected at a later time, the scores can be correlated to determine the extent to which high test scores of the measure are correlated to the high performance criterion.

As an example, Banki and Latham (2010) conducted a concurrent sample of employees examining the utility of the SI and SJT in predicting job performance. While the purpose of the study was a concurrent validity study, the participants were informed that the results of the study would be utilized to predict future performance of job applicants.

In a separate study, Bauer et al. (2001) conducted five phases of research to assess applicant reactions to selection utilizing a Selection Procedural Justice Scale (SPJS). The process of validating the SPJS scale consisted of developing and generating the items for the scale, reducing the number of items using exploratory factor analysis, validating the results from the previous phase using a confirmatory factor analysis, assessing convergent and discriminant validity of the items on the scale, and replicating the results using a sample of students. The first few phases involved the use of actual job applicants to refine the scale. They found support for the first few phases, and in phase five, they sought to replicate their previous findings utilizing individuals that *fail* as well as *pass* a selection hurdle. Over 400 students were surveyed utilizing two samples utilizing the results from the previous phases to assess the impact that the SPJS has on applicant reactions. They found support for the ability to differentiate between SPJS and applicant reactions for participants that pass and fail selection hurdles.

CHAPTER SUMMARY

- Validity and reliability are two concepts that are integral to improving the results of the experiment by ensuring the findings are both consistent and reliable. For results to be accurate they must be consistent, but results can be consistent and not accurate. There are four main categories of validity: statistical conclusion and internal, external, and construct validity.

- External validity is concerned with the generalizability of the cause and effect relationship from the current experiment to other experiments based on changes in the participants, settings, treatments, or outcomes.

- Construct validity is concerned with the operationalization of the variables included in an experiment. There are many threats to construct validity, and they can be categorized three ways: definitions of variables, researcher/participant issues, and implementation of design.

- Face, content, and criterion-related validity are other types of validity that may be discussed in relation to experiments. These validities can all be traced back to being related to construct validity. Each one of these validities is concerned with the information contained within the test or measure but not with how each one of the variables is operationalized.

- There are four different types of criterion-related validity: convergent, discriminant, concurrent, and predictive. All types are related to the accuracy of being able to assess a criterion or measure whether these measures are similar (convergent) or different (discriminant) or benchmarked against the same (concurrent) or different (predictive) population.

DISCUSSION QUESTIONS

- Think of an example of a study within a nonprofit organization of your choice and explain a scenario where all four threats (variation in participants, settings, treatments, and outcomes) to external validity may be plausible.

- Create your own operational definition for employee performance. Share this definition with another individual and identify potential threats to construct validity.

- What are some potential issues that you see with the ability to measure variables within an organizational setting?

CHAPTER KEY TERMS

Compensatory Equalization
Compensatory Rivalry
Confounding Constructs
   With Levels of Constructs

Construct Confounding
Experimenter Expectancies
Inadequate Explication of
   Constructs

Mono-Method Bias
Mono-Operation Bias
Novelty and Disruption
   Effects

Reactive Self-Report Changes
Reactivity to the Experimental
    Situation
Reliability
Resentful Demoralization
Treatment Diffusion

Treatment Sensitive
    Factorial Structure
Validity
Validity, Concurrent
Validity, Construct
Validity, Content

Validity, Convergent
Validity, Criterion-Related
Validity, Discriminant
Validity, External
Validity, Face
Validity, Predictive

Research Designs

CHAPTER 7

Experimental Research Designs

After speaking with five to ten current practitioners in the field, there was one interesting commonality between them. Not many of them mentioned the term *experimental design* as being conducted within their organization. This leads to the question of why. Is it because these practitioners are working with propriety organizational information that cannot be published? Is it because these practitioners do not think about conducting or publishing research due to being consumed with performing and delivering? Perhaps the review of more than 700 articles conducted by Scandura and Williams (2000) that suggests empirical research is in fact shifting away from experimental design and moving more toward field studies is a potential reason for not conducting experimental designs. This isn't to say that field studies cannot be experimental in nature but rather a shift toward field studies creates a sense of realism that is not present in the laboratory where experimental designs are easier to conduct. While the practitioners we spoke with may not have used experimental design, there are many studies conducted in the field or applied settings that are in fact considered experimental design or other types of designs.

The purpose of this chapter is to discuss the fundamental concepts of research design and the various components that are related to experimental design. Prior to discussing experimental design, it is important to briefly review the four main types of research design that are discussed in the next four chapters. Each design has its own advantages and disadvantages, but no one design is better than the other. At this point, you may be wondering how all the concepts and topics discussed in the previous chapters fit together. One of the most common questions raised by a researcher is what type of research design should be utilized to answer the question. As mentioned in previous chapters, no one research design is better than the other. Each research design has its own advantages and disadvantages. The critical aspect to choosing a methodology is through understanding the differences between each one as well as being able to choose the most efficient and effective design to answer the question.

| Box 7.1 | Research Designs |

1. Experimental Design – utilizes random assignment and purposely introduces a manipulation to observe an effect.

2. Quasi-Experimental Design – utilizes other design features to account for lack of random assignment to study the impact of a cause and effect relationship.

3. Nonexperimental Design – utilizes primary analysis, secondary analysis, or meta-analysis to describe data, examine relationships or covariation between variables, and compare groups.

4. Survey Design – utilizes experimental, quasi-experimental, or nonexperimental designs to study a cause and effect relationship or examine relationships between variables.

REQUIREMENTS OF EXPERIMENTAL DESIGN

Beginning with experimental design research, there are three conditions that are required for a study to be considered experimental:

1. Both the cause and effect covary

2. Cause must precede the effect

3. No other factor should cause a change in the effect

The first requirement that both the cause and effect covary should remind you of the discussion on **statistical conclusion validity** in Chapter 5. By definition, statistical conclusion validity is the covariation of the cause and effect relationship. All experiments require data analysis to some degree, so this particular condition is determined during the statistical analysis of the data or through determining an appropriate sample size prior to data collection.

The second requirement that the cause must precede the effect should remind you of the ambiguous temporal precedence threat of internal validity. Ambiguous temporal precedence is a threat when it becomes unclear whether the cause preceded the effect. When a researcher conducts an experimental or quasi-experimental design, the independent variable is manipulated before the effect occurs. Therefore, with these two types of designs, this condition is easily controlled for. In regards to nonexperimental and survey research, the researcher must exercise caution with the design to ensure the cause precedes the effect. However, one caveat to these two designs is that a cause and effect relationship may not be the ultimate goal but rather an exploration of the relationship between variables. Keep in mind that not all research is experimental in nature because some research can be qualitative or exploratory.

statistical conclusion validity:
Covariation of the cause and effect relationship through the appropriateness of the statistical procedure used for the analysis

The third requirement that no other factor should cause a change in the effect becomes a critical issue for internal, external, statistical conclusion, and construct validity threats. This is the condition where a researcher is required to develop a sound methodology because the purpose of conducting research is to explain a phenomenon. A researcher conducts research with the purpose of stating that the **independent variable** had the intended impact on the **dependent variable** or implementing a cause is going to result in an effect. The problem arises when an alternative explanation can provide an explanation for the relationship between the independent and dependent variable because a statistically significant causal relationship may not be present.

> **independent variable:** A variable in research that is manipulated or changed
>
> **dependent variable:** A variable in research that is measured

KEY ELEMENTS OF EXPERIMENTAL DESIGN

While the focus of this chapter is on experimental design, the designs and components are not only relevant for experimental design. The designs can also be quasi-experimental, nonexperimental, or survey research designs, but the limit to a design is your own creativity. Each design discussed in this book has unique features that define how to use this technique. However, the requirement to determine whether the design is experimental, quasi-experimental, nonexperimental, or survey is what differentiates between them. The purpose of experimental design is to determine a cause and effect relationship. In order conduct an experimental design or evaluate existing research as being an experimental design, there are four key important elements that qualify all research as experimental design:

1. Random Assignment

2. Control

3. Manipulation

4. Measurement

The key elements are also discussed with quasi-experimental research in Chapter 8 because they apply to these designs as well. The only distinction between experimental design and quasi-experimental design is random assignment.

Random Assignment Versus Random Selection

The first key element is **random assignment**. This concept is discussed with random selection because the two are similar but different. Throughout our experience, the terms *random selection* and *random assignment* are mentioned many times and may create confusion due to both concepts having the word *random* in them. The key to differentiating them is to know how

random assignment: A technique in experimental designs used after a sample is selected to increase internal validity by assigning participants to conditions by chance

random selection: A sampling technique used in research to select participants from a population based on chance before a sample is determined

external validity: Generalizability of the cause and effect relationship across changes in the participants, settings, treatments, or the outcomes

internal validity: Covariation of the cause and effect relationship

the participants are being used. **Random selection** takes place *before* the sample is determined and random assignment takes place *after* the sample is determined.

With random selection, every participant in the population has an equal chance of being selected to participate in the study. The overall purpose of random selection is to better select a sample that is representative of the population. This would ultimately increase **external validity** or enhance the ability to infer the results with other settings because every participant in the population would have an equal chance of being selected for the study. Random assignment is when participants are randomly assigned to different conditions in the experiment after a sample is already selected. Random assignment is utilized to increase **internal validity** because the rationale is that all participants have an equal chance of being assigned to each condition. Therefore, individual differences between participants would be equally distributed between conditions.

Although random assignment may seem beneficial for experiments, organizations may not understand the utility of random assignment, or there may be ethical reasons precluding random assignment from being used. To properly make a determination to utilize random assignment, it is recommended that a researcher has a thorough understanding on the utility of random assignment. Readers interested in a further discussion on advantages and disadvantages of random assignment are recommended to refer to Shadish, Cook, and Campbell (2002, p. 269).

Control

The second important feature of experimental research is that the researcher is required to exercise control over the variables or variability within the experiment. The purpose of control with respect to experiments is to exercise the ability to reduce variability or variation within an experiment. Through a reduction in variability, a researcher can have a clearer understanding of the causal relationship between the independent and dependent variable. When the term *control* is discussed in relation to experiments, some researchers may include a control group in which there is one condition in an experiment where the participants do not receive the independent variable or certain variables may be held constant. Secondly, through the use of control, a researcher may be able to reduce threats to validity that compromise the accuracy of the results.

For example, Hardre and Reeve (2009) conducted a 6-week experimental design on training corporate managers in a large, multinational Fortune 500 company. The goal was to determine whether or not a training intervention would be the reason for a manager adopting an autonomy-motivating behavior toward employees. The final sample consisted of using a random sample technique as well as randomly assigning the managers to either a training intervention group or a delay-training control group. The control in this experimental design was delivering a delayed-training group 1 week after the training group.

In another example, Sitzman and Johnson (2012) conducted a 2×3 experimental design offering a free 4-hour course on Microsoft Excel to examine the impact a planning intervention would have on learning and reducing attrition. Participants were randomly

control variable: A variable in research that is designed to remain constant

assigned to two levels of a planning intervention and three levels of self-regulation prompts. They included multiple aspects of control within their design such that the Excel content was set in a predetermined order with a requirement of completing the course 2 weeks after enrolling. As an added level of control, they also implemented age as a **control variable**.

These two examples are both experimental designs conducted in a field setting, but the use of control slightly varied. The type of control exercised in a study whether it is a control group (Hardre & Reeve, 2009) or a control variable and a controlled intervention (Sitzmann & Johnson, 2012) does not matter. The important point is that both researchers exercised control within their study design.

Manipulation

The third feature of experimental research is manipulation. This is a required feature of an experiment and can often be categorized as a true experiment (Shadish et al., 2002). Similar to the requirement that the cause must precede the effect for a study to be considered experimental research, the manipulation component of experimental design specifically ensures this condition is met. A manipulation is the researcher's way of exercising control over the intervention (i.e., independent variable) within the research being conducted.

For example, Egan and Song (2008) conducted a pretest-posttest randomized field experimental design in a U.S.-based Fortune 500 health care organization to examine the impact that a 6-month mentoring program has on measures of job satisfaction, organizational commitment, and person-organization fit. The manipulation, also known as an independent variable, in this experimental design was three levels of the mentoring program where participants were randomly assigned to a high-level-facilitated, low-level-facilitated, or a control group. The control group consisted of participants that were unable to participate in the program at that given time but were offered the opportunity the following 6 months. To differentiate between the high- and low-level-facilitated conditions, the high-level-facilitated condition involved a 1-hour monthly meeting with a 15-minute structured discussion by a human resource development practitioner.

Measurement

The fourth feature of experimental research is measurement. This measurement, also known as a dependent variable, was discussed in Chapter 2. Similar to the manipulation, a researcher has the flexibility of measuring any variable of interest. Keep in mind all the potential threats to construct validity when operationalizing a variable to measure. As mentioned in the required conditions for experimental research, the measurement or effect must come after a manipulation or cause.

For example, Johnson and Chang (2008) conducted an experimental design utilizing a survey on undergraduate students enrolled in a psychology or business course. The purpose of the study was to manipulate working self-concepts to determine if differences in three levels (relational, collective, and individual) would have an impact on measures of organizational commitment, perceived organizational support, organizational justice, supervisor satisfaction, company satisfaction, outcome satisfaction, and demographic variables that served as covariates and control variables. For this to be considered experimental design, the requirement is that these measures must occur after the working self-concepts were implemented. To ensure this occurred, each participant completed a reading of a vignette and written descriptions of working self-concepts prior to completing the survey.

EXPERIMENTAL RESEARCH AND VALIDITY

The aforementioned discussion on the key components that qualify a study as being experimental in nature would not be complete without a discussion on validity. During the process of creating an experiment, you should have already defined what your variables of interest are and what your potential hypothesis or research question is. The next step, if your decision is to conduct an experimental design, is to focus on developing a sound research methodology.

Beginning with threats to construct validity, these threats should be avoided prior to the start of the experiment, but it is possible that issues with measurements can be found after data have been collected. To ensure construct validity, it is important to select measures that have been shown to be valid and reliable through replication of previous research. As an example, all dependent variables measured by Johnson and Chang (2008) contain references from previous research where these measures have been used as well as reliability coefficients associated with each scale used. We recognize that the main challenge faced by researchers is not having a good measure or blindly relying on measures lacking construct validity (Rogelberg & Brooks-Laber, 2004) and that the most commonly reported threat to construct validity is a *less than ideal* way of measuring it (Brutus, Gill, & Duniewicz, 2010). We know that not everything you want to do already has a validated measure. When situations arise where new measures are needed, there are techniques, such as **content analysis** (Morris, 1994), **exploratory factor analysis** or **confirmatory factor analysis** (Scandura & Williams, 2000), **multitrait-multimethod analysis**, and **variance partitioning analysis** (Bowler & Woehr, 2009), that can be used to validate the constructs.

Statistical conclusion validity is related to the statistical analysis of the data and should be taken into account after data is collected with the exception of ensuring the sample size is sufficient to ensure statistical power is high enough to determine significance. A power analysis should be

content analysis: A computerized technique used by researchers to analyze text to classify variables

exploratory factor analysis: A multivariate statistical technique utilized to examine underlying structure of a data set

confirmatory factor analysis: A multivariate statistical technique utilized to determine if the constructs or factors are consistent with a researcher's understanding of a variable

multitrait-multimethod analysis: A technique used to establish construct validity by examining correlations of two or more traits by two or more methods

variance partitioning analysis: A technique based on generalizability to examine different sources of variance conducted prior to collecting data to ensure the sample size is large enough to detect statistical significance. The remaining threats to statistical conclusion validity are dealt with during the data analysis. We recommend reviewing a statistical textbook to ensure a thorough understanding of the assumptions to each statistical analysis and how to properly analyze the results. Any addition of experimental design features may have no impact on reducing threats to statistical conclusion validity. On the other hand, they may actually increase the plausibility of threats because additional design features may require an increase in the number of participants required to participate in the experiment. Interested readers are recommended to consult a statistical textbook for further knowledge on conducting quantitative and qualitative analyses.

External validity threats are taken into consideration from a global perspective to identify what the generalizability will be with the results of the experiment. These threats can be addressed prior to the start of collecting data by determining what the goals of the experiment are and through selecting an appropriate sampling technique to obtain a sample that is representative of the population, but design features may not reduce the plausibility of these threats. The most efficient and effective method to reduce external validity threats is through proper sampling techniques to ensure the sample is representative of the population of interest or through conducting validation studies (i.e., Anderson, Lindsay, & Bushman, 1999; Mitchell, 2012).

While all threats to validity are important to consider, at this stage of development, the main threats to consider are internal validity threats. The reason internal validity is critical with research design is because this is where the causal relationship can be explained by alternative variables. Prior to beginning the discussion on reducing threats to internal validity, it is important to note one caveat to experimental design: random assignment. The thought is that by virtue of random assignment the threats to internal validity are less plausible because the individual differences between participants are randomly assigned to all conditions and may not be considered plausible. However, this thought may not always be true, but the one threat to internal validity that is less plausible with random assignment is selection. This is because a selection threat implies that there was a bias with how participants were selected to participate in the experiment. With random assignment, this is not plausible since every participant had an equal chance of being assigned to each group, and therefore, no bias exists.

Applicability of Random Assignment

While there may be benefits to utilizing random assignment, when doing applied research in an organizational setting, the ability to randomly assign participants to conditions may be reduced. This is not to say that random assignment within the applied setting cannot be accomplished but rather some organizations may not understand the benefits of random assignment, or for ethical, legal, or logistical reasons, random assignment cannot be conducted, or the person conducting research or developing an intervention may not consider random assignment as a plausible design component. In order to reduce threats to validity, a researcher can incorporate different design features within an experiment. However, remember that no one design feature is better than another and each one has its own advantages and disadvantages.

Experimental Design Features

When thinking about designing the methodology of an experiment, a researcher has the ability to add design features that can reduce the plausibility of validity threats. These design features are

1. Pretests/Posttests,

2. Control Group, and

3. Between/Within Subjects Design.

Each one of these features enhances the existing design and rules out threats to validity but at the same time introduces additional threats to validity. A goal of conducting research and evaluating research is to be aware of threats to validity that can be introduced to compromise the results of a study. Internal validity is the most common threat to experiments, but other types of validity threats to the design of a study are also reported (Brutus et al., 2010).

Similar to creating variables to measure, developing a methodology for a study is limited to your own creativity. There are many different types of experimental designs that can be developed such as designs with or without pretests, designs examining variables over time, designs with multiple variables, designs with control groups, or designs that are referred to as between or within subjects. These design features can be used independently or in conjunction with each other. Each one of the aforementioned experimental designs has their own advantages, disadvantages, and threats to validity.

Throughout the discussion of these additional experimental design elements, we provide research that utilizes each one of these design components. Each experimental design provides a section on limitations to their research. As a consumer of information, it is your responsibility to think beyond what is provided to evaluate the research design. We provide additional threats to the experimental research provided below to demonstrate that other threats that were not discussed may be present in the existing research. Researchers may not be aware of all threats present in their research or for space requirements, do not have the ability to elaborate on every possible limitation.

Pretests and Posttests

The first type of experimental design feature consists of pretests or posttests. A researcher can add these measurements to the design in an effort to provide a baseline measurement and enhance the ability to state that the change in behavior was a result of the manipulation. Keep in mind that there generally is no limit to the amount of pretests and posttests that can be administered in an experiment. These additional measurements may serve as a means to strengthen the causal relationship through providing baseline measurements that can be compared to posttest measurements. On the other hand, multiple measures may also introduce threats to internal validity, such as testing effects or regression to the mean.

In a series of three experimental studies, Grant (2008) examined the relationship that task significance has on job performance in two fund raising organizations and a community recreation center. In particular, study two involved data collection from an aquatics center where supervisors and lifeguards completed pretests and measures were collected throughout the intervention as well as on performance and job dedication. Despite the positive findings of these studies, it is important to recognize the validity threats associated with this design. Although random assignment was utilized, the participants in the study were relatively young; therefore, a possibility exists that there was a selection threat and Grant (2008) recognizes that future research should examine these effects on older and more experienced employees.

Furthermore, the addition of multiple tests adds the complexity of the results due to internal validity threats. Specifically, he mentions regression to the mean as a plausible but unlikely threat to the performance level. Since this was a longitudinal experiment with multiple tests throughout, it is possible that testing effects may have primed participants to respond in a certain way or maturation could have occurred regardless of the intervention. With longitudinal designs, the chance of attrition can occur given the fact that participants are required to participate in an experiment over time. One threat not mentioned within the article but worth taking a look at is attrition. This information can be found in the statistical analysis section for the **degrees of freedom** provided in the **analysis of variance** results. In study two, there were a total of 32 lifeguards that were selected for the study. You will notice that the degrees of freedom provided range from 20 to 25. While attrition may not be a threat

in this study, it is important to note that you have the ability to examine a research study beyond what is provided in the limitations section to evaluate and critique what is provided. Given the complexity of the design and utilization of three experiments that all support a common finding, these additional threats are unlikely. However, as a consumer of information it is your responsibility to be able to critically evaluate research beyond the limitations that are presented in the literature article.

> **degrees of freedom:** The number of values in a statistical test that are free to vary
>
> **analysis of variance:** Also known as ANOVA. A statistical technique utilizing an F ratio to determine if an independent variable has a statistically significant effect on a dependent variable

Control Group

A second experimental design feature that can be added to enhance the existing design by allowing for the elimination of threats to validity is a control group. Control as mentioned above is a requirement of experimental design. In this regard, control is being used in relation to a control group in which a group of participants that do not receive the treatment can be compared to participants that do receive the treatment. This control group is designed to reduce variability within the experiment and to reduce the plausibility of threats to validity.

Recall the Egan and Song (2008) experimental design examining three levels of a mentoring program where participants were randomly assigned to either a high or low facilitation group or a control group. In this particular study, the control group consisted of participants that were unable to participate in the mentoring program at that time. The issue with a no treatment control group is the possibility that participants may engage in compensatory rivalry or feel resentful demoralization, which are threats to construct validity. In this case, Egan and Song (2008) were aware of this and did post hoc evaluations, and control group participants felt the mentoring program was part of several new employee development activities and did not have any negative views. Furthermore, the control group also had the option to participate in the mentoring program at a later time. Despite the positive findings from this experimental design, they recognize limitations to the generalizability or external validity of their current study to other industries and suggest future research focus on replicating the results in different organizations. Additionally, the delayed treatment control group may have resulted in reducing any resentful demoralization or compensatory rivalry between the groups. It is also possible that a threat of history or selection may be present that could explain why the participants were unable to participate in the treatment group.

Although Egan and Song (2008) utilized a delayed treatment control group, another possible use of a control group is through a no treatment control group. The use of a no treatment control group would strengthen the causal relationship between the independent and dependent variables through reducing the plausibility of threats to internal validity. This happens when any potential changes occur in one group but not the other.

As an example of a no-treatment control group, Hulsheger, Alberts, Feinholdt, and Lang (2012) conducted two experiments examining the impact of mindfulness on emotion regulation, emotional exhaustion, and job satisfaction. In particular, study two consisted of 203 participants recruited from a broad range of jobs in the medical and educational industry in Germany that required participants to keep a diary for 10 work days. The goal of this field experiment was to determine if a mindfulness intervention group was statistically different from a control group on trait mindfulness, surface acting, emotional exhaustion, and job satisfaction. The control group did not receive any intervention during the course of the 10 work days, but at the conclusion of the experiment, they were provided with the same self-training intervention as the treatment group.

At the conclusion of data collection, the final sample consisted of 64 participants. A total of 37 participants were excluded from the analysis, and 102 participants dropped out of the study, which should trigger the question of attrition. Additionally, you should also be thinking about the possibility that these 102 participants could be different than the remaining 101 participants in the study. Likewise, they also provided additional analysis within the method to account for the participants that dropped out, and no statistically significant differences were found. This additional information means that they took into consideration the plausibility of attrition and selection to demonstrate that there may not be a plausible explanation for the results.

However, this may trigger the question of whether history, maturation, regression to the mean, resentful demoralization, reactivity to self-report, or compensatory rivalry could be plausible threats to the validity of the experiment. You may also be thinking about differential effects between selection and other threats to internal validity as possible explanations for the results in the Hulsheger et al. (2012) field experiment. While most of the threats to internal validity are reduced with the addition of a control group, differential effects between the groups, such as selection and history, selection and attrition, or selection and maturation, may be able to explain the relationship found between the control and treatment group. Differential effects are when the treatment group and control group advance at different rates.

Between and Within Subjects

The last design feature of an experimental design is the use of between and within subjects experiments. A **between subjects** design is where all participants are exposed to only one condition. A **within subjects** design is where all the participants are exposed to all levels of the independent variable. A between or within subjects design can be a viable option to include in an experiment, but this depends on the independent variable. Egan and Song (2008) used a high level and low level of facilitation group. It may not make sense to have participants go through both conditions, so a within subjects design may not work. On the other hand, Derous, Ryan, and Nguyen (2012) utilized a within subjects design to have college students review resumes of two potential applicants.

> **between subjects:** A research design component where participants are exposed to only one condition in a study
>
> **within subjects:** A research design component where participants are exposed to all conditions in a study

The challenge to choosing a between or within subjects experiment is complex and is left entirely up to the researcher. However, all legal and ethical issues must be considered prior to determining which design to utilize in the experiment (refer to Chapter 3 for more information). There are advantages and disadvantages to both designs, and it is important to understand the implications of each design. The main issue for a between subjects experiment is the impact that individual differences have on threats to validity. While random assignment in experiments reduces the plausibility of a selection threat, a possibility exists that there still may be individual differences between the groups. As you know, every person is unique and their intelligence, gender, education, work experience, etc. are possible differences that could create an issue for the causal relationship. On the other hand, a within subjects design eliminates individual differences because every individual participates in all experimental conditions and can serve as their own control. However, the main issue the researcher needs to consider is the order in which participants receive the different levels of the independent variable.

Between Subjects Experiments

As previously mentioned, a between subjects design consists of participants being exposed to only one level of the independent variable with the main issue of assessing individual differences between groups. Though individual differences between groups in an experiment using random assignment are reduced, there are threats to validity that may still be plausible.

McElroy and Crant (2008) conducted a $2 \times 2 \times 2$ between subjects experimental design utilizing 246 working adults to determine the impact that performance outcome, source of handicapping, and frequency of handicapping had on assignment of credit and blame, interpersonal affect, and credibility. In total, there were three independent variables (i.e., performance, source of handicap, and frequency of handicap) with two levels each, so participants were randomly assigned to one of eight conditions in which they read a scenario and responded to survey questions. All dependent variables used in the current study were based on previous research findings that demonstrated reliability and validity of those measures. As Brutus et al. (2010) mention, an issue with construct validity is that variables are operationalized in a *less than ideal* way. To demonstrate construct validity of the measures used, McElroy and Crant (2008) analyzed the measures through confirmatory factor analysis to demonstrate the construct validity of each dependent variable.

Despite the promising results, McElroy and Crant (2008) recognize that a mono-method bias or reactive self-report changes may exist within their research because the current study utilized one method (i.e., a survey) requiring self-reported dependent variables. Additionally, the external validity of the results may be questionable due to the nature of the study taking place in the lab. Additionally, they recognize limitations to the operationalization of their handicapping variable. From a construct validity perspective, this is critical to consider. While the operationalization of their definition was appropriate, the definition of handicapping could be a result of inadequate explication of constructs, construct confounding, or confounding constructs with levels of constructs. These threats were not specifically mentioned, but as an outside reader consuming this information, you have to know the operationalization of the construct used. Recognize that the operationalization was appropriate for this study but could use further development by looking at other aspects of handicapping behavior. From an internal validity perspective, despite the use of random assignment, the selection of participants may be a threat to the validity of the results. McElroy and Crant (2008) mention that the broad sample of participants in various jobs and industries prevented them from examining differences in sales professions compared to nonsales professions.

In another example, McAuliff, Kovera, and Nunez (2009) conducted a 4 × 2 fully crossed factorial experimental design to determine if jury-eligible participants in a southern California community were able to recognize four manipulated levels of internal validity and two levels of ecological validity on quality and credibility. This particular design incorporates random assignment through randomly assigning participants to one of eight conditions and exercises control through manipulated levels of internal and ecological validity occurring before the measurement of quality and credibility.

In another experimental design, Cojuharenco, Patient, and Bashshur (2011) conducted three survey designs to examine the effects that temporal perspective or a perspective that participants can be influences by context and individual differences can have on perceptions of unfair treatment at work. In particular, study two consisted of 416 U.S. employees completing an online survey where they were randomly assigned to one of four between-subjects conditions. The four conditions were defined as distant past (over a year and at least two months), recent past (over the past two weeks), distant future (over the next year and not earlier than two months from now), and near future (over the next two weeks). Additionally, in study three, 640 U.S.-based employees were randomly assigned to one of four conditions in a 2 × 2 between subjects design assessing abstract versus concrete cognitions about employment while holding temporal perspective (i.e., next two weeks versus past two weeks) constant. Sample demographics were obtained from each of the three studies to allow for a comparison of participants based on gender, age, work experience, occupation type, college education, and ethnicity. They note that the results are limited by asking participants to recall an actual past event and anticipate a future hypothetical event and relying on participant recollection to past or future events they consider unjust. This brings to question the individual differences between each participant and their ability to recall past and future events.

Dealing With Individual Differences

The main issue with between subjects designs are individual differences between participants. There are techniques researchers can utilize to reduce the plausibility of these differences when they are known to exist prior to beginning an experiment. Even though random assignment is a requirement of experimental designs, random assignment alone may not be sufficient enough to control for these differences, but it is a potential solution. With that said, there are three potential solutions to reducing individual differences:

1. Random Assignment

2. Holding Variables Constant

3. Matched Design

Random assignment is a required condition for experimental design and the only internal validity threat that is reduced is selection. Although selection may be reduced from the examples provided above, selection could be an issue if the participants selected differ from the population of interest. Random assignment does not reduce the selection threat if the sample differs from the population. However, random assignment may eliminate a selection threat from the participants in the study because all participants have an equal chance of being assigned to conditions, which may limit the confounding of individual differences. Another way to reduce individual differences is to hold as many variables constant as possible. For example, Cojuharenco et al. (2011) utilized two variables of control. On the other hand, Johnson and Chang (2008) collected data on four self-reported demographic variables that could serve as control variables or covariates.

The last alternative for individual differences would be to use a matched design. The purpose of a matched design would be to determine specific characteristics that the sample has in common and randomly assign these sets of participants to different independent variables. What this means is that a researcher concerned that tenure, age, gender, ethnicity, and so on, would impact the results of the independent and dependent variables could match participants on this. For example, Egan and Song (2008) could have used a matching design for assigning the participants to mentors on the basis of personality, needs, or participant input, but they did not utilize a matching process. As a result of not matching participants, they recognize that the mentoring effects found represent the lower bound and that matching participants may result in higher effects.

Within Subjects Experiments

A within subjects experiment may also be referred to as a **repeated measures design**. This design feature is used when all participants receive all levels of

> **repeated measures design:** Also known as a within subjects design. A research design component where participants are exposed to all conditions of a study.

order effects: Occurs when a participant is exposed to more than one condition and the results from one condition can influence the next condition

power: A statistical term in research that determines the extent to which a statistically significant effect can be found

counterbalancing: A process utilized to counter order effects of a within subjects design where conditions to which participants are assigned are systematically varied

the independent variable. This means that each participant serves as their own control and all potential issues with individual differences between groups is eliminated. The use of random assignment in a within subjects experiment is used to randomly assign participants to the order in which they receive the levels of the independent variable to counter potential **order effects**. The advantage to a within subjects experiment is that fewer participants are needed in an experiment, which means the cost associated with conducting the experiment is reduced. Additionally, there is an increase in statistical **power** because each participant serves as their own control. The main disadvantages to within subjects designs are order effects of when participants receive the different levels of the independent variable.

Although the issue of individual differences is eliminated, the use of a within subjects experiment introduces other complexities and issues to consider. The first issue to take into consideration is to determine if it is ethically and legally possible for participants to receive all levels of the independent variable (refer to Chapter 3 for a discussion on ethics and legal issues). Another issue for within subjects experiment is the order effects or the order in which participants receive the levels of the independent variable. Since all participants receive all levels of the independent variable, a possibility exists that different levels may influence a participant's response to the dependent variable.

To reduce the plausibility of order effects, the researcher can enact **counterbalancing** as a method for eliminating order effects. Counterbalancing is a methodology for a within subjects design to systematically assign participants to different orders of the levels of the independent variables. This method becomes challenging when there are more than three conditions because for counterbalancing to be effective, all possible orders must be used. For example, if a researcher was conducting a training program with three conditions that consisted of participating in the training in a classroom setting (C), self-directed setting (S), or a virtual setting (V), the researcher would have a total of six possible conditions. The six possible combinations are as follows: CSV, CVS, SCV, SVC, VCS, and VSC. When experiments have more than three conditions, full counterbalancing becomes increasingly complicated.

DESIGN FEATURES COMBINED

The aforementioned discussion of the different design features of pretests and posttests, control groups, and between and within subjects designs are not independent of one another. In fact, the experiments mentioned in those sections combine multiple aspects of each design component. Grant (2008) used multiple pretests or posttests combined with a control group. Egan and Song (2008) utilized a pretest and posttest, control group, and a between subjects design. Hulsheger et al. (2012) utilized multiple pretests or posttests, control group, and a between subjects design. Lastly, Derous and colleagues (2012) conducted a mixed-factor design that included a within and between subjects factor utilizing a counterbalancing technique to account for order effects. While each one of these design components aids in reducing threats to validity, the complexity of design also introduces additional threats to validity that may not have been present if these design components were not included. As an example, multiple posttests or measures throughout the experiment create a longitudinal design and introduce the threat of attrition compared to a study not containing multiple posttest measures.

EXPERIMENTAL DESIGN SUMMARY

When conducting or evaluating research to determine if it is experimental, you must ensure that three requirements are met. Keep in mind that these requirements are generally

1. Both the cause and effect covary,

2. Cause must precede the effect, and

3. No other factor should cause a change in the effect.

Once this has been established, the next step is to ensure that the following four items are built into the design:

1. Random Assignment

2. Control

3. Manipulation

4. Measurement

Once all this has been established, you can be fairly certain that the research you are conducting or evaluating is experimental in nature. Keep in mind that a researcher(s) generally states within the methodology section or the abstract that the research is experimental. You may not have to critically evaluate most of these components, but it is helpful to have an underlying understanding of these concepts.

Once establishing the design is experimental, you have to begin to think about the validity of the results. If you are in the beginning stages of conducting or evaluating research, then you may take what the researchers write as being valid. However, once your knowledge of research design advances, you can begin to critically evaluate the effectiveness of the experimental design and propose alternatives to enhance the existing design. As we mentioned, it is possible that some design features (i.e., pretests/posttests, control groups, or between/within subjects design) reduce the plausibility of threats to validity. These design features may introduce additional threats that may not have been a threat. All research designs are susceptible to validity threats, not all researchers have to account for every threat, and not all journals allow for the space to explain every threat. Therefore, whether you are consuming information or creating a research design, you will be able to better evaluate existing research.

CHAPTER SUMMARY

- Experimental design is the first type of four research designs discussed and requires three conditions to be an experiment, which are both the cause and effect covary, the cause must precede the effect, and no other factor should cause a change in the effect.

- In addition to those requirements, there are specific elements that are required for a design to be categorized as experimental. A research design is considered experimental if there is random assignment, control, manipulation, and measurement.

- To conduct an experimental design, three design features can be incorporated independently or combined. The design feature options are pretests/posttests, control groups, and between/within subjects design, and as many or as few design features can be conducted in conjunction with each other.

DISCUSSION QUESTIONS

- Compare and contrast the differences between random assignment and random selection and the impact on the different types of validity.

- What are some advantages and disadvantages of experimental designs when conducting applied research?

- Develop an experimental design that utilizes all three experimental features (pretest/posttest, control group, between/within subjects design), and discuss the threats to validity that are both plausible and reduced.

CHAPTER KEY TERMS

Analysis of Variance
Between Subjects
Content Analysis
Counterbalancing
Degrees of Freedom
Experimental Design
Factor Analysis,
    Confirmatory
Factor Analysis,
    Exploratory
Factorial Design

Longitudinal Design
Multitrait-Multimethod
    Analysis
Nonexperimental Design
Order Effects
Power
Quasi-Experimental Design
Random Assignment
Random Selection
Repeated Measures Design
Survey Design

Validity, Construct
Validity, External
Validity, Internal
Validity, Statistical
    Conclusion
Variable, Control
Variable, Dependent
Variable, Independent
Variance Partitioning
    Analysis
Within Subjects

CHAPTER 8

Quasi-Experimental Research Designs

As with experimental designs, we approached the same five to ten current practitioners to ask them about their experience with conducting quasi-experimental designs within their organizations. Almost all of the practitioners had experience conducting quasi-experimental designs. The next challenge we had was deciding which practitioner to sit down with to gather more information as to how a quasi-experimental design was used within their current organization. Since we had no compensation to offer them, we felt that the least we could do would be to tell you about what we learned!

We were fortunate enough to coerce, through freewill, a current practitioner at a large international consumer packaged goods organization that utilizes an assessment center. The purpose of the assessment center is to select employees that were considered high potential for a general manager position in each region and country the organization operates. This example is considered quasi-experimental in nature because **random assignment** is not used but utilized other design features to qualify it as a quasi-experiment. All high potential employees, which is believed to consist of between two to ten internal candidates or 0.05 % of the total organizational population, receive a battery of assessments to assess cognitive ability, 360 degree feedback, personality, and resilience. Before going further, the **statistical conclusion validity** threat of restriction of range should jump out as a plausible threat because only a specific level of internal candidates is being considered. By utilizing this methodology, the practitioner conducting the assessment has the ability to behaviorally and experientially compare equivalent criteria required for success in the job.

Internal candidates may be moved from one country to another country. Despite the fact that the instruments used in the assessment center have been globally validated, an issue of problem solving may be the top priority for one country and the least important in another country. Another potential issue identified by the practitioner was that even though the construct of a given competency is defined the same way globally, this does not 100 % account for differences in interpretation in which one leader may place their own subjective interpretation of problem solving when rating the competency. You can never fully account for individual rater subjectivity. This may bring up questions related to threats to **construct validity**. Despite these potential threats, the organization determines that this

random assignment: A technique in experimental designs used after a sample is selected to increase internal validity by assigning participants to conditions by chance

statistical conclusion validity: Covariation of the cause and effect relationship through the appropriateness of the statistical procedure used for the analysis

construct validity: Generalizability that the variables used in a study represent the variable they intend to measure

external validity: Generalizability of the cause and effect relationship across changes in the participants, settings, treatments, or the outcomes

quasi-experimental: Utilizes other design features to account for lack of random assignment to study the impact of a cause and effect relationship

validity: The accuracy of the results of a research study

type of assessment process is extremely useful for adding greater degrees of objectivity to succession planning decisions. With that said, due to the global nature of the organization and constant evolution, a lot of these decisions may be made without assessments. As a means to improve the validity to the assessment, internal validation studies should be conducted to more rigorously assess the predictor-criterion relationship.

Take a step back beyond this particular example provided and begin to think about this business problem from a research methodology perspective. Sometimes we get so caught up in work and what is going on that we do not take the opportunity to think about what is happening. A few threats were discussed above and other problems identified by the practitioner were mentioned, but there are many other issues with this particular assessment center. Do you recognize any other threats to internal validity, **external validity**, or construct validity?

When random assignment cannot be utilized in research, then research designs can be **quasi-experimental**. A lot of the concepts and features discussed with experimental design in Chapter 7 are also conducive to quasi-experimental design with one caveat. The term *quasi* indicates a resemblance to something, and in this case, a quasi-experimental design is similar to an experimental design. The main difference between quasi-experimental design and experimental design is random assignment. You are probably already thinking that with the lack of random assignment there is an increase in threats to **validity**. Therefore, to accommodate this lack of random assignment, a quasi-experimental design must utilize design features to reduce the plausibility of threats to validity when making a causal inference.

REQUIREMENTS OF QUASI-EXPERIMENTAL DESIGN

While a lot of the concepts and features discussed in Chapter 7 may also apply to quasi-experimental design, the purpose of this chapter is to not restate the same design features and different types of experiments again. Our purpose is to demonstrate the flexibility of research design through a creative solution to a problem. All research designs require a careful thought process and quasi-experimental design is no different. The requirements for causal inference and elements to create an experiment as discussed with experimental design also apply to quasi-experimental design and they are as follows:

1. Both the cause and effect covary

2. Cause must precede the effect

3. No other factor should cause a change in the effect

Both the cause and effect covary is by definition statistical conclusion validity, which was discussed in Chapter 5. The second requirement that the cause must precede the effect indicates that any **independent variable** in an experiment must come before the **dependent variable**. When an experimental or quasi-experimental design is used, the independent variable is intentionally manipulated before the effect occurs. Therefore, with these two types of designs, this condition is easily controlled for. The last requirement that no other factor should cause a change in the effect is slightly more complicated for quasi-experimental design. Quasi-experimental designs require increased creativity to reduce the plausibility of threats to internal, external, statistical conclusion, and construct validity because these designs do not utilize random assignment. When an alternative explanation can provide an explanation for the independent and dependent variable, then a statistically significant causal relationship may not occur.

> **independent variable:** A variable in research that is manipulated or changed
>
> **dependent variable:** A variable in research that is measured

KEY ELEMENTS OF QUASI-EXPERIMENTAL DESIGN

Once a causal relationship is determined and the decision is to conduct a quasi-experimental design, then there are three important elements to conducting a quasi-experimental design. These elements are the same as experimental design and are as follows:

1. Control

2. Manipulation

3. Measurement

As with experimental designs, quasi-experimental designs require that the researcher exercises control over the variables or variability within the experiment. In terms of control, a researcher has the flexibility of including a control group in which there is one condition in an experiment where the participants do not receive the independent variable or add additional design features to the experiment to exercise control over the variability. The use of control in an experiment provides a clearer understanding of the causal relationship between the independent and dependent variable and reduces the plausibility of threats to validity. The idea behind this is that when variation occurs in one group and not the other, there is less of an opportunity for there to be a threat to internal validity. The second feature of quasi-experimental research is manipulation. The purpose of a manipulation is to deliberately introduce an independent variable to a participant prior to observing an effect. By doing this, it is a way for the researcher to exercise control over the intervention that is introduced in the quasi-experiment. The third feature of experimental research is measurement. After a researcher elicits a manipulation in an experiment, a type of measurement must exist. The purpose of the measurement is to observe what happens after a manipulation.

Quasi-Experimental Design and Validity

Up to this point the only differentiating factor between a quasi-experimental design and an experimental design is the absence of random assignment. With all the benefits that random assignment has at reducing the plausibility of threats to validity, one may wonder why a researcher would choose a quasi-experimental design over an experimental design. One of the main reasons for not using random assignment when conducting research in an organization is due to legal or ethical reasons (see Chapter 3 for a discussion on ethics and legal issues). When doing research in an applied setting, organizations may not allow their participants to be randomly assigned to conditions. This could be due to the fact that they are not aware of the benefits of random assignment or that they will not allow random assignment to be done.

Whether you are conducting quasi-experimental designs for research purposes or evaluating an existing quasi-experimental design, there are techniques that can be incorporated to improve the validity of a design. Since quasi-experimental design does not utilize random assignment, the plausibility of groups in the experiment being different at the start of the experiment is highly probable. Without the use of random assignment, quasi-experimental designs may be subject to all threats to internal validity. However, with a well thought out methodology, the plausibility of internal validity threats can be reduced. In addition to internal validity threats, other types of validity threats (i.e., external, construct, and statistical conclusion validity) also have the potential to provide alternative explanations for the causal relationship. Likewise, when evaluating a quasi-experimental design, there is not one way to conduct them, so keep that in mind when critically evaluating quasi-experiments.

To briefly revisit validity, external validity deals with the generalization of the quasi-experimental results to other settings, participants, interventions, or outcomes to ensure that the results of the current experiment apply in other situations. Construct validity is concerned with the operationalization of the variables within the quasi-experiment. The purpose is to ensure that the variables included in the quasi-experiment are well defined and thoroughly describe the intended variables. Statistical conclusion validity deals with the covariation of the causal relationship and is taken into consideration during the analysis of the data. Lastly, internal validity is focused on the covariation with the relationship between the independent and dependent variable. In other words, did the independent variable have the intended effect on the dependent variable or was there some other variable that could explain this relationship?

Sometimes alternative explanations may not be apparent during the design of the methodology but became obvious after the quasi-experiment was conducted. This is why it is critically important to understand the nuances of the different types of validities and determine creative ways to optimize research designs that reduce the plausibility of threats to validity. Regardless of how creative you are or the researchers that conducted the quasi-experiment you are evaluating, there is no way to remove 100% of threats to any research design. The challenge then becomes, What threats are present in the current research or what threats are you willing to have in your existing research?

Consider the following quasi-experimental field study with a control group. Luthans, Rhee, Luthans, and Avey (2008) examined the impact that the use of money, social recognition, and feedback had on employee performance for 133 employees in broadband Internet access in a Korean organization over the course of one month. This study is considered quasi-experimental even though random assignment was used. The component that makes this quasi-experimental is the fact that the four conditions used in the study were randomly assigned but the individual participants were not. They recognize the following threats to external, internal, and construct validity as limitations and strengths:

1. The study took place with a very specific organizational setting that may be unique and limit generalizability to other settings (external validity).

2. The workforce was mainly comprised of young females, so the generalizability to other individuals may be limited (external validity).

3. Attrition was not an issue because no one left the organization. While this may be true, attrition is also related to participants withdrawing from the study. Since data was captured longitudinally and degrees of freedom were provided, you can examine the sample size used in each analysis to determine if this was a threat. You will notice that no participants withdrew from the study, which confirms their statement (internal validity).

4. Maturation is deemed as a threat that is not plausible because all participants had similar experiences (internal validity).

5. Instrumentation may be a threat due to the use of the same pre- and post-test being used in all conditions (internal validity).

6. Diffusion of treatment was not a threat because the four conditions took place in different geographical locations in Korea (construct validity).

7. Resentful demoralization was not a threat because the participants were not in the same geographical location.

While Luthans et al. (2008) recognize many strengths and limitations to the current research, there is a possibility that other threats to validity may be present in the study.

1. Performance was based on service quality and number of calls handled. While number of calls may be straightforward, the operationalization of service quality was not explicit. This leads to the question of inadequate explication of constructs, construct confounding, confounding constructs with levels of constructs, or mono-operation bias (construct validity).

2. Selection may be a threat because the participants were not randomly assigned to conditions. The participants were also in four different geographic locations that may make them different (internal validity).

3. History could be a plausible threat if there was a situation that happened in one geographic location and not the other (internal validity).

4. Maturation may be a threat even though Luthans et al. (2008) state participants had similar experiences. Participants may have had naturally occurring changes throughout the month of the intervention that may have resulted in a change (internal validity).

5. Since the same pre- and posttest was provided to participants, a testing threat or regression to the mean may be present. Although this is unlikely due to the quasi-experiment lasting a month (internal validity).

6. Restriction of range may be plausible because all participants were defined as being young and female (statistical conclusion validity).

The purpose of reviewing one quasi-experimental design in relation to threats to validity was to highlight that not all threats are reported in the limitation section. As a consumer of information, you have the ability to critically evaluate a research study to draw your own conclusions regarding threats to validity. This short review served as a way of demonstrating ways to think outside the realm of what is provided and critically evaluate research.

Through a proper understanding of the threats to validity, a researcher can know beforehand what potential problems may exist and how to eliminate them. Although the different variables may not be common sense when creating a research design, it is imperative to think about each threat individually to understand any potential impact the threat may have on the research design. It is also possible that these threats may become clearer after a study has been carried out, so future research can focus on the areas that were overlooked during the first research design. While all threats to validity are important, from a research methodology perspective, threats to internal validity are the most problematic but can be addressed through different quasi-experimental design features.

Quasi-Experimental Design Features

The design features discussed with experimental designs in Chapter 7 also apply to quasi-experimental designs. These different design features can be incorporated alone or in combination with other features to reduce threats to validity. Through creatively designing a quasi-experiment, a researcher can incorporate different design features to reduce these alternative explanations. By reducing the plausibility of alternative explanations, the researcher can be certain that the independent variable had an effect on the dependent variable and no other variables could explain this relationship. Recognize that not every threat to validity will be reduced because no study is free of all threats.

Each of the following design features can be utilized independently or in conjunction with other design features to reduce the plausibility of threats to validity. The number of designs/design features that can be created is limited to your own creativity. Similar to experimental designs, quasi-experimental design features are as follows:

1. Pretests and posttests

2. Nonequivalent control groups

3. Between and within subjects

These design features not only improve the validity of quasi-experimental designs by eliminating threats to validity but also introduce new threats to validity. These design features can be used independently or in combination with one another.

Pretest and Posttests

The first design features that can be added are pre- and posttests. The addition of pretests allow for additional measures that act as a baseline prior to the implementation of the independent variable. Posttests would measure the consistency of the effect after the independent variable to determine the long term effects of the intervention. Overall, pretests and/or posttests would strengthen the relationship between the independent and dependent variable through reducing multiple threats to validity.

For example, Oostrom, Bos-Broekema, Serlie, Born, and Van der Molen (2012) conducted a pretest and posttest quasi-experimental design on 205 applicants from various organizations that utilized a psychological assessment at a Dutch consultancy firm. The purpose of the study was to compare the effects of a paper-and-pencil versus a computerized version of an in-basket exercise on perceptions of face validity, predictive validity, and fairness. This design qualifies as a quasi-design because random assignment was not possible. They state the reason is because applicants "tested at the same location could be competitors for the same job or promotion" (p. 100).

Oostrom et al. (2012) recognize that there was a difference in difficulty between the paper-and-pencil test and the computerized test on measures of test performance. This difference may be due to the amount of time required to complete the computerized version and learning the different functions. Ideally, these two tests should be designed to have **parallel** or **equivalent forms reliability** because the idea was to test the differences between two modes of in-basket testing. They recognize in the limitations that it would be unfair to assess competitors for the same job or promotion with different versions.

Therefore, you may wonder if these two modes of in-basket testing truly assess the same constructs. A possibility exists that inadequate explication of constructs, construct confounding, or confounding constructs with level of constructs is occurring that may explain these differences between the two forms. Additionally, in terms of construct validity,

parallel forms reliability: Also referred to as equivalent forms reliability. The extent to which two tests are developed to measure the same construct of interest.

equivalent forms reliability: Also referred to as parallel forms reliability. The extent to which two tests are developed to measure the same construct of interest.

they used one item to measure belief in tests and fairness perceptions. One item may not sufficiently assess the construct of interest, and more items may be needed to fully operationalize this variable. There may also be a threat to the unreliability of measures because of the variability of coefficient alpha with this one measure. Lastly, for construct validity, the responses to the measures were self-reported measures, which increase the chance of a reactive self-report change threat. Lastly, with respect to construct validity, data were collected from different locations, and each office only utilized one form of the in-basket test, so compensatory rivalry, resentful demoralization, or treatment diffusion may not be plausible.

To address the selection threat, Oostrom et al. (2012) conducted a test between the paper-and-pencil and computerized version of the in-basket test and found no significant differences between "gender, age, education level, years of working experience, experience with psychological assessments, experience with the use of e-mail software programs, frequency with which they use e-mail software programs, computer skills, cognitive ability, and Big Five personality dimensions" (p. 101). Although a variety of variables were compared to determine if there was a selection threat in the study, you cannot fully rule out selection as a threat. They state that not finding significant differences between demographic variables would allow for stronger inferences if participants could be randomly assigned to conditions. Therefore, despite being able to assess variables to examine selection threats, this threat is still plausible. The study assessed pretest measures and posttest measures over the span of the 70-minute intervention. Since the pre- and posttest measures were assessed in a relatively short time, regression to the mean and testing threats may be plausible and explain the differences found. On the other hand, attrition is not a plausible threat to validity because the sample began with 206 participants and the final results consisted of 206 participants.

As you can see, there are threats to validity that researchers acknowledge in their study. You have the ability to critically evaluate any existing research to determine if it is possible for other threats to validity to explain the results. By identifying these threats within a study, you can develop or recommend a future study to reduce these threats to validity and enhance the accuracy of the results.

Nonequivalent Control Group

The second design feature that can be added to a quasi-experimental design is a nonequivalent control group. The concept of a nonequivalent control group is similar in scope to the control group discussed in Chapter 7. However, the difference is that participants are not randomly assigned to conditions, which increases the challenge of ensuring that the groups are similar at the start of the quasi-experiment. This is also why this design feature is referred to as a nonequivalent control group as opposed to the control group terminology used in experimental design. The one caveat to an introduction of addition conditions and especially with a nonequivalent control group is to ensure that all ethical and legal precautions are taken to ensure that a treatment or intervention can be withheld.

For example, Hahn, Binnewies, Sonnentag, and Mojza (2011) conducted a quasi-experiment with a training group and a nonequivalent control group with a total of 135 employees from diverse organizations (i.e., two public service, two private companies, and one university) in Germany. The purpose of the study was to examine the effects that a recovery training program had on recovery experiences, recovery-related self-efficacy, emotional exhaustion, perceived stress, state negative affect, sleep quality, and learning about recovery through a pretest and two posttest measures over the course of 1 week. Random assignment was not possible due to the fact that participants selected the dates they wanted to attend training based on their schedule. The control group in this case was a waitlist control group such that they received the training after the study. However, this control group was included for the purpose of reducing threats to validity by comparing results to the treatment group.

To address testing effects, Hahn et al. (2011) conducted two posttest measures collected 3 weeks apart. This data collection point may be considered short and possibly may influence the results of the test. They suggest future research examine longer time frames between data collection to demonstrate testing effects are not plausible. Since multiple measures were assessed at three points in time, the plausibility of a maturation, regression to the mean, or testing effects are possible. Although, the two post measures following the intervention may provide support for reducing the plausibility of these threats.

Since random assignment was not possible, selection is a plausible threat. This is because the participants self-selected the date of training based on their schedule. Therefore, it is possible that there may be a difference between the two groups. Additionally, attrition may not be a plausible threat, but you examine this by knowing that 135 participants started the study but 114 completed the study. Of the 114 completing the study, 95 of the participants completed all three data collection time periods. They tested for this and found no differences between the participants completing the study compared to the ones that dropped out.

The training program consisted of four modules assessing different components. Although the results are promising, there could be a potential of threats to confounding constructs with level of constructs, construct confounding, and inadequate explication of constructs to fully understand what components of the module had the impact. Hahn et al. (2011) suggests that future research address this issue. With respect to the construct validity of the dependent measures, all measures were provided with literature articles that utilized the measures in the past and supplemental confirmatory factor analysis was conducted with a three factor model to confirm the validity of the measures.

To complete the training, there were a total of five different trainers with each session being run by one or two trainers. Although a detailed procedure for implementing the training was provided, it is important to consider a plausible threat of unreliability of treatment implementation. Treatment diffusion, resentful demoralization, or compensatory rivalry are plausible threats to consider based on the 13 different training programs offered.

The use of a nonequivalent control group would strengthen the causal relationship between the independent (i.e., training program) and dependent variables (i.e., recovery experiences, recovery-related self-efficacy, and well-being outcomes) by reducing the plausibility of threats to validity. While some of the threats to validity were discussed by Hahn et al. (2011) in the article, as an outside reader critically evaluating the study you have the ability to examine all threats to validity as plausible explanations. The purpose of adding a nonequivalent control group is to allow for the reduction of threats to validity by allowing for a group of participants that do not receive the treatment or training program to be compared to participants that attend the training program. The thought is that if there is a statistically significant difference between the nonequivalent control group and the treatment group, then the difference could potentially be due to the intervention. Therefore, with this nonequivalent control group, a researcher can compare measurements taken in both groups to assess any potential differences that occur in one group and not the other that could be related to alternative explanations for the relationship between the intervention and the effect. The downside to nonequivalent control groups is that random assignment is not used and there is a possibility that the two groups differ at the start of the experiment, which may result in differential effects between threats to validity.

Between and Within Subjects

The final design feature discussed for quasi-experimental designs are **between subjects** and **within subjects** designs. To review, a between subjects design is when every participant in the quasi-experiment only received one condition or intervention, whereas a within subjects design is when every participant in the quasi-experiment receives every condition or intervention. This design feature differs from a nonequivalent control group because all groups within the quasi-experiment are exposed to some type of intervention.

between subjects design: A research design component where participants are exposed to only one condition in a study

within subjects design: A research design component where participants are exposed to all conditions in a study

A between and/or within subjects design can be utilized in quasi-experimental designs, but this depends on the independent variable and the plausibility of a participant being exposed to all conditions. The decision of choosing a between or within subjects quasi-experiment is left entirely up to what the researcher will be allowed to do. It is important to take into consideration all legal and ethical issues prior to determining which design to utilize in the experiment.

Between Subjects Experiments

As previously mentioned, a between subjects design consists of participants being exposed to only one level of the independent variable with the main issue of assessing individual differences between groups. Peterson and Luthans (2006) conducted a quasi-experimental longitudinal between subjects design assessing the impact that three groups had on gross profitability, drive-through time, and employee turnover in 21 fast food restaurants. This design is considered quasi-experimental because the randomization was not at the individual level but rather randomly assigning groups to one of the three interventions. Interventions consisted of a financial training group, a nonfinancial training group, or a control. This particular study would not benefit from a within design because it is not practical to assign each group to all three conditions. As an added feature of control, participants were asked to rate managerial style differences before the intervention occurred.

Peterson and Luthans (2006) recognize threats to validity within their study. The sample size consisted of 21 different units and may result in low statistical power. Since the study took place in the field, they had no way to increase the sample size to achieve an adequate power. Another threat that was acknowledged was in regards the external validity of the results. This particular study took place in a fast food restaurant that these findings may not generalize to other settings. Additionally, the sample consisted of young employees with a low complexity job that these findings may not generalize to other individuals. The design of the quasi-experimental design was developed to address threats to internal validity. Selection was taken into consideration by obtaining demographic measures from each of the three groups to statistically test for significant differences. Maturation, regression to the mean, history, and testing can be addressed through the comparison of the control group to the 3, 6, and 9 month data collection points as well as pretest measures.

Additionally, the objective nature of their dependent measures reduces the plausibility of reactive self-report changes. The study design does not explicitly mention the location of the store or if multiple stores are used, so there may be a possibility that compensatory rivalry, resentful demoralization, or treatment diffusion is present in the study. Interestingly, the effects of the financial incentive group post intervention had a greater effect on the outcomes, but over time, the financial and nonfinancial incentives were similar. Could this effect be a result of the novelty or disruption threat?

Dealing With Individual Differences

The main issue with between subjects designs are individual differences between participants. There are techniques researchers can utilize to reduce the plausibility of these differences when they are known to exist prior to beginning an experiment. Since random assignment is not an option for quasi-experimental designs, researchers have two potential solutions for reducing individual differences between groups:

1. Holding Variables Constant

2. Matched Design

Through holding variables constant, a researcher has the ability to reduce alternative explanations. For example, Hahn et al. (2011), Oostrom et al. (2012), and Peterson and Luthans (2006) dealt with the individual differences between groups by assessing demographic variables and previous experience to statistically determine if differences existed between the control and treatment group. In all three quasi-experiments, no statistically significant effects were found for these variables, which demonstrates that collecting and analyzing demographic variables allows researchers to assess potential differences that may exist as a means to account for lack of random assignment.

Another method to control for individual differences is through a matched design. For example, Latham, Ford, and Tzabbar (2012) utilized an interrupted-time series quasi-experimental design with mystery shoppers rating performance measures of servers in three different restaurants. The procedure put in place involved matching the mystery shopper with the demographics of customers in a restaurant on variables such as age, education, dining out preferences, and salary. Matching mystery shopper demographics to the restaurant can enhance the validity of the study results because these mystery shoppers were designed to be reflective of a *typical* customer.

Within Subjects Experiments

A within subjects experiment may also be referred to as a repeated measures design. This design feature is used when all participants receive all levels of the independent variable. This means that each participant serves as their own control and all potential issues with individual differences between groups is eliminated. The advantage to a within subjects quasi-experiment is that fewer participants are needed: (1) It is easier to achieve the recommended level of statistical power to detect an effect, and (2) each participant serves as their own control. This also means that the cost associated with conducting the experiment is reduced.

One of the main issues to within subjects designs are order effects of when participants receive the different levels of the independent variable. Since all participants receive all levels of the independent variable, a possibility exists that different levels may influence a participant's response to the dependent variable, which is referred to as order effects. When participants are required to participate in a within subjects design experiment, they may experience fatigue or boredom from participating in all levels of the independent variable. While order effects may not correspond specifically to threats to validity, they still create potential problems that may in turn increase the probability that threats to internal validity can explain the causal relationship. To reduce the plausibility of order effects, the researcher can counterbalance the levels of the independent variable to eliminate order effects. Counterbalancing is a methodology for a within subjects design to vary the order in which participants are exposed to the various levels of the independent variables.

Banki and Latham (2010) conducted a concurrent validity study that was a within subjects quasi-experimental design. A total of 101 employees from a sales department in an Iranian automobile company completed a situational interview and a situational judgment test to assess the impact that these selection tests had on an employee's perceptions of fairness, performance, anxiety, and motivation. Since participants were given both the situational interview and the situational judgment test, Banki and Latham (2010) counterbalanced the order in which each interviewee received the two selection tests. Additionally, as a means to reduce experimenter expectancies and reactivity to the experimental situation, the first rater "was blind to the interviewee's job performance and the manager was blind to the identity of the interviewee" (p. 131). To reduce the threat of testing effects, there was a time lag of 1 week between the administration of both tests.

Banki and Latham (2010) recognize that there are limitations to the existing study. The first is construct confounding and confounding constructs with levels of constructs when comparing validity coefficients. This is because when different predictors (i.e., the situational judgment test and situational interview) are used, the conclusion drawn between the two predictors has the potential to be theoretically or conceptually uninterpretable. However, they state this threat is not plausible because of the difference in the way each test required an answer. The situational interview required the employee to provide an answer, and the situational judgment test required the employee to choose an answer. Since both tests assess the same job-related situations using two methods, the threat of mono-method bias may also be less plausible. They mention five other limitations that are worthwhile to consider when evaluating the research results.

External validity threats were not mentioned, but the results may not be generalizable beyond the Iranian automobile company where the study took place. This is mainly due to the assessment of the performance measure because performance was assessed by the manager using the company's performance appraisal instrument. Additionally, the specifics of the development of this performance appraisal instrument was not included in the article, so you may want to question if there is a threat of inadequate explication of constructs, construct confounding, or confounding constructs with levels of constructs with regards to the performance construct. They provide demographics on gender, which consisted of approximately 75% male and 25% female, and company tenure, which was an average of 4 years. The distribution of male to female should be examined carefully as a potential limitation to generalizing the results to other employees.

Design Features Combined

Each of the three previously mentioned design features can be independently implemented in a quasi-experiment or pretests and posttests, control groups, and between and within subjects designs can be conducted in conjunction with one another. Although some design features reduce the plausibility of threats to validity, there also is a possibility that these design features may introduce additional threats that may not have been a threat. The only limit to what type of quasi-experimental design you can conduct is your own creativity and the resources, ethical, and legal obligations to complete the research study. It is worth noting that the addition of multiple design features may increase the costs and time associated with conducting the experiment as well as add to the complexity of interactions between threats.

As an example, May, Reed, Schwoerer, and Potter (2004) conducted a naturally occurring quasi-experimental longitudinal field study that incorporated a control group and pre- and posttest measures. They utilized employees in a large Midwestern city in the United States to examine the effects that an office workstation ergonomics intervention program would have on measures of workstation ergonomic characteristics, persistent pain, eyestrain, workstation satisfaction, workstation ergonomic change, age, job tenure, and positive affectivity.

A total of 230 surveys were distributed at time 1, which was 4 months before the intervention, with 180 being returned, and a total of 87 employees responded to the second survey, which was 4 months after the intervention. Therefore, the final sample consisted of 87 employees with an experimental group of 61 employees and a control group of 26 employees. To address a potential issue of low statistical power as a result of a small sample size, they utilized a power analysis for each group and determined that power ranged between 0.55 and 0.56. The experimental group consisted of four major groups of workstation ergonomic interventions that consisted of seating enhancements, keyboard-related improvements, computer relocations, and computer screen modification. The control group was determined based on the employees that did not report any form of physical enhancement on the second survey.

May et al. (2004) recognize many strengths and limitations to the existing research. They state potential threats to internal validity as selection, selection-maturation interaction, instrumentation, attrition, local history, differential regression to the mean, and a construct validity threat of reactive self-report change. While these threats are plausible, they state that these threats are not plausible because there were few differences between the control group and treatment group and between the respondents and nonrespondents. They state that this finding also reduces the selection-maturation interaction and attrition. Selection is a plausible threat because the naturally occurring quasi-experiment was voluntary. The same questionnaire separated by 8 months can potentially reduce the threat of instrumentation, reactive self-report changes, and regression to the mean.

As a consumer of information, you have the ability to either reject or accept their explanations for reduction of those threats through interpreting the methodology and results section. There may still be a question related to threats to statistical conclusion and construct validity, although a power analysis was conducted and the medium effects in the study with a power of 0.55–0.56 may question the possibility of low power. Cohen (1988) recognizes a power of 0.8 or above. However, since the study was a naturally occurring experimenter, May et al. (2004) did not have the ability to increase sample size. Extraneous variance in experimental setting is plausible on the basis of employees receiving more than one ergonomic intervention. Although only one ergonomics expert was used, there may have been variability and unreliability of treatment implementation by this expert when providing interventions to each employee in the study. Novelty and disruption effects may explain the relationship based on the ergonomics expert creating a specific intervention for the employee. Since each intervention may have been individual, there is a potential for a threat of treatment sensitive factorial structure.

With regards to internal validity, May et al. (2004) recognize selection may be a threat based on voluntary participation. This is plausible, but an additional question is related to the control group. It appears as if employees self-select whether they are in the control or treatment group. Therefore, despite the findings, no significant differences were found between measures of persistent pain or eyestrain. If the employees self-select, then the possibility exists that the control group may have not required an intervention. Lastly, threats to external validity must also be considered. The question you should ask yourself is, Can these results from a large organization in a Midwestern city of the United States consisting of mainly female employees with various administrative responsibilities apply to other settings, people, or treatments?

QUASI-EXPERIMENTAL DESIGN SUMMARY

When conducting or evaluating research, there are many steps that you need to go through. If the decision is to conduct a quasi-experimental design, then it is important to understand the advantages and disadvantages of the design so that you can include the appropriate design features to strengthen the causal relationship. On the other hand, if you are evaluating a quasi-experimental research design, then there are many opportunities to critically evaluate the methodology beyond what the researchers provide. Regardless of whether you are evaluating or conducting a quasi-experimental design, every decision you make along the way has important implications on understanding or enhancing the validity of the results.

CHAPTER SUMMARY

- Quasi-experimental designs qualify as an experiment because both the cause and effect covary, the cause must precede the effect, and no other factor should cause a change in the effect. To do this, the elements of control, manipulation, and measurement are built into the design.

- The main differentiating factor between quasi-experimental and experimental design is the fact that random assignment is not used in quasi-experimental designs. To accommodate the lack of random assignment, design features such as pre- and posttests, nonequivalent control groups, and between and within subjects designs can be utilized.

DISCUSSION QUESTIONS

- What are some advantages and disadvantages of quasi-experimental designs when conducting applied research?

- Develop a quasi-experimental design, and discuss the threats to validity that are both plausible and reduced.

- If you had to convince an organization to use a quasi-experimental design over an experimental design, then how would defend your position that a quasi-experimental design is more advantageous compared to an experimental design?

CHAPTER KEY TERMS

Between Subjects	Validity	Variable, Dependent
Quasi-Experimental	Validity, Construct	Variable, Independent
Design	Validity, External	Within Subjects
Random Assignment	Validity, Internal	
Reliability, Equivalent Forms	Validity, Statistical	
Reliability, Parallel Forms	Conclusion	

Nonexperimental Research Designs

When we think about *experimentation*, we typically conjure up ideas that involve independent variables and some form of manipulation of treatments or conditions, measurement of their effects on dependent variables, and design elements that enable randomization of participants and a degree of control of extraneous variables. This method of inquiry is critical to us as researchers if we are interested in making a causal inference and, as we have discussed, this type of research is quite common using a variety of experimental and quasi-experimental designs. However, there are a multitude of research designs that do not incorporate the same elements as the experimental or quasi-experimental approaches, and these are referred to as nonexperimental designs.

In reality, most (if not all) of us have used some form of informal nonexperimental research methods at some point in our lives! We are sure many of you can recall *people-watching* at a shopping mall or airport and attempting to understand various individual and group behaviors, or asking targeted questions to gather information on specific areas of interest, or perhaps searching through archived files to answer questions or formulate a picture about past behaviors or try make predictions about future events based on trends that have appeared over time. These are all considered nonexperimental research methods, and even though you may have used them in an informal and unstructured manner, applied researchers often use methods such as these in a more systematic manner as they conduct formal research studies.

Nonexperimental research designs provide value in exploring certain types of research questions on their own and can be strategically integrated into a research methodology along with an experimental or quasi-experimental design. However, nonexperimental research designs are typically not appropriate for use on their own in the examination of research questions involving causal inference (though some exceptions exist), and we will explain this in greater depth as it is a very important factor to consider when designing a methodology that is appropriate to the research question(s) under examination. So, let's explore nonexperimental research methodology, its purpose, its key design elements, and its appropriate use—the *how-when-why* factor.

WHAT IS NONEXPERIMENTAL RESEARCH?

Nonexperimental research is unique in that its methods may fall into the categories of primary analysis, secondary analysis, and meta-analysis. *Primary analysis* is the term used to describe the analysis of data that were collected by the actual researcher. Examination of data collected by someone other than the researcher is referred to as *secondary analysis*. *Meta-analysis* is the statistical analysis of results from a collection of relevant studies (Glass, 1976). This is an important distinction, as researchers conducting experimental or quasi-experimental research are using primary analysis, but a researcher conducting nonexperimental research may be using either type of analysis or the various types in some combination. In particular, secondary analysis, or the use of previously collected data, can be used to answer new research questions with existing data (Glass, 1976) and may be a valuable alternative for applied researchers to consider when situational constraints do not permit real-time data collection by the researcher. We will discuss all of the different approaches within nonexperimental research in this chapter.

primary analysis: the analysis of data that were collected by the actual researcher

secondary analysis: the examination of data collected by someone other than the researcher

meta-analysis: the statistical analysis of results from a collection of relevant studies

Nonexperimental methods are used primarily for describing data, examining relationships or covariation between variables, and comparing groups. Researchers also describe data and examine relationships using experimental and quasi-experimental methods, but they can go further to examine causal relationships with these methods as well. Nonexperimental designs do not incorporate the manipulation of a treatment or condition as experimental and quasi-experimental designs do, which means causal relationships cannot be examined. It is important to remember that nonexperimental designs do allow for the measurement of variables. A researcher can employ measures on two or more variables of interest and collect data to analyze (e.g., exercise frequency and blood pressure, gender and stress management techniques), but without some degree of controlled manipulation of an independent variable by the researcher conducting the study, causality cannot be inferred. There is no way for a researcher to determine if a causal relationship exists between the specific variables being examined or if other extraneous variables affected the outcome or the order (temporal precedence) of the variables in producing the outcome.

Let's consider the example of a study that examines the effects of exercise frequency on stress reduction. In an experimental design, a researcher could randomly assign participants to different conditions of exercise and follow up with a stress measure. Through this method, a researcher could infer the strength of a causal relationship between exercise and stress level. In a nonexperimental design, a researcher could still collect data on exercise behaviors (e.g., frequency, type) and individuals' stress levels. However, without experimental controls in place, the manipulation of the independent variable, and creation of precise conditions prior to the measurement of stress levels, it is impossible to determine (a) if exercise behavior causes a change in stress level, (b) if stress level causes a change in exercise behavior, or (c) if a causal relationship between these two variables exists at all, or if some other variable is affecting the change (e.g., caffeine consumption). The data obtained may still be quite useful but will have limitations for appropriate inference.

Although this may seem like a serious disadvantage, nonexperimental designs are appropriate in many field settings and can be a valuable option for researchers, which we will discuss next. As identified by social researchers (Babbie, 2004; Lofland & Lofland, 1995), research in field settings is often appropriate for obtaining information such as the following:

- individual behaviors and actions
- group behaviors, practices, norms
- variations in cultures or large social settings
- roles and relationships
- single events and episodes
- recurring events and trends
- comparisons between two or more variables

Remember, the selection of the research design is dependent on the research questions of interest and the data needed for a particular study. The more design options a researcher is aware of and clearly understands in terms of when and how to implement, the more effective a researcher can be in conducting a study in an applied setting with unique and sometimes challenging parameters and constraints.

ADVANTAGES AND DISADVANTAGES OF NONEXPERIMENTAL DESIGNS

Advantages

Perhaps the most valuable aspect of nonexperimental research designs is their degree of adaptability. The different nonexperimental designs that we will discuss in this chapter can be used in a variety of situations, in a short- or long-term time frame, in combination with each other and preceding or following an experimental/quasi-experimental design. As applied researchers and field professionals can attest, adaptability is a valuable feature due to changing research needs and expectations, settings, conditions, and parameters. Nonexperimental designs can be incorporated into a breadth of applied research contexts.

Disadvantages

The most critical disadvantage to consider when exploring nonexperimental design options is the inability to make a causal inference with any nonexperimental design used as a stand-alone method. Data obtained through these methods can be examined to better understand history, trends, relationships, preferences, and behavioral tendencies, but we as researchers cannot determine causality through our findings using a nonexperimental approach. Without inclusion of an independent variable that is manipulated along with the measurement of a dependent variable, it is impossible to determine the direction of a cause and effect finding and the possible impact of extraneous variables on the perceived causal relationship.

Some common examples of how applied researchers use data obtained through non-experimental methods include the following:

- The collection of rich, descriptive data to gain insight about a construct of interest and develop a theory for future examination, referred to as *grounded theory*

- The exploration of relationships between variables to develop a hypothesis(es) for a study

- The analysis of archival data used as a baseline measure prior to conducting an experiment or a quasi-experiment when the inclusion of a pretest is not feasible

- The analysis of archival data used as a follow-up measure after conducting an experiment or a
  quasi-experiment when the inclusion of a posttest is not feasible

- The analysis of trends over time, across individuals and groups, and in various settings and contexts

---

grounded theory: the collection of rich, descriptive data to gain insight about a construct of interest and develop a theory for future examination

---

The most common nonexperimental methods used by researchers in applied settings include observation (obtrusive and unobtrusive), archival data analysis, survey designs, case studies, and meta-analysis. We will focus on each of these methods next.

OBSERVATION

Observation, sometimes referred to as field research or field observation (Lofland & Lofland, 1995), is used extensively across a breadth of disciplines and applied settings because it enables researchers to obtain real-time data about subjects' behaviors, interactions, and experiences from the actual environment in which they naturally occur. The field setting can range in scope from a process involving just one individual (e.g., grocery shopping), to an interaction involving a few individuals (e.g., a business meeting), to a gathering in which hundreds of individuals are participating (e.g., a protest rally). A researcher can be examining one behavior or several, or examining differences in behaviors observed between different individuals (e.g., males and females). The research question will be the most important factor in determining the context and special field circumstances to incorporate into the observational method conducted.

Observation is perhaps the most basic of all nonexperimental methods. After all, we observe behaviors and phenomena every day in many different contexts. The main difference between our normal *people-watching* and research-oriented types of observation is in the systematic identification, documentation, description, and interpretation of selected behaviors of interest. The goal with observational research is to develop a comprehensive picture of a specific area or phenomenon of interest through interpretation of data collected, or field notes, within a particular period of time. Description is the first objective in observational research followed by analysis and interpretation.

It is important that the research question(s) of interest be the focus when collecting data through observation; the method of observation, type of data collected, and coding protocol are all influenced by the questions the researcher is interested in examining. If you consider how much information you take in during the course of a typical day, it is clear that most of us have information overload! Quite a lot of this information is usually irrelevant to us as well, so we need to develop filters in order to retain valuable information and discard information we do not need. The same filters are needed to conduct observational research, again, developed from the research question of interest.

Obtrusive and Unobtrusive Observational Designs

A researcher can conduct an observation using a variety of methods and degrees of participation ranging from complete immersion and interaction in a setting to none at all—observing while remaining outside the setting and removed from any interaction with those individuals within the setting. Also, the individuals in the setting can be cognizant of the researcher's presence and know they are being observed or completely unaware that an observation is taking place. In an obtrusive observation, the individuals in the setting are aware of the researcher's presence, whether or not the researcher is actually in the setting or observing from outside the setting. In an unobtrusive observation, the individuals in the setting are not aware of the researcher's presence or that they are being observed. The researcher and the observational activity are concealed. Ethical considerations and the needs of the research study must be carefully weighed and included in the decision to proceed with either method.

It is important that a researcher carefully consider the construct or topic of interest when determining the degree of involvement or immersion in an observational setting because this can either benefit or hinder the results. For example, a researcher who is interested in examining an area that is controversial or sensitive in nature (e.g., racism and discriminatory behaviors) might not be as successful conducting an observation in a setting in which individuals are aware of the researcher's presence and intention. Individuals being observed will likely be *on their best behavior* in the presence of the researcher, a behavioral phenomenon studied in the context of impression management and social desirability, and demonstrate behaviors that are often not honest and realistic, thus compromising the validity of the data obtained and their interpretation. In a situation like this, a researcher may decide to conduct an unobtrusive observation. However, a researcher who conceals his or her presence while conducting an observation must be aware of any ethical considerations with regard to privacy and anonymity. As we previously discussed, the Belmont Report and professional codes of ethics state that researchers are required to respect all persons involved in research and protect the dignity and privacy of individuals who are part of a study. This is an especially important factor to consider when observing individuals in applied settings such as schools, hospitals, and businesses in which specific legal requirements protect students, patients,

> **obtrusive observation:** the individuals in the setting are aware of the researcher's presence, whether or not the researcher is actually in the setting or observing from outside the setting
>
> **unobtrusive observation:** the individuals in the setting are not aware of the researcher's presence or that they are being observed

and employees from any act that is considered a violation of their privacy or confidential personal information.

A less commonly used but effective approach to observation in certain circumstances involves a hybrid of obtrusive and unobtrusive observation, in that the researcher's presence is known to the individuals being observed, but the researcher is actually observing and collecting data in another location through use of video and audio recording equipment. An example of this technique is an observational approach that consumer products companies and market researchers may use to collect information about consumers' use of certain products in their actual homes. Participants volunteer to participate and receive recording equipment to place in their specific rooms in their homes, such as the kitchen or living room. While the participants know their behaviors are being observed and recorded for analysis, the notion of *out of sight, out of mind* shifts the participants back into their normal everyday routines without feeling the need to act unnaturally. This type of observational research can yield a wealth of information about product usage, such as the number and type of individuals in a household that consume a certain beverage, how a certain food item is prepared (e.g., microwave or conventional oven), and any issues that a consumer may have with a product (e.g., difficult packaging to open).

Box 9.1   Obtrusive Versus Unobtrusive and Reactivity: Remember the Hawthorne Studies?

Observational methods can be obtrusive or unobtrusive. Unobtrusive observation is typically the preferred approach because individuals will often alter their behaviors—often referred to as *reactivity* — when they believe or know they are being observed. This is posited to be what happened during the Hawthorne Studies, in which researchers were commissioned by Western Electric to obtrusively observe employees performing their jobs at the Hawthorne Works plant (Mayo, 1949). The purpose of the study was to determine if the amount of light in the work area affected workers' productivity. The subjects increased their productivity, and it was later proposed that the attention they were receiving from the researchers may have influenced the increased productivity, not necessarily changes in lighting, also referred to as demand effects (Orne, 1962).

However, ethical concerns regarding concealment or deception may necessitate that researchers make their presence known to participants. In addition, unobtrusive observation is often difficult for researchers to conduct for any extended length of time. An unobtrusive observation of shoppers in a grocery store, individuals socializing at a party, or fans at a sporting event may be feasible, but a lengthy observation or one in which repeated observations are necessary in a social or workplace setting is a challenge to accomplish without being identified, or at least noticed, as an outsider.

Naturalistic and Controlled Observational Settings

While a large amount of observational research is conducted in naturalistic field settings, an observational design can also be implemented in a controlled environment. A controlled setting is appropriate when naturalistic observation is not feasible or when a more systematic and precise observation of fewer, more specific behaviors is necessary.

<table>
<tr><td>**Box 9.2**</td><td>**Advantages and Disadvantages to Naturalistic and Controlled Observation Settings**</td></tr>
</table>

Naturalistic Setting

Advantages

Behaviors occur in the context of their natural setting, so the picture a researcher gets through the observation will likely be more accurate—all the contextual factors occurring in the actual setting provide a more realistic and comprehensive backdrop. It may also be more cost effective and practical in many situations to simply observe in a naturalistic setting rather than create a simulated setting that incorporates all necessary parameters and contextual factors in a controlled environment such as a lab.

Disadvantages

It is often difficult for a researcher to be completely immersed in a setting for an extended period, with time commitment and logistical factors being common impediments.

If a researcher must conduct the observation unobtrusively, it may be not be feasible in certain settings, such as a workplace or social setting, where the researcher's presence would be obvious.

Controlled Setting

Advantages

An observation that takes place in a simulated lab setting may provide the researcher with a greater degree of control of the environmental parameters. Conditions can be held constant so a more focused observation can take place on a specific set of variables without digression or fluctuation.

Disadvantages

In a controlled observation setting, there is the chance that the environment did not get created exactly as it occurs in its natural setting, and in many situations, it is not possible to introduce every natural element in a controlled setting.

There are different advantages and disadvantages to each approach, which should be taken into consideration when designing the study.

There are a variety of ways to collect and record the information, often referred to as *field notes*, we obtain through observation, and the techniques we choose largely depend on the focus and needs of the study as well as time and resource constraints. The process of observing and recording data can be a time consuming and arduous task, whether a researcher is working alone or even with a team of assistants. A researcher must determine the best method for collecting and recording observational data that will yield accurate and reliable data through the most effective and efficient approach possible. For example, if a researcher is interested in nonverbal communication, or body language, or differences among men and women in a business meeting, it may be necessary to video the meeting. A video recording would enable the researcher to replay the scenario as many times as necessary to capture all evidence of

> **archival data:** qualitative or quantitative data in the form of hard copy and electronic documents, multimedia sources such as audio and video recordings, or public and statistical records

nonverbal communication that occurs among all of the participants—no simple task. It would be very difficult to document everything through note taking alone, and an audio recording would be irrelevant in the examination of this particular construct. Clearly, the research questions, breadth and complexity of data, participant characteristics, and context of the observational setting are factors to consider when determining an appropriate observational design.

ARCHIVAL DATA ANALYSIS

Archival research involves the use of existing data that have been collected and stored for a variety of needs. Archival data may be used to establish a historical background relevant to a current research question or issue, to examine trends, and to establish a baseline for an experimental or quasi-experimental study when it is not feasible to conduct a pretest. Archival data can be qualitative or quantitative and be used in the form of hard copy and electronic documents, multimedia sources such as audio and video recordings, or public and statistical records.

Archival Data: Hard Copy, Electronic, and Multimedia Sources

The vast majority of archival data have typically been in the form of hard copy documents and records. As technology has advanced in recent years (and will continue to rapidly evolve and advance), not only have more data been created and stored in electronic forms, but a great deal of existing hard copy archived data records have been converted to an electronic format through scanning and data entry. This is a laborious process, but it can be worthwhile if the data will be needed and accessed regularly or if the data are an important piece to a particular analysis.

Examples of archival data sources commonly used in nonexperimental research include the following:

- letters, memos, e-mails, and forms of correspondence

- journals, diaries, and logs

- periodicals such as magazines and newspapers

- presentations and speeches

- research publications

- web-based communications such as social networking forums, message board posts, and blogs

- radio broadcasts

- television and news programs

- documentary films

Archival Data: Statistical Records

Statistical records are collected by both public and private organizations, and while some data is private and not accessible to the public, an extensive amount of public data does exist. U.S. Census data records are often used by researchers to examine trends in demographics across the country.

Statistical data collected through polls are also commonly used, though it is important for a researcher to be aware of the margin of error associated with polling data. A good example of the importance of this factor can be found in political poll data interpretation, such as public opinion polls on the popularity statistics and ranking of U.S. presidential candidates, or the favorability rating of the incumbent U.S. president. While these statistical records can vary tremendously based on timing, events, and other influencing variables, reasonable trends can often be extrapolated after examining polling statistics over time.

While archival data can be a rich and valuable source of information, there are two points of caution in its use. Archival data, especially very old hard copy records, can be difficult to obtain in their entirety. A record could have been moved from one file cabinet or box and never properly returned or refiled in the wrong place. The result is an otherwise useful data set that contains gaps or is misfiled, and this becomes a reliability issue for the researcher. Another issue with archival data lies in its accuracy. Data that lack construct validity are not only useless but also damaging to our research. A researcher who was not involved in the data collection process really has no way to verify that the methodology supported the collection of appropriate data that actually reflected the construct of interest. Also, the older the data are, the more difficult it becomes to be able to track the source and validate. While these concerns do pose a real issue to researchers using archival data, they are not *deal breakers*. Archival data can be used effectively provided the researcher understands the limitations of this type of data and potentially problematic areas to watch out for and identify before becoming too immersed in inaccurate and/or inconsistent data.

SURVEY RESEARCH DESIGNS

The use of survey research designs is a common approach in a great deal of applied research as this is a method that can yield a large amount of data despite the typical constraints of data collection in field settings, specifically limited financial resources, assistance, and time. While we discuss survey research in greater depth in Chapter 10, it is appropriate to also include here in the context of nonexperimental methods.

Survey designs include questionnaires, which can be hard copy or electronic, and interviews, which can be in person or by phone. Technology tools and online social networks have significantly improved the techniques for collecting survey data though they are not always the best approach and should be implemented with careful consideration of question content, setting, and respondent characteristics.

CASE STUDIES

A case study is an in-depth exploration of a particular individual, group of individuals, or entity, such as a team, family, organization, special interest group, or neighborhood. The purpose of the case study is to examine a single case that is relevant to a specific focus of interest and collect the most detailed and comprehensive data possible in a determined time frame. In the context of the case study design, the term *case* is used broadly as it can be defined in myriad ways within the context of applied research. To illustrate, an individual involved in educational research could conduct a case study on an individual student, a class, a grade level, or a school, and these would all be reasonable types of case studies. The research question and level of detail needed are key factors in determining how narrow or how broad to make a case study's focus. For example, for a comprehensive examination of the benefits and challenges of an after-school wellness program for future comparison to schools without such a program, a broader case study of an entire school would be appropriate. However, if the goal is to examine the benefits of such a program on a certain grade level or type of student, a more narrowly focused case study would be more appropriate to obtain that level of detail.

A case study is not limited to a set of established parameters, rules, or criteria; the manner in which case studies are conducted and the data that are collected will vary across research studies. A researcher must define the parameters of the case, such as time, place, and situational factors, to put the case study in its proper context. Clearly, external events and influences of the particular time period (e.g., a natural disaster, a presidential election, a stock market crash) in which the case study is being conducted will affect its documentation and therefore its interpretation, and this information should be carefully recorded and included to provide this necessary context.

Findings obtained from a case study are often more descriptive and offer a deeper understanding of a construct or phenomenon compared to other types of nonexperimental research designs but less likely to offer any degree of generalizability to a larger group or population since a case study is much more narrowly defined than a typical sample. Another limitation of case study findings is the inability to determine a causal explanation for any of the phenomena and observations obtained through the case study. However, a researcher can certainly use findings derived from a case study to develop a theory and hypothesis that can be tested through experimental or quasi-experimental methods for making a causal inference. This is a common approach among applied researchers.

META-ANALYSIS

A meta-analysis is a nonexperimental method that enables a researcher to integrate findings from a large number of studies in a particular area of interest or relevant to a particular research question (Glass, 1976). Rather than interpreting results from an individual data set, a researcher conducting a meta-analysis is essentially interpreting results derived from multiple data sets across many studies. A meta-analysis may consist of as few as 10 studies or as many as hundreds of studies. This method is most often used by researchers to make comparisons, examine relationships between variables, and generalize findings across different populations and settings (Cozby, 2001).

Researchers in certain fields, such as medicine and the physical sciences, have long used the meta-analytical approach to validate and provide substantive support for clinical procedures, treatments, and theories (Rosnow & Rosenthal, 1993). Today, the meta analytical approach has emerged as a useful method in applied fields as well, including business, law, health care, and education. A meta-analytic research study examining the psychometric properties of employee performance ratings from different sources found important differences in interrater reliability and correlations between ratings from incumbents (self-ratings), supervisors, and peers (Conway & Huffcutt, 1997). Through examination of findings from 177 samples ($n = 28,999$), the researchers found that supervisors demonstrated the highest interrater reliability (.50), followed by peers (.37), and lastly, subordinates (.30). Correlations between sources indicated that, with the exception of higher correlations for performance ratings for incumbents in nonmanagerial jobs of lower complexity, the different raters had different perspectives on performance expectations in interpersonal and cognitive dimensions (Conway & Huffcutt, 1997). What does this type of meta-analysis mean for field settings? Well, for any organization that implements rating systems for employee performance measurement, this meta-analysis provides a body of evidence from multiple studies indicating differences in ratings based on the rating source, the type of job, and the performance dimensions being evaluated. Such differences in reliability may likely affect outcomes, including performance appraisal feedback, training plan recommendations, promotions, performance improvement actions, and other high-stakes employment decisions.

A researcher conducting a meta-analysis will gather relevant published studies and examine the results and key findings across all the studies. Provided the meta-analysis is conducted correctly, incorporating precise steps and measures and also including appropriate research studies, which we will discuss next, it can enable a researcher to have a greater degree of confidence in the strength of validity and causality of findings derived from individual studies because they come together as a collective body of research.

A researcher conducting a meta-analysis is required to follow a sequence of steps. Even though the studies being considered for inclusion may be relevant in construct or topic area, they will consist of different hypothesis statements, types of participants, measures, and other methodological variations. Because of these variations, it is critical to create a type of standardization that creates homogeneity and applies to all the studies included in the meta-analysis to ensure the researcher is comparing *apples to apples*.

The first step is quite basic—a researcher must develop a hypothesis before proceeding. Of course, this is an important step in any research study, but it becomes especially critical with a meta-analysis. Why is this? Before immersing oneself in dozens of research studies, it is important that a well-constructed hypothesis serve as a basis for a clear articulation of the construct and variables of interest. Even though the measures, participants, methods, and statistical analyses may vary across studies, it is necessary that the construct, the variables themselves, and their operational definitions are in alignment across studies. If the hypothesis is ambiguous and these components are unclear, the researcher may be more likely to include irrelevant studies in the meta-analysis that should not be included.

The next step involves the development of criteria of inclusion for the studies being considered. The criteria should be developed based on the research question and the hypothesis. For example, a researcher may be interested in examining study findings across cultures, time periods, or another type of parameter. In this example, these needs will influence the determination of the type of journal (e.g., country-specific journals, international journals) and publication date range of the studies to examine. This step will facilitate the appropriate selection of studies in an efficient and standardized manner.

Lastly, a researcher must conduct specific statistical procedures for analyzing and comparing results from many different studies in a standardized manner. The most common statistical calculations used in a meta-analysis involve transformation of the different values into standardized metrics such as Z scores and effect size. The overall significance level of the studies is examined using Z scores and enables the researcher to derive the degree of inferential statistical power. The effect size, or strength of the results, can be derived using the correlation coefficient r or using d values that represent the standardized difference between means. Each of these types of standardized calculations answers a different but equally important research question in a meta-analysis. Significance levels and effect sizes yield unique and necessary values about the overall statistical power and strength between variables, and a researcher needs this information for making a confident determination regarding the alignment of findings across studies.

A challenge for a researcher conducting a meta-analysis is to search for and include only the most credible and relevant studies. This may not sound too difficult, but consider this task in an everyday context: web surfing. How many of you have entered a keyword or phrase into an Internet search engine and located several appropriate and seemingly credible resources . . . along with dozens of irrelevant and *sketchy* resources and websites? How many of you have wasted hours clicking on those questionable links, leading you to more questionable links, and eventually found yourselves completely off track of your intended search (or worse, using irrelevant or bad information)? This can also occur in a meta-analysis as a researcher must search and sift through sometimes hundreds of studies! A technique that can alleviate this issue includes the use of a weighted checklist that consists of all the necessary criteria for a study to have in order to be included in the meta-analysis.

A meta-analysis can be very informative, though it is often a time-consuming process. The selection and statistical standardization of the studies determined appropriate for the meta-analysis are critical, and both of these steps require a great deal of detail-orientation and critical thinking skills as one irrelevant study or set of inaccurate results can contaminate the entire meta-analysis.

NONEXPERIMENTAL DESIGNS AND QUALITATIVE DATA ANALYSIS

Research methods involving nonexperimental designs can yield quantitative or qualitative data. The collection and analysis of qualitative data is especially common through the use of nonexperimental methods as we examine such sources as observation notes, letters, speeches, interviews, and narratives. Qualitative data offer a richness and depth of detail in the information that are not characteristics of quantitative data. While this is certainly beneficial, the use of qualitative data comes with a price—the time and effort needed to categorize and code the data in order to analyze and derive findings.

Content Analysis

Content analysis is a commonly used systematic technique for coding and categorizing qualitative data. This is an approach that requires the researcher to examine content from credible data sources relevant to the research question with an awareness of the potential for missing data or inconsistencies and to categorize the data based on a structured coding system for accurate interpretation. Content analysis can be a time-consuming effort and may require research assistance, which further emphasizes the need for a systematic approach among all individuals involved in the process.

Content analysis can be conducted manually or through technology applications that automate the process for electronic content. While conducting content analysis manually can be a labor-intensive process, it can be helpful for a researcher to get a sense of the context in which the data are presented, which can sometimes get lost in translation with an automated program (especially in the English language, with our many homonyms and words with multiple meanings!). A researcher can also incorporate both approaches in the content analysis process, perhaps manually analyzing materials to determine what the categories, subcategories, and method of classification should be first. Many times the necessary categories do not emerge until the data are examined quite thoroughly. This step would be followed by the researcher programming an automated content analysis tool with these specifications and then running additional data source materials through the program.

Regardless of the approach, the content analysis process and resulting coding system for qualitative data interpretation should be as simple as possible and allow for ease of use not only for the researchers but for any other research assistants and contributors involved in gathering, reviewing, categorizing, and entering data for analysis of findings.

The Coding System

A researcher must develop a coding system before qualitative data can be statistically analyzed and interpreted. The coding system developed should be as simple as possible, and it should be *parsimonious*, which means it should not consist of either too many or too few categories. Categories must be clearly defined so there is no confusion about the type of data that should be placed in each category. The numbers, or quantifiers, that each category receives should be logical and orderly. Many researchers develop codebooks, either hard copy or electronic, to record and keep their coding systems well-organized. The following table is an example of a codebook that a researcher might develop for observational research of consumer characteristics and behaviors in a grocery store.

Table 9.1 Sample Codebook for Consumer Behavior Observation

Data Description	Variable Label	Coding System
Primary Shopper Gender	Variable Label = SEX	Male = 1; Female = 2
Children Under 10 yrs With Primary Shopper	Variable Label = KIDS	Yes = 1; No = 2
Purchase Size	Variable Label = SIZE	Hand-held Basket = 1; Shopping Cart = 2

(Continued)

Table 9.1 (Continued)

Data Description	Variable Label	Coding System
Produce Purchase	Variable Label = PROD	Yes = 1; No = 2
Frozen Meal Purchase	Variable Label = FROZ	Yes = 1; No = 2
Packaged Snacks Purchase	Variable Label = SNACK	Yes = 1; No = 2
Coupons Used	Variable Label = COUP	Yes = 1; No = 2
Payment Type	Variable Label = PAY	Cash = 1; Credit/Debit = 2; Check = 3

A strategy that a researcher can use for standardization of data coding is the development of tools, including checklists, matrices, and tally sheets (Rosnow & Rosenthal, 1993). Instruments such as these can facilitate systematic observation of specific behaviors and their frequency and be especially helpful when multiple observations are conducted or when a researcher uses assistants for data collection to ensure consistency across time periods or observers.

Box 9.3 **Practitioner Spotlight: Using Nonexperimental Designs in Human Resource Management Practices**

An example of the strategic use of nonexperimental designs in HRM practices is provided to us by a Senior Human Resources Generalist, Coach, Trainer, and Speaker with more than 10 years of industry corporate experience focused on employee relations/employee engagement, training/development, coaching/counseling, recruitment, selection, and performance management. In the current role, this position manages the HR function for one of the company's facilities to support 175 employees.

As HR practitioners, we want to partner with our managers and better prepare them for potential employee relations cases so that we can appropriately and immediately handle these cases in the best way possible. When issues arise, the acceptable approach to initially take is to first find out exactly what is really bothering the employee(s) and work through their concerns while at the same time gather the critical facts that relate to that particular situation. Two methods often used to better understand and remediate employee relations issues are the analysis of archival personnel data and the conducting of face-to-face interviews. In my experience, I have used these methods successfully and recommend several key steps for effectively researching and resolving employee relations issues:

- Review the employee's personnel file to get familiar with past performance history and past issues that may have been addressed and the associated disciplinary action taken. Take notice if there is a pattern of behavior that has been recognized.

- Consult with other members of the HR team and management to discuss any additional relevant information to that issue and to discuss the approach to take especially when it's a new or sensitive employee relations matter—such as an employee is a member of a protected group, the employee has filed a similar complaint in the past or recent complaint for something else, or the employee has filed a complaint against management/company to the Department of Human Rights or to the Equal Employment Opportunity Commission (EEOC).
- Review past practices and company policies in the Employee Handbook.
- Review past similar employee relations matters and the disciplinary actions taken in those situations. The key is to be consistent and fair across the organization and for all levels of employees.
- Conduct fair employee relations investigative interviews or hold conversations with the employees involved, any witnesses to the situation reported, and management. Never make assumptions about the situation without confirmation through reliable information sources.
- Consult with other members of the HR team and management before making a final decision on the appropriate course of action.
- Ensure you have obtained all the necessary facts and concerns by summarizing your findings with the employee(s) involved, members of the HR Team, and management. Ask for a commitment for the behavior you are seeking from an employee.
- Follow documentation best practices as these narratives and notes to file can later be reviewed for HR/management decisions and possibly may be requested for legal review.
- Coach and teach your management on how to effectively manage employee relations and document incidents for archival record keeping and investigative interviews.

HR practitioners and management should manage employee relations together to proactively encourage employee performance and engagement, to ensure fairness of practices across the workforce, to minimize escalation of problems, and to avoid legal ramifications. Careful personnel documentation and record keeping will ensure accurate archival data analysis when it's necessary to conduct research and investigate issues, and data collected through targeted interviews will help to validate existing information and fill in the gaps.

CHAPTER SUMMARY

- Nonexperimental methods are used primarily for describing data, examining relationships or covariation between variables, and comparing groups. While nonexperimental designs do not incorporate the manipulation of a treatment or condition as experimental and quasi-experimental designs do, which means causal relationships cannot typically be examined, they can be strategically integrated into a research methodology along with an experimental or quasi-experimental design. Nonexperimental designs also allow for the measurement of variables.

- Nonexperimental research methods may fall into the categories of primary analysis, secondary analysis, and meta-analysis. Primary analysis is the term used to describe the analysis of data that was collected by the actual researcher. Examination of data collected by someone other than the researcher is referred to as secondary analysis, and meta-analysis is the statistical analysis of results from a collection of relevant studies.

- Nonexperimental designs are appropriate in many field settings and can be a valuable option for researchers in obtaining information on individual and group behaviors and norms, variations in cultures or large social settings, roles and relationships, single events and episodes, recurring events and trends, and comparisons between two or more variables. The most common nonexperimental methods used by researchers in applied settings include observation (obtrusive and unobtrusive), archival data collection and analysis, survey designs, and case studies.

- Research methods involving nonexperimental designs can yield quantitative or qualitative data. The collection and analysis of qualitative data through nonexperimental designs is common with such data sources as observation notes, letters, speeches, interviews, and narratives. Qualitative data offer a richness and depth of detail in the information that are not characteristics of quantitative data, though the use of qualitative data does require time and effort to categorize and code the data in order to analyze and derive findings. Content analysis is a commonly used systematic technique for coding and categorizing qualitative data.

DISCUSSION QUESTIONS

- Why should a researcher consider using nonexperimental research methods if causal inference cannot be made? How can a researcher integrate nonexperimental methods in a study and still have the ability to infer causality from the findings obtained?

- What is the difference between primary analysis, secondary analysis, and meta-analysis? Why is this distinction important with nonexperimental research designs?

- What factors should a researcher consider when making a determination between conducting observational research as unobtrusive, obtrusive, or a hybrid approach? How might the typical parameters and constraints in many field settings influence this decision?

- How can qualitative data be a valuable source of information when conducting nonexperimental research? What technique is used for analyzing and deriving findings from qualitative data?

- Consider the following scenario:

  An educational consulting firm has recently introduced a short-term remedial reading package for elementary schools. This program, "Quick Literacy," is 1 week in length. The consulting firm states that the 1-week program significantly improves the reading ability of children of average development in the third through fifth grades.

You are an advisor to a school system's Board of Education, and they have asked you to propose a strategy to evaluate the program. There are three classes at each grade level, and you have access to archival records that includes monthly reading aptitude test scores, annual intelligence test scores, and quarterly progress reports.

How can you use the resources available to conduct a program evaluation using a nonexperimental approach? What are the strengths and limitations of such an approach? How could you integrate a nonexperimental method with another research method to make a causal inference regarding the effectiveness of this program?

CHAPTER KEY TERMS

Archival Data	Field Notes	Qualitative Data
Case Study	Interview	Reactivity
Codebook	Meta-Analysis	Secondary Analysis
Coding System	Naturalistic Observation	Unobtrusive Observation
Content Analysis	Parsimonious	Z Score
Controlled Observation	Primary Analysis	
Effect Size	Obtrusive Observation	

CHAPTER 10

Survey Research Designs

Throughout our experience, we have noticed that a lot of our colleagues believe the solution to a problem can be solved using a survey. While this may be true in some situations, our colleagues sometimes do not understand the complexity and nuances of developing a reliable and valid survey. Just because software organizations have made it easier for you to create a survey at the click of a button does not necessarily mean that you should go out and administer surveys. Simply being an expert in the field is a necessary, but not sufficient, condition for developing a high quality and valid survey. It is always advisable to consult a survey methodology expert in addition to the subject matter experts during the survey development process. Writing survey items is complex, and it is important to understand the nuances of item writing. Think about this for a minute. Both of your textbook authors have experience with survey design and development but no experience flying a plane. However, we have the ability to read books and learn about flying a plane. Would you feel comfortable getting on a plane knowing that one of us would be your pilot? The moral of the story is that you wouldn't want us flying your plane and we wouldn't want a pilot developing a survey!

AN INTRODUCTION TO SURVEY RESEARCH

Survey research is perhaps the most commonly used type of research design by applied researchers and practitioners. Survey research methods include self-report measures such as questionnaires and assessments as well as interviews and are mainly used for collecting data on attitudes, beliefs, preferences, and behaviors from a representative sample of a population.

Researchers use different survey research methods for a variety of needs in applied settings. These are just a few examples:

- A polling organization sends a questionnaire to residential homes in a geographic location to learn about citizens' views on candidates for an upcoming mayoral election.

- A researcher in a shopping mall approaches shoppers to ask them questions about the stores they shop in most often and the purchases they typically make in each store.

- A market research firm conducts a focus group for a client in the beverage industry to obtain feedback on a proposed new packaging design for their line of bottled water.

- A Human Resources function for a global organization develops and distributes an anonymous online questionnaire to determine employee satisfaction with the current benefits offerings and compare feedback among regional business sites.

Data collected through survey research can be used for descriptive, comparative, and explanatory purposes. As we have discussed in the previous chapter, survey research methods are one type of nonexperimental research method commonly used for describing behaviors and phenomena, for examining relationships and covariation among two or more variables, and for examining changes and trends in people's attitudes, behaviors, and preferences over time. However, survey research methods should not be considered solely nonexperimental, and here is the reason: A researcher can create different versions of a questionnaire and use these versions as conditions, or levels of an independent variable, to measure differences in a dependent variable across conditions. For example, a researcher interested in examining the effect that the gender of a restaurant server has on a customer's service perception following a bad meal may create three different versions of a questionnaire: one version with an opening scenario that includes a female server name, one with an opening scenario that includes a male server name, and one that includes a gender-neutral server name. Yes, this is a type of survey research, but because there is manipulation of an independent variable in this example, it is considered experimental.

> **respondent:** an individual providing information through a survey research method

Survey research is unlike other types of research methods in that the accuracy of the data lies predominantly with the individuals providing it. These individuals, referred to in survey research as *respondents*, are expected to be willing and able to provide honest and accurate information. In some cases, respondents purposely give inaccurate information, and in some cases, the respondents simply do not remember the information correctly. For example, if you were asked the question, "How many hours of television did you watch in the last week?" would you be able to recall the exact number of hours you watched television? It is highly unlikely. Researchers can construct items that can facilitate more accurate recall of such details, which we will discuss in more detail in the context of questionnaire construction. Researchers can employ various techniques for determining the accuracy of responses, such as comparing data between similar samples of respondents, or including dummy items that can *red flag* a less than truthful, biased, or forgetful respondent.

Box 10.1 Survey or Questionnaire . . . Tomato or Tomahto?

While the terms *survey* and *questionnaire* are used interchangeably quite often, there is actually a difference between them. The term *survey* is used to describe the type of research, and the term *questionnaire* is used to describe the actual document or form containing questions and items developed by a researcher to obtain the necessary data.

QUESTIONNAIRE CONSTRUCTION

When constructing a questionnaire, a researcher should develop items that will be easily and consistently interpreted by all respondents in the sample. The questionnaire layout and design also requires focus in terms of the overall look and appeal. Visual elements, such as color of paper or web page background, font style and size, and pictures, figures, and graphics, are an important consideration when developing a questionnaire. A questionnaire should not look bland and dull nor should it look cluttered and complicated. In addition, the questions should be straightforward and appear nonthreatening so the respondents will actually want to answer them. To accomplish this, a researcher must word items simply, objectively, and in as nonoffensive of a manner as possible. As you can imagine, this is no easy effort as individuals vary tremendously in terms of language comprehension and reading skills, attention span, and personal values and attitudes. Survey researchers can integrate a variety of question design elements to suit the needs and content of the questionnaire, which we will discuss next.

Types of Questions

There are several types of questions and items that are most commonly included in the different forms of survey research: questions about attitudes, beliefs, and preferences; questions about behaviors; and fact and demographic-based questions. A questionnaire may incorporate any combination of these item types depending on the construct and research question under examination.

No matter what types of questions are included, they should follow some basic rules. Questions should be written in complete sentences. Respondents will likely comprehend, "What is your age?" more clearly than an item that merely states the word "Age." Researchers should write in active sentences rather than passive sentences. What does this mean? The following are examples of active and passive sentences:

> **jargon:** terminology that is specific to a population, industry, organization, or group, and is not well known or understood by anyone outside that entity

Active Sentence:

Your school's teachers select textbooks that are interesting.

Passive Sentence:

The textbooks that are selected by the teachers in your school are interesting.

Also, the words selected for each question should be as simple as possible, and a researcher should consider average reading level in the sample, perhaps by age, grade/education, or literacy, to approximate the level of wording that will be appropriate and not too advanced. A researcher should be careful to not include words that are highly specialized, or jargon, which is terminology that is specific to a population, industry, organization, or group, and is not well-known or understood by anyone outside that entity. The only situation in which jargon may be a reasonable inclusion in a questionnaire is when it is necessary and relevant to the answers provided by respondents *and* it is determined that all individuals included in the sample will understand the terminology and the context in which it is being used. However, if this determination cannot be made with a reasonable degree of certainty, it is best to stick with simple and generic words.

While simplicity is an important consideration when developing questions, an equally important consideration is clarity versus ambiguity. A researcher walks a fine line between keeping question wording simple and becoming vague as a result of wording questions too simply without necessary detail and context. One way a researcher can address this need is to allow outside readers, who possess a reading and language level close to the individuals in the expected sample but are not part of the research, to read through the questions and provide their interpretation of each one. A researcher will be able to determine the extent to which the questions are being read and understood as intended and make any adjustments to wording before administering the questionnaire to the actual sample.

Open-Ended and Close-Ended Questions

An open-ended question is one in which the respondent may answer freely and provide a response in any length or detail. An advantage with the use of open-ended questions is they may yield a greater level of detail and put the response into a certain context that a researcher may not be able to obtain through close-ended questions.

The following is an example of an open-ended question:

What are the main reasons for your decision to resign from your position with our organization?

Response:_____

A close-ended question is one in which the respondent must provide an answer from a limited number of responses, such as yes or no. The main advantage of using close-ended questions is their simplicity for data collection and analysis, and researchers often use close-ended questions when they are interested in targeting a specific response set or if they do not have the time or resources to set up a coding system.

The following is an example of a close-ended question:

Is the main reason for your decision to resign from your position with our organization compensation related?

_____ Yes

_____ No

While both open- and close-ended questions offer unique benefits, they also have certain disadvantages. A researcher may have to spend a great deal of time and effort in coding/categorizing responses to open-ended questions and discarding irrelevant information. With close-ended questions, a researcher may not be providing all possible response options suitable to all the respondents in the sample. This may result in a respondent skipping a question or providing an answer that is not really accurate.

Forced Choice Items

A forced choice response set is an option that offers a bit more flexibility than the close-ended question yet retains more limitation in response than the open-ended question. A questionnaire item that incorporates a forced choice response set provides respondents with a short list of items from which to select the most appropriate response to that item. A researcher could also decide to include an "Other" option in the event a respondent does not see an appropriate choice among those listed. The use of the "Other" choice should be carefully considered before implementation as it does require content categorization and coding before the responses can be analyzed.

A researcher may choose to allow respondents to select multiple choices from the response set provided or restrict respondents to selecting just one option. Either approach is reasonable and depends on the intent of the questionnaire item and the researcher's specific data needs.

An example of an item with a forced choice response set that restricts the respondent to just one answer may look like this:

What is your main reason for shopping online? Please select one response that best represents your perspective.

__ I don't have time to travel to stores to shop.

__ I can find out if a particular item is in stock immediately.

__ I like the ease of making online purchases.

__ I receive coupons and shopping rewards the more I shop online.

__ Other _____

An example of an item with a forced choice response set that allows the respondent to select multiple options may look like this:

What do you prefer about shopping online instead of shopping in a physical store? Please feel free to select all responses that represent your perspective.

__ I don't have time to travel to stores to shop.

__ I can find out if a particular item is in stock immediately.

__ I like the ease of making online purchases.

__ I receive coupons and shopping rewards the more I shop online.

__ Other _____

Response Scales

For certain types of forced choice questions, researchers will use response scales that provide respondents with options that fall along a continuum. Depending on the questionnaire item, the options on a response scale can be provided as numbers, words, phrases, and even graphics. Though any options that are nonnumeric must still be coded as numerals for data analysis, the coding is a relatively simple process.

Perhaps the most commonly used type of response scale in survey research is the Likert scale, named for its developer Rensis Likert (1932), which can be customized based on the appropriate response needed for a questionnaire item and the level of detail needed from the response. The scale anchors are numbered or coded, and each anchor represents a degree of attitude that ranges from extremely favorable on one end to extremely unfavorable on the other end of the scale.

A commonly used Likert scale incorporates anchors of agreement and is often used with questionnaire items dealing with attitudes about certain topics or issues (e.g., legalization of marijuana, hands-free cell phone laws).

An example of an agreement type of Likert scale may look like this:

1	2	3	4	5
Strongly Disagree	Disagree	Neutral	Agree	Strongly Agree

Another scale commonly used in survey research is the Thurstone scale, named for its developer L.L. Thurstone (1929). This type of scale is used to assess attitudes and is constructed using Thurstone's method of equal-appearing intervals.

Researchers typically use response scales that consist of five to seven anchors, or points, along the scale that represent the response choices. A response scale that includes too few anchors may not offer respondents with an adequate number of choices, and respondents may be forced to choose between two less than accurate options.

An example of this issue might look like this:
How often do you floss your teeth?

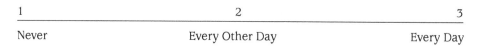

1	2	3
Never	Every Other Day	Every Day

Clearly, this scale is not adequate because it does not offer enough response options. A respondent who flosses once or twice a week, for example, would be forced to choose an inaccurate response, thus contaminating the data.

Conversely, a response scale that includes too many anchors may not provide a clear differentiation between the anchors.

Frequency Response Scales

A researcher who is interested in the number of occurrences respondents behave in a particular manner (as in the previous example of flossing) may design a frequency scale. Frequency scales are commonly used in questionnaires, though a researcher must construct the anchor labels carefully. It is important that (1) the anchor labels are not vague, (2) the anchor labels represent all time/frequency options necessary to examine, and (3) the progression from one end of the scale to the other should follow a logical sequence and reasonably equal distance between anchor points.

Unipolar and Bipolar Response Scales

Bipolar response scales incorporate cue words that are connotative, or represent subjective meaning, of a construct of interest. This is known as *semantic differential* and enables researchers to examine how respondents subjectively perceive constructs from one end of a spectrum to the other (Rosnow & Rosenthal, 1993). Researchers form bipolar cue response scales using the most common dimensions of subjective meaning: evaluation,

> **semantic differential:** cue words that represent subjective meaning of a construct of interest, enabling researchers to examine how respondents subjectively perceive constructs from one end of a spectrum to the other

potency, and frequency. The evaluation dimension is comprised of such cue words as good-bad, fair-biased, beautiful-ugly, and smart-stupid. The potency dimension encompasses such cue words as light-heavy, small-large, shallow-deep, and soft-hard. Lastly, the frequency dimension is comprised of cue words such as always-never and fast-slow. It is critical that respondents all have a unified understanding of the cue words and their definitions in the context of the questionnaire item and scale.

The following are some examples of bipolar and unipolar response scales:

Bipolar Scale

1	2	3	4	5
Poor	Fair	Average	Good	Excellent

Unipolar Scale

1	2	3	4	5
Not at all Fair	Somewhat Fair	Neutral	Moderately Fair	Completely Fair

Different items on a questionnaire can have response scales with different types of anchors, and in fact, this is a fairly common design. However, the scales used should include the same number of anchors (e.g., all 5-point scales) for consistency and simplicity for the respondent. Scales that vary throughout the questionnaire, for example, a 3-point scale followed by a 7-point scale, may be confusing for the respondents and increase the likelihood for inaccurate answers or fewer completed questionnaires.

Graphic Response Scales

A researcher may wish to design a response scale that is easily or universally understood by all respondents regardless of language and reading ability. For example, a customer service questionnaire may be sent to all customers in a store's database, but the customers may differ in their level of literacy. Another example of this need is the distribution of an employee input questionnaire within a global organization that has business units in several countries. In these types of situations, the use of a scale that incorporates graphical depiction of the response options rather than words or phrases can be an effective approach.

Graphic response scales use pictures to represent the meaning of each anchor. A common scale is the "Faces" scale (Kunin, 1955), which incorporate smiling, neutral, and frowning faces to represent degree of happiness or satisfaction in response to that particular questionnaire item. Similarly, the use of a thermometer graphic, with response options along its length, may be a useful and recognizable picture associated with responses of degrees, literal temperature, figurative temperature (one's feelings of hot or cold about a topic), or some movement along a low-high spectrum.

Item Quantity and Progression

The number of questions or items on a questionnaire should be carefully considered as the length of a questionnaire can affect the number of completed submissions and also the accuracy of the answers provided. A questionnaire that is too long may disinterest respondents who may decide to quit before completing the entire questionnaire, make up answers just to get through it quickly, or decide not to participate at all if the length of the questionnaire is known before beginning. Any items that are not relevant to the research question should be omitted. However, a researcher should ensure that all necessary items are included because respondents cannot be sent follow-up questions if they are inadvertently excluded in the first questionnaire. The bottom line for a researcher is to make sure there are items representing every area in which data are required to examine the research question, no more and no less.

Items on a questionnaire should be positioned in a way that appears as a logical progression to respondents. Typically, a researcher will position broader and more general questions first, in the beginning of the questionnaire, followed by more specific questions. Some questionnaires are designed to address several themes or topics, for example, favorite stores and their key attributes, followed by items typically purchased in those stores, followed by likelihood of purchasing those items from a competitor. When this is the case, a researcher can incorporate structured topic sections or groupings so the respondent can easily see where one topic's items end and a new topic's items begin. A respondent may become confused and frustrated when attempting to complete a questionnaire in which the questions bounce around between specific and general or between topics. This will result in either inaccurate responses or lowered response rate as a result of respondents quitting before completion.

QUESTIONNAIRE IMPLEMENTATION

Sampling and Sample Size

Determining the correct sample of relevant cases from a population that includes all the necessary characteristics for a study is critical to the validity and reliability of survey research. Obviously, it is not feasible to conduct survey research on an entire population, and the good news is that it's not even necessary with the appropriate sample. A sample is a representative group of cases from the population, and this means that the sample consists of all the characteristics of the population as a whole. A sample can consist of individual persons, such as registered voters, college students, teachers, and senior citizens, and this is the most common type of sample. A

> **sample:** a representative group of cases from the population, ideally consisting of all the characteristics of the population as a whole

sample can also consist of entities such as households, companies, schools, labor unions, churches, and so on. Sometimes cases are also referred to as elements.

However a sample is comprised, its representativeness of the population and relevance to the research question of interest are the most important

> **confidence interval:** a value used to depict the degree of a sample's representativeness to the population from which it was derived

considerations. With a representative sample, a researcher can have confidence that the inferences made about the sample can also be extended, or *generalized*, to the population. The type of generalization that a researcher is seeking will vary based on the unique research goals. A researcher may seek to generalize findings across (U)nits, (T)reatments, (O)utcomes, (S)ituations, or a combination of these elements, which we will revisit in more detail in Chapter 12. A confidence interval is a value used to depict the degree of a sample's representativeness to the population from which it was derived. The higher the value (a 95% confidence interval is considered an adequate value), the greater the likelihood that the sample provided data that is a valid estimate of data that the entire population would have provided and the lower the likelihood of measurement error. In survey research, this type of error is referred to as sampling error and depicts the degree to which a sample is irrelevant or *veered off* from the population.

Sampling Techniques

Two techniques used by researchers are referred to as probability sampling and nonprobability sampling. We will define these sampling techniques and discuss the specific methods within each one next.

Probability Sampling

With probability sampling, each member of the population has a specifiable probability of being included in the sample. Probability sampling includes the following methods:

- *Simple random sampling*, in which each member of a population has an equal probability of being included in the sample. This is the most basic of the probability sampling designs, and it is the most straightforward. Essentially, simple random sampling is similar to picking names (cases) from a hat (population). Up until fairly recently, the process was rather arduous because researchers had to conduct the random sampling manually—imagine opening up a hard copy phone book to a random page, closing your eyes, picking an entry, and recording the contact data . . . several hundred times! Thankfully, technology has facilitated simple random sampling, and researchers can use applications that automatically randomly identify and record cases based on preselected criteria from large pools of population data, such as phone numbers or store rewards account numbers.

- *Stratified sampling*, in which the population is divided into subgroups, or strata, and a researcher selects members from each subgroup to be included in the sample. Strata are determined by their relevance to the research question and area of interest.

- *Cluster sampling*, in which a population is divided into groups by geographical location. Some examples of common cluster groups in applied research include schools and school systems, individual businesses, business units/sites within a large organization, hospitals, and towns in a district or county. A researcher will obtain information on all the geographic clusters in a population to determine selection of representative cluster groups.

Nonprobability Sampling

With nonprobability sampling, a researcher cannot determine the probability of any one member of the population being included in the sample. Nonprobability sampling includes the following methods:

> **probability sampling:** a sampling technique in which each member of the population has a specifiable probability of being included in the sample
>
> **nonprobability sampling:** a sampling technique in which a researcher cannot determine the probability of any one member of the population being included in the sample

- *Convenience sampling*, in which the researcher gathers individuals for a sample using whatever mode is feasible given time, location, and resource constraints.

- *Snowball sampling*, in which a researcher requests referrals of additional individuals to contact from existing respondents. Snowball sampling is another type of convenience sampling method often used in situations in which desired respondents are difficult to locate within the population based on scarcity or lack of identifying information.

- *Quota sampling*, in which a population is divided into subgroups, similar to stratified sampling, but the researcher gathers individuals for the sample's subgroups in a nonprobability manner. When the quota for a subgroup is filled, the researcher focuses on gathering individuals to include in the other subgroups.

- *Purposive sampling*, in which the researcher specifically selects the cases judged to be most typical of the population and should be included in the sample. A researcher using a purposive sampling approach will determine the cases to include in the sample based on how relevant they are to the research question and also the quantity and quality of information they are likely to provide.

Delivery Modality

Survey research methods can be conducted through a variety of delivery approaches. Questionnaires can be distributed by hard copy mail and electronically by e-mail and web links. Questionnaires can also be delivered by telephone interview and conducted through either a live person-to-person conversation or an automated touch-tone or voice-response system. Lastly, questionnaires can be administered face-to-face through a live interviewer who asks the questions and records responses on a structured form. There are advantages and disadvantages to all of these modalities, which we have summarized in Box 10.2.

A mixed mode approach in which two or more different delivery techniques are implemented is ideal in many situations that require outreach to a diverse sample that may not be able or willing to provide information through certain modes. Here are several examples of common issues:

Box 10.2 Advantages and Disadvantages of Survey Research Delivery Modes

Hard Copy Mail

Advantages

Ability to reach a large number of individuals

Random selection can be easily handled through zip codes

Individuals without telephones or computers can be included

Disadvantages

Can be time consuming to put together mailings

Response rate can be low

E-mail & Web Links

Advantages

Ability to reach a large number of individuals

Cost efficient to distribute

Disadvantages

Individuals without computer access or proficiency cannot participate

Development of questionnaire can be time consuming and require technical skills

Telephone

Advantages

Random selection can be easily handled through area codes

Real-time data collection

Disadvantages

May be perceived as inconvenient or intrusive

Response rate—respondents must answer the phone and be available to participate at that time

Language barriers

Complex questions with many response options may be difficult to process without visual

Face-to-Face

Advantages

Real-time data collection

Researcher can provide clarification to questions if needed

Disadvantages

Can be time consuming

Respondents may feel pressure to answer a certain way

- An individual who is not computer literate or does not have access to a computer with Internet will not be able to provide information through an e-mail or web-based questionnaire.

- An individual who cannot read well or at all will not be able to provide information through a questionnaire in any written format, hard copy or electronic.

- An individual who is busy and always on the go will be much less likely to respond to a questionnaire that arrives in their hard copy mail (snail mail) or must be conducted by calling a certain telephone number.

Interviews

Researchers often use interviews to gather information in applied settings and can be conducted one-on-one or in groups depending on the situation and need. In place of a questionnaire, a researcher will develop an interview script to facilitate data collection and keep each interview on track by enabling delivery of the same questions in the same order. There are unique advantages to each approach as well as disadvantages.

Individual Interview

A one-on-one, or individual, interview is a useful method when a lack of trust exists among interviewees—a common issue in applied settings. Interviewees may not trust each other and they may not trust the organization or institution, which will likely result in interviewees refusing to offer information and answers to questions in the presence of others for fear of misrepresentation or retaliation. One way to build trust and reduce an interviewee's hesitancy to give information is to conduct the interviews one-on-one in a confidential environment that puts the interviewee at ease. Remember, inaccuracies and omissions will render the data that a researcher worked so hard to collect corrupt and invalid, and it is critical to take steps to reduce this possibility. The main disadvantage with the individual interview approach is that it can be quite time consuming, particularly if a large number of interviews must be conducted.

Group Interview

A group interview is an efficient method for collecting data from multiple individuals at the same time. Group size can vary but should not be so large that responses from all interviewees are not possible.

A common type of group interview is referred to as a focus group, which is commonly used in business settings and for market research to explore consumer preferences and opinions. Focus groups are typically video recorded and led by a facilitator with a panel of researchers observing from another room. Focus groups are strategically designed and conducted to gather group and individual responses to structured questions, multimedia clips and pictures, and products as well as to observe nonverbal cues and behaviors.

A disadvantage with the group interview technique is that interviewees may distort responses to conform to the group or to make a certain impression on the group and/or interviewer.

It can be especially helpful to provide interviewees with a list of questions or topics that will be covered to ensure they can provide the appropriate information or bring any important materials or resources to the interview session. This strategy not only facilitates the collection of specific and relevant information but it can also save valuable time and need for follow-up action.

Another useful interview approach is referred to as the critical incident technique. This is considered an open-ended question, and the interviewee is asked to provide an example of a real situation that is relevant to the construct of interest. For example, if the topic of customer service is the focus area for the interview, a critical incident question may be, "Describe a time when you received excellent customer service in your favorite store, and what specifics of this experience made it excellent in your opinion?"

Survey Research Issues

Response Rate

The percentage of individuals selected for a sample that actually completes a questionnaire or interview is referred to as the response rate. If a researcher sends a web link to an online questionnaire to 1,000 individuals and 500 of them complete and submit the questionnaire, the response rate is 50%. There are many factors that may negatively affect a response rate, including timing of distribution and time required to respond, required effort to respond, ability to respond based on distribution method, and interest in responding.

> **response rate:** the percentage of individuals selected for a sample that actually completes a question or interview

Survey researchers can use different types of incentives and rewards in an attempt to increase response rate, and they can be monetary or nonmonetary. For example, researchers may include a small token monetary reward such as a one-dollar bill or product coupons with a hard copy questionnaire that is distributed via mail.

Honesty

The extent to which a respondent is providing honest answers is always a concern in survey research. Even the most accurate, objective, and well-designed questionnaires may be subject to inaccuracies from dishonest responses ranging from *white lies* to dramatic falsification. One common issue regarding honesty in survey research is impression management, which is the tendency of individuals to alter their behaviors based on their perception of what will make a good impression to others. In survey research, self-report questions are often subject to impression management, especially with questions that are sensitive in nature such as habits like smoking/alcohol/drug use, personal ethics, and unfavorable personal opinions. Though challenging to identify at times, a researcher may be able to decrease the likelihood of impression management and honesty issues by ensuring respondents that the information provided will be confidential (or anonymous) and that the wording of the questions does not appear judgmental. Another approach that a researcher can take to identify dishonest responses is to integrate dummy questions that may *red flag* a questionnaire potentially containing dishonest answers. An example of a dummy question is, "Have you ever told a lie at any point in your life?" Obviously, we have all told a lie at some time during our lives, and a respondent who answers "no" to this question may also answer dishonestly to other questions.

Memory and Recall

Researchers strive to obtain the most accurate information possible from respondents and must be able to design survey research items that respondents can answer simply and without much difficulty. A researcher should determine the extent to which a respondent will be able to recall the information requested as this will vary based on a variety of factors such as level of detail and preciseness of information, quantity of information, and the recency of the information (Dillman, 2007). Obviously, respondents will be able to answer certain questions such as one asking for their age rather easily and without assistance as this is personal information well known to us and easily recalled. However, other pieces of information may be more challenging to recall with any degree of accuracy. To facilitate recall, questionnaire items can be designed to assist respondents with cues that are especially helpful with frequency and time ranges.

The following questions are examples of a question without assisting recall cues and a question that provides a recall cue in the form of frequency ranges:

Question without a recall cue

In the past month, how many hours have you used a smartphone to check your e-mails?

_____ times

Question with a recall cue

In the past month, how many hours have you used a smartphone to check e-mails?

_____ More than 20 hours

_____ Between 11–20 hours

_____ Between 1–10 hours

_____ Less than 1 hour or never

_____ I do not own a smartphone

Wording Issues

A researcher must be careful to word questionnaire items in the most objective way possible. This is especially critical with topics that are sensitive or likely to elicit strong emotions from respondents. It can be easy for a researcher to inadvertently frame questions in a way that can be construed as biased or misleading; sometimes this can occur with a mere addition of one word or phrase. An example of a question with bias is, "Do you believe that your organization's senior managers make far too many insensitive budget cuts in areas that negatively affect employees?" In this question, the phrase "far too many" and the word "insensitive" together create a tone that can come across as biased against senior managers. A more objectively worded question would be, "Do you believe that your organization's senior managers make budget cuts in areas that negatively affect employees?"

Negative words, such as "not" and "no," should also be avoided because the use of negative words can be confusing to respondents when reading a questionnaire item. An example of a statement with negative wording is, "I believe the airline industry should not ignore the need for ongoing training for security personnel." A better way to word this sentence is, "I believe the airline industry should continue to provide ongoing training for security personnel." Another example of negative wording is called a double negative in which a researcher uses two negative words in one questionnaire item to actually reflect a positive because the two negatives cancel each other out. An example of a statement with a double negative is, "I do not believe that the airline industry should not implement extra security measures in airports during holiday travel." This sentence is basically stating, "I believe the airline industry should implement extra security measures in airports during holiday travel," but the use of the double negative in the wording often results in confusion, which may affect the accuracy of the response provided.

Lastly, a double-barreled question is another common wording issue. A double-barreled question is one that includes two questions or is comprised of two topics in one question. An example of a double-barreled question is, "Are you in favor of the proposed income tax increase and educational budget cuts?" Because it is impossible to determine whether

> **double-barreled question:** an item that includes two questions or is comprised of two topics in one question

the response provided is for one or both items in the question, researchers must be careful to ensure that each question addresses only one area of focus. If both items are important to include in the questionnaire, they should be addressed in two separate questions.

Survey Research Errors

Coverage Error

When a researcher's sampling effort does not allow all the individuals in a population to have an equal chance of being included in the sample, coverage error is a likely result.

Sampling Error

Sampling error may occur when a researcher has not randomly selected an adequate number of representative individuals from the population. The sample does not represent all of the categories or groups within the population that should be included to participate.

Measurement Error

Measurement error may occur as a result of question wording that is confusing, vague, inaccurate, or unintelligible. Respondents may interpret the question in different ways because the question is not clearly and accurately presented, and this will likely affect the answers provided.

Nonresponse Error

When survey research respondents are different in some way to individuals who were included in the sample but did not respond, nonresponse error is an issue. Individuals may choose to respond or not respond for a number of reasons, including time constraints, topic interest, desire for a participation incentive/reward, or feelings of obligation.

Rating Error

Rating errors may occur when respondents' answers are provided based on inappropriate judgments, bias, and other perceptual distortions. There are a variety of rating errors, including the following:

- Halo effect may occur when a respondent forms an overall impression based on a favorable perception of just one attribute.

- Leniency error occurs when a respondent provides responses that are overly favorable.

- Central tendency error may occur when a respondent provides responses around the center or middle of all the options provided rather than the extremes at either end of the response scale.

ANALYZING, REPORTING, AND APPLYING SURVEY FINDINGS

Survey research can yield data that is versatile and can be analyzed from a multitude of different perspectives, depending on the actual data collected and the source. The scope and direction of the analysis are important considerations as the modality itself (e.g., questionnaire items, interview questions) is developed. Demographic data that are collected, such as gender, education level, department, job title, and years employed with the organization, can be integrated as needed to fine-tune a broad *big picture* analysis or provide another layer of detail to the responses obtained.

We must emphasize the importance of only collecting data that are absolutely necessary, and this is a critical point for several reasons. Respondents faced with a lengthy and overly probing series of questions may feel exposed and hesitant to provide complete or accurate information, which negatively affects the analysis. Administrators (e.g., Human Resources professionals, managers, consultants) trying to deliver a complex and elaborately detailed interview or questionnaire, be it face-to-face or electronically conducted, may find the development and process more time consuming than it needs to be, and this can become a frustrating effort that is not likely to be considered for future needs (i.e., the "We're not going through that again!" mindset). In addition, respondents and stakeholders alike may have a certain set of expectations on the application and outcome of the survey data based on the items included. We have learned through our experience that if you do not intend to do anything with a certain piece of data, do not include an item asking for information or input on it! If a questionnaire item is included that asks respondents for their interest level on the possible implementation of a new wellness program and there is no budget allocation or support for such a program, do not ask about it because its inclusion on the questionnaire will create an expectation that a wellness program is being planned. This will ensue disappointment and create or add to a sense of skepticism and distrust in the survey research process, the outcomes, or both.

Regarding the reporting of data, findings from survey research can be presented in a variety of ways depending on the needs of the practitioners involved. Let's take a common organizational practice administered by a Human Resources department as an example: the employee exit interview. This modality for collecting data from an employee voluntarily terminating employment can be conducted as an interview or administered as a questionnaire. Items typically include reasons for leaving the organization and suggestions for increased focus for improvements to be made that may benefit the workforce. The interesting thing is most people are quite candid in their responses, and this is likely due to the fact that they are not concerned with the consequences of providing negative feedback because they are leaving. The data collected can be valuable to numerous stakeholders as long as it's reported and presented with their needs in mind. A report on the overall number of voluntary terminations and their respective departments, perhaps presented as a quarterly or annual trends report, may be relevant to senior management and Finance department stakeholders to better understand how employee turnover affects overhead costs and the organization's bottom line. A report summarizing the myriad reasons for leaving provided by the former employees will be useful for Human Resources department stakeholders as they examine needs from which to propose changes or initiatives. For example, a consistently reported "low salary" reason for leaving an organization may be evidence that a salary benchmarking project is needed, or a "no opportunities to learn new skills" reason may signal a need to assess existing training programs and the extent to which supervisors encourage and support their staff to participate in developmental opportunities.

Our final point on the utility of survey research concerns the application of findings to meet organizational needs. The purpose of the survey research, if clearly discussed and supported by key stakeholders right from the beginning of the process through a needs assessment and implementation plan, should be directly aligned with the specific decisions and

---

Box 10.3	**Practitioner Spotlight: Organizational Survey Research/Correlational Research**

The goal of this research initiative was to assess the satisfaction of employees in a public sector agency in New York with their job and the workplace. Survey/correlational research was the method chosen to carry out this research study. It was hypothesized that employees of this public sector agency would be satisfied with their job and the workplace.

The dependent variable in this study was job satisfaction. For studying job satisfaction, an attitude-based model was applied according to which job satisfaction was defined as the positive or negative evaluative judgments employees make about their job or job situations.

Extensive review of the existing literature on job satisfaction was conducted where five components were identified. As a result, the dependent variable was clearly specified and construction of the instrument to be used started. In designing the questionnaire, it was decided that none of the instruments available suited the needs of this study. Hence, the first draft of the questionnaire was written following guidelines regarding the wording and ordering of questions. The questionnaire was reviewed by experts in survey research and members of the administration to ensure that the items were not confusing or biased. Then, a pretest was carried out where the questionnaire was administered to a

(Continued)

(Continued)

small number of respondents to assess their reactions to each question and to the questionnaire as a whole. Three items appeared somewhat ambiguous to the respondents, and edits were made to resolve this problem. Another pretest was performed to determine whether the changes made were adequate. It appeared that the items were now clear, specific, and unambiguous.

The questionnaire consisted of 31 items and responses were given on a 5-point Likert-type scale with options ranging from 1 (strongly disagree) to 5 (strongly agree). An open-ended question was also included in the questionnaire where participants were asked to offer practical suggestions for improving employee satisfaction. In addition to the items that assessed components of job satisfaction: (1) satisfaction with the work/job (e.g., autonomy, job design), (2) relationship with the supervisor (style of supervisor and type of participative climate), (3) relationship with coworkers, (4) compensation (pay and benefits), and (5) opportunities for growth and learning, a few demographic questions were added such as occupational group, work location, and length of employment with the agency. These questions were included to allow for comparisons by type of office/division and occupational group as well as to enable meaningful interpretation of the data obtained.

The reliability and validity of the measurements made using this questionnaire were assessed. Reliability analysis (Cronbach's alpha) was performed on the measure used in this study, and results indicated that the measure had satisfactory internal consistency reliability ($\alpha = .965$). The validity of the measure was assessed using a construct validation approach. The items on the questionnaire were factor analyzed using direct quartimin rotation and five major components were identified, a finding consistent with the structure of the questionnaire.

In order to reduce research costs and to enlarge sample size, the survey was administered via the agency's Intranet. The survey form was created using an electronic survey platform and access to an Intranet server for posting the materials and for processing incoming data was granted. Before going *live* with this web-based survey, extensive pilot testing was conducted to ensure the proper appearance and functioning of the survey web page. The survey was also available in paper-and-pencil format to include employees who did not have access to a personal computer.

Using the contact information of all of the agency's employees, a census survey was planned and conducted. An e-mail from the agency's administrative director was sent out inviting all employees with access to the organization's e-mail system ($n = 700$) to participate in the survey and give the administration a first-hand account of their experiences working for the agency. The e-mail also included a link to the survey and an attached paper version. An additional 50 employees who did not have access to the agency's e-mail system were distributed a paper version of the survey. Employees were told that they could obtain a paper version of the survey from their supervisor and were assured that their responses would remain confidential. They were also informed that the survey would take approximately 15 minutes to complete. Those filling out the paper-and-pencil versions of the survey were instructed to return them by mailing them to a P.O. Box. A month past the original e-mail, a follow-up e-mail was sent by the agency's administrative director inviting those who hadn't already responded to participate and informing them that the final day to respond was a week later.

A total of 272 employees responded to the survey online or by a paper submission resulting in a 36.3% response rate. Following an initial analysis of the survey results, 93 employees were randomly selected and invited to participate in one of seven focus group sessions. Participants for the focus groups were selected using a stratified random sample where employees were divided into subgroups based on their job grade and the office/division they worked in. Participants were drawn on a proportional basis to ensure representativeness. Each of the focus groups had employees from different Offices/Divisions but were separated into two groups, by type of position, either supervisory or nonsupervisory. Employees in managerial or security-related positions were not part of the focus group sessions. The purpose of the focus groups was to elicit additional perspectives about the survey results as well as to gain a better understanding of the comments and suggestions that were put forth by survey participants. Completion of the survey was not a requirement for focus group participation. Approximately 65% of those invited to the focus groups attended one of the sessions.

The survey results indicated that there were both widespread satisfaction working for the agency as well as the desire on the part of many employees to make it a better place to work. There were a number of places were employees function particularly well and were truly content. The overwhelming majority of survey respondents indicated that they were proud to work for the agency and were satisfied with the kind of work they do. However, there were other places where severe discontent was present. The results highlighted three main areas in need for improvement: job advancement, training, and performance management. A number of employees expressed interest in learning more about job advancement opportunities within the agency and communicated their hope that their supervisors would be supportive of efforts to pursue other opportunities, particularly within other units of the agency. Employees responded in the survey that they would welcome additional training, particularly training opportunities to help them develop and advance within the agency; a similar need for focused training for managers and supervisors was also identified. In addition, employees expressed interest in receiving increased feedback from their supervisors on their performance.

Participants were clerical, secretarial, drivers/messengers, nonsupervisory and supervisory analysts, attorneys, auditors, IT-database/network analysts and programmers, security, and managerial personnel.

As soon as the survey results were analyzed, they were presented to the agency's administrators, then to the managers and supervisors. Several meetings were held in order to identify and discuss potential solutions and future courses of action. Then a memo from the agency's administrative director was sent out via e-mail to all employees informing them of the survey's results and of the steps that would be taken. Implementation of some of these steps commenced a few months later.

Potential problems: Response bias; social desirability

actions that are made based on the key findings of the research. Detail orientation and focus on the objectives identified are important for keeping everyone involved on the same page and the various steps in the process well organized. Timeliness is also a critical factor in this stage of moving forward, and a lag in time can result in a disconnect between the research effort and any observable outcome. In addition, stakeholders may come and go; key players may shift due to promotion, retirement, or other types of termination; or members may rotate on committees and project teams. As applied researchers or practitioners tasked with conducting survey research and coordinating appropriate change efforts, our effort to sustain momentum and move forward to meet the objectives of the entire project is a *make or break* responsibility. We must strive to turn our findings into real-world, tangible strategies and practices quickly and transparently; this will enable the success of the initiative and enhance our reputation as trusted experts in transforming data into meaningful, visible results.

CHAPTER SUMMARY

- Survey research methods include self-report measures such as questionnaires and assessments as well as interviews and are mainly used for collecting data on attitudes, beliefs, preferences, and behaviors from a representative sample of a population.

- Survey research methods are one type of nonexperimental research methods commonly used for describing behaviors and phenomena, for examining relationships and covariation among two or more variables, and for examining changes and trends in people's attitudes, behaviors, and preferences over time. However, survey research methods should not be considered solely nonexperimental because a researcher can create different versions of a questionnaire and use these versions as conditions, or levels of an independent variable, to measure differences in a dependent variable across conditions.

- Individuals who provide information through survey research methods are referred to as respondents, and the accuracy of the data is contingent upon respondent honesty, correct interpretation of the items, and memory of the information being requested of them to recall. Researchers can employ various techniques for determining the accuracy of responses, such as comparing data between similar samples of respondents.

- When constructing a questionnaire, a researcher should develop items that will be easily and consistently interpreted by all respondents in the sample and design a layout that is visually appealing. Items should be clear, straightforward, and appear nonthreatening, and to accomplish this, a researcher must word items simply, objectively, and in as nonoffensive of a manner as possible. Survey researchers can integrate a variety of question design elements to suit the needs and content of the questionnaire, including appropriate integration of open and close-ended questions, forced choice items, and items that include a corresponding response scale.

- Determining the correct sample of relevant cases from a population that includes all the necessary characteristics for a study is critical to the validity and reliability of survey research. A sample is a representative group of cases from the population, and this means that the sample consists of all the characteristics of the population as a whole. With a representative sample, a researcher can have confidence that the inferences made about the sample can also be extended, or generalized, to the population. The two broad categories of sampling techniques are probability and nonprobability sampling.

- Survey research methods can be conducted through a variety of delivery approaches. Questionnaires can be distributed by hard copy mail, electronically by e-mail and web links, by telephone interview, and conducted through either a live person-to-person conversation or an automated touch-tone or voice response system. Questionnaires can also be administered face-to-face through a live interviewer who asks the questions and records responses on a structured form. A mixed mode approach in which two or more different delivery techniques are implemented is ideal in many situations that require outreach to a diverse sample that may not be able or willing to provide information through certain modes.

DISCUSSION QUESTIONS

- How can survey designs be used in both experimental and nonexperimental research methodology? Give an example of how a survey design element, such as a questionnaire, could be used in an experimental research method and an example of how one could be used in a nonexperimental research method.

- What are some respondent characteristics that researchers must take into consideration when constructing survey research questions and items? What general rules should researchers follow when constructing survey research items regardless of respondent demographics?

- Why do you think that many applied researchers working in field settings must rely on nonprobability sampling techniques? What are the challenges that they must contend with concerning the representativeness of the sample obtained through a nonprobability technique?

- Why would a survey researcher choose to conduct interviews with respondents instead of administering questionnaires? What are the benefits and challenges of conducting interviews to collect data with both individual respondents and groups of respondents?

- Consider the following scenario:

    You are the Director of Student Life for a large liberal arts university. Enrollment has become unstable in the past few years, in particular with the freshman class continuing on into their sophomore year. There are many drop-outs and transfers from the first year to the second year, and this is becoming progressively worse. As a result, the Provost has asked you to revisit the use of a *first year experience* questionnaire that was given to students several years ago at the end of their freshman year. The questionnaire addressed such factors as the availability of class sections, the quality of the instructors, the helpfulness of advisors, the comfort of the residence halls, the dining services, and the overall interest in campus clubs, extracurricular activities, and sports.

    The existing questionnaire was constructed completely in open-ended questions, such as "What is your opinion of the quality of your professors?", "What do you like about the residence hall you live in?", and so on. You determine that the questionnaire is going to have to be restructured because this design is too cumbersome and time consuming to analyze in order to present findings and recommendations to the Provost for improvements to be made before the start of the next academic year. Design a new questionnaire, integrating open-ended, close-ended, forced choice, and response scale items appropriately in order to obtain the most accurate respondent information in the simplest and most efficient way possible.

CHAPTER KEY TERMS

Bias	Interview	Recall
Case	Jargon	Response Rate
Close-Ended Question	Likert Scale	Response Scale
Cluster Sampling	Nonprobability Sampling	Sample
Confidence Interval	Open-Ended Question	Sampling Error
Convenience Sampling	Population	Snowball Sampling
Double-Barreled Question	Probability Sampling	Stratified Sampling
Element	Purposive Sampling	Survey
Forced Choice Question	Questionnaire	Thurstone Scale
Generalize	Quota Sampling	

PART III

Research Interpretation and Application

Integration of Statistical Terminology With Validity and Statistical Analyses

Throughout our lives, we will be faced with a lot of data or facts to examine that we are required to make sense of. The way the data is given to us can vary based on the data source, but the end result of determining something meaningful still applies. At work, you could be trying to determine how to compare resumes from potential applicants in a meaningful way, how effective a training program is on improving performance, how engaged employees are through completing a survey, etc. At home, you could be trying to figure out which mode of transportation to take to get to work, how much time you would save by taking an alternate route to work, etc. Regardless of the type of information you are given, the challenge is to figure out how to create something meaningful from the mound of data you are given.

Now that you have read through a variety of different research designs and learned about the importance of validity, validity threats, and reliability, you may be wondering where to go next. Regardless of the decision to read and evaluate a literature article or develop a research study, think about taking your knowledge to the next level through interpreting statistics. Although the intent of this book is to provide the knowledge to provide a thorough understanding of research design, it is imperative to provide an overview of statistical concepts. The purpose of this chapter is to provide you with the tools needed to begin the analysis of data or to understand how to evaluate a results section.

There are many different types of research designs to choose from, and there are many different statistical analyses to choose from. We do not intend to provide an in-depth discussion of statistics within this book. This chapter is packed with statistical concepts and terminology. Theoretically, it can be taught as two chapters with the first break after "Closing Thoughts on Statistical Terminology" and the second chapter beginning with "Statistical Analysis and Scales of Measurement." The structure of this chapter begins with a review of integrating the composition of a variable or measure with **construct validity** and **statistical conclusion validity**

> **construct validity:** Generalizability that the variables used in a study represent the variable they intend to measure

statistical conclusion validity: Covariation of the cause and effect relationship through the appropriateness of the statistical procedure used for the analysis

nominal scale: A qualitative scale of measurement used to provide a categorical response to a variable

ordinal scale: A qualitative scale of measurement used to rank order categorical responses

interval scale: A quantitative scale of measurement that have equal numeric intervals between values that does not have a true 0

ratio scale: A quantitative scale of measurement that have equal numeric intervals between values that does have a true 0

validity: The accuracy of the results of a research study

reliability: The extent to which a measure or process is consistent, dependable, precise, or stable

Classic Test Theory: Also referred to as True Score Theory. A measurement error theory derived from the thought that a raw score consists of a true and random component.

True Score Theory: Also referred to as Classical Test Theory. A measurement error theory derived from the thought that a raw score consists of a true and random component.

criterion variable: Similar to dependent variable. A variable in regression that is measured.

using statistical terms. Then the middle section discusses the relationship between statistical terminology and tests with scales of measurement (i.e., **nominal**, **ordinal**, **interval**, and **ratio** scales). Lastly, we provide an overview of questions designed to assist in selecting the correct statistical analysis.

CONSTRUCT VALIDITY AND CONSTRUCTS

Throughout the discussion on constructs, we have recognized the fact that researchers commonly report that constructs are operationalized in a *less than ideal* way (Brutus, Gill, & Duniewicz, 2010) that has an impact on the construct validity of a measure. Specifically, in organizational settings we are faced with a challenge that we do not have good measures or we are blindly relying on measures that lack construct validity (Rogelberg & Brooks-Laber, 2004). The logical question to ask is, Why? The easy answer to this is that constructs are made up of highly complex information. When we try to measure or understand human behavior or interactions, there is always some degree of measurement error associated with any variable. This variability can impact the overall **validity** and **reliability** of a variable. When a measure is developed to assess a construct, this variability can be a result of an error in measurement. Errors in measurement may consist of a true component, and an error is theorized by **Classical Test Theory** or **True Score Theory** (refer to Chapter 4). Regardless of your beliefs on why error exists in measurement, there will likely be some degree of variability between what you are measuring and what you think you are measuring. When examining this variability within a construct, the measurement can be examined two ways from the perspective of the **criterion variable** or the **predictor variable.** With respect to the criterion, there are three possibilities of measurement:

1. Criterion Deficiency

2. Criterion Relevance

3. Criterion Contamination

Figure 11.1 is a graphical representation of these concepts utilizing three measures (i.e., in-basket test, cognitive ability test, and personality test) in an assessment center to

Figure 11.1   The Story of Criterion Measurement

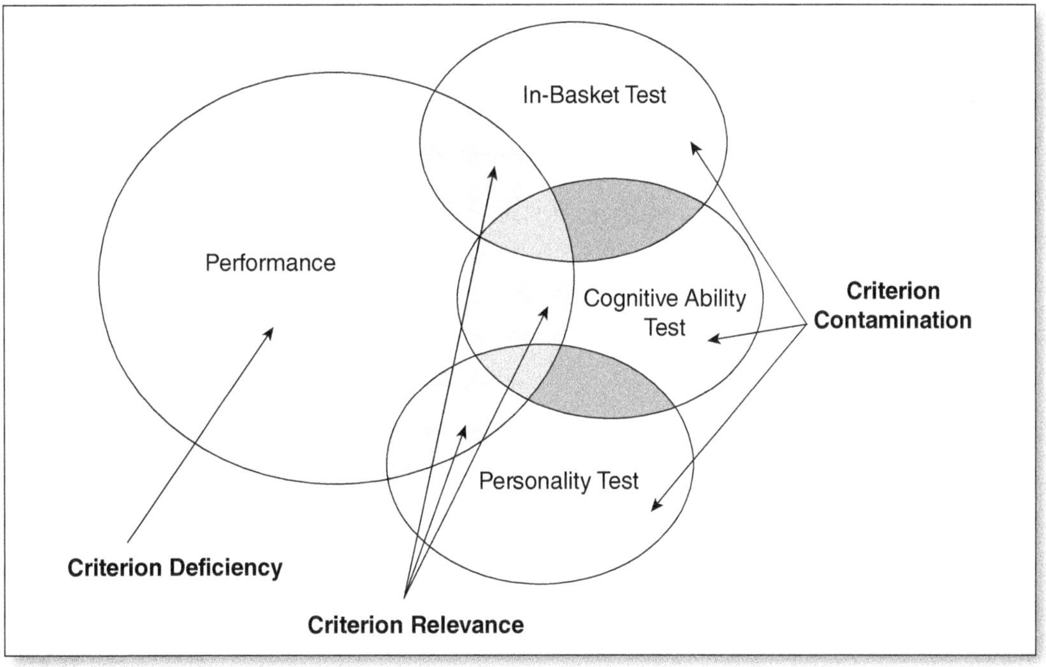

predict the criterion of performance. The main focal point in Figure 11.1 is the circle around performance. This is because performance is the criterion variable designed to be measured by the three predictor variables. In this example, the performance criterion or measure is captured by only a small portion of the three measures. The unshaded area is

> **predictor variable:** Similar to an independent variable. A variable in regression that is manipulated by the researcher.

what is referred to as criterion deficiency. What this means is that the three measures (in-basket test, cognitive ability test, and personality test) selected to predict performance only account for a small portion of performance and do not entirely capture performance.

On the other hand, within the performance circle, the light gray circles indicate criterion relevance. This means that each test or measure designed to predict performance accounts for a portion of the performance criterion. The portion of the circle in medium gray indicates an overlap between the measures and occurs when a portion of a test shares the same predictive power as the other variable. In other words, the personality test and cognitive ability test share a portion of the predicted performance measure and a portion of the cognitive ability test and in-basket test also account for a portion of predicted performance.

Lastly, we have what is referred to as criterion contamination. Criterion contamination is the area of the predictor that appears outside of the performance circle. This occurs when the predictor measure(s) (i.e., personality test, in-basket test, and cognitive ability test) accounts for another variable that it was not desired to predict. In this case, portions of the personality test may measure personality variables, the cognitive ability test may measure intelligence, and the in-basket test may measure time management. This is viewed as criterion contamination because each measure may also account for another variable that was not intended to be predicted at that time.

Of equal importance is the mention of the term **variance** and what it means. Variance is a measure of variability that occurs within your measure. It is expected that not all measures will account for 100% of the criterion measure and there will be some overlap between them. With regards to variance, there are three possible scenarios for a predictor variable:

1. Unexplained Variance

2. Uniquely Explained Variance

3. Common Explained Variance

Figure 11.2 is the same graphical representation of an assessment center to predict a performance criterion using three measures (i.e., in-basket test, cognitive ability test, and personality test). In this example, rather than focus on the criterion and its measurement,

Figure 11.2 Explaining Validity in Measurement

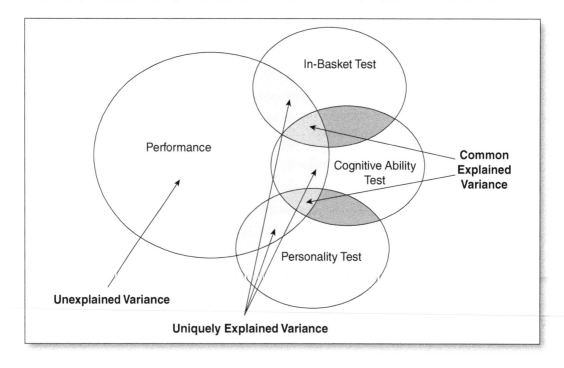

we discuss the variance accounted for by each predictor. In this example, the first type of variance with predictors is referred to as unexplained variance. This is indicated by the white space in the criterion or performance measure. This means that this is variability that the predictor variables or personality test, in-basket test, or cognitive ability test do not measure, which is similar to the criterion deficiency mentioned in relation to the criterion variable.

The second type of variance in predictor variables is referred to as uniquely explained variance. This is the part of the performance circle that is highlighted in light gray. What this indicates is the amount of variance that each of the predictor variables account for in relation to the performance criterion.

The last type of variance is referred to as common explained variance. As you know, there may be some degree of overlap between individual measures or predictors. This is typically because no one predictor may be designed to measure only one criterion. This common explained variance is highlighted in medium gray to show the overlap that each measure may account for. This particular variance is similar to criterion relevance in the sense that this variability is accounted for as part of the

criterion deficiency: The part of a predictor that is not measured by the criterion

criterion relevance: The part of the predictor that is measured by the criterion

criterion contamination: The part of the criterion that measures a different predictor

variance: A statistical term that measures the variability of data

unexplained variance: Variability within the criterion variable that the predictor variables do not account for

uniquely explained variance: Variability within the criterion variable that the predictor variables do account for

common explained variance: Variability that is shared between two predictors that both explain the same variance in the criterion

performance measure. However, this also means that portions of the personality test and cognitive ability test as well as the cognitive ability test and in-basket test account for the same component of the performance criterion.

Regardless if you are conducting or evaluating research, it is critical to know how much variance the variables are designed to measure. In another example, Figure 11.3 indicates a scenario that you may desire for a measure. The information contained within the large performance circle highlighted in light gray and dark gray indicates the criterion relevance of how much variability each measure (personality test, in-basket test, and cognitive ability test) accounts for in the performance criterion. The information in light gray also indicates the uniquely explained variance of each predictor variable. You will also notice that the information highlighted in dark gray is minimal. This means that there is only a small portion of overlap or common explained variance between each measure in predicting performance. The white spaces within the performance circle accounts for the criterion deficiency or unexplained variance. This means that this portion of variance is not accounted for by the three measures. The white space outside the performance circle of each predictor variable is the criterion contamination. This means there is a small portion of variability that each test measures outside the performance criterion. Regardless of how you view a construct or measure or variable, it is important to know and understand the makeup of a measure.

Figure 11.3   An Idealized State of Variable Measurement

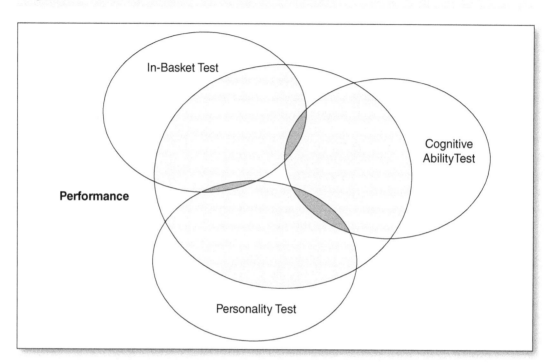

STATISTICAL CONCLUSION VALIDITY AND STATISTICAL TERMS

In addition to understanding the relationship between constructs and measurements, there is a relationship between statistical conclusion validity and statistical terms within research. Upon defining your construct of interest, the next phase of the development or evaluation process is to begin to understand where statistics fit into the equation. This understanding can range from an introduction to statistics terms and techniques from univariate to multivariate statistical analyses. The next few sections take you through common statistical and research terms you will encounter. To provide a road map of the next few pages, the following topics are covered:

1. An overview of the relationship between **alpha**, **beta**, and **power**.

2. Introduction to the **descriptive statistics** and **inferential statistics** and the terminology associated with them.

3. The relationship between scales of measurement and qualitative and quantitative analysis where we provide a review of some statistical analyses that can be utilized.

Each concept presents a unique challenge to the evaluation of research and is important in respect to the validity of the results. Keep in mind that this chapter only serves as an overview of statistical terms to begin the discussion of analyzing data or choosing an appropriate statistical test. We do not intend to cover all statistical concepts, and we strongly encourage you to consult an appropriate textbook designed for statistical analyses for further guidance and review.

Alpha and Type I Error

To begin the statistical discussion, the first statistically related terms you will encounter are in regards to setting up a study. When conducting or evaluating research, the end goal is to determine if there is a statistically significant effect found in the results of the study. Statistical significance is determined when the results of a study meet certain criteria at a specified significance level that is set by the researcher. The significance level is also known as alpha, alpha level, p value, or α. Alpha is defined as the likelihood or probability that the results of the experiment are due to chance. These alpha levels are set by the researcher and must be reported when presenting results on an experiment. The most common acceptable alpha levels are 0.05, 0.01, and 0.001. These levels can be converted to a percentage to equal 5%, 1%, or 0.1%. Alpha is based on probability, so the levels can range from 0 to 1 in which a 0 would be 0% and a 1 would be 100%.

More importantly, you will notice that these levels are not 0, which means that a level of variability or error in measurement is taken into consideration. When there is an error in measurement due to the alpha level set, then this is referred to as a **Type I error**. The level set by the researcher at a 0.05, 0.01, or 0.001 is equal to the Type I error expected in a study. This means that a researcher has a 5%, 1%, or 0.1% chance of making an incorrect decision with the hypothesis. A Type I error occurs when a researcher states that the cause and effect covary when they do not. In other words, the researcher determines that the independent variable did have an effect on the dependent variable when this relationship does not exist.

Beta and Type II Error

In addition to alpha, there are additional statistical concepts that are related to making a decision about the results. These concepts are interrelated and are referred to as Beta or β and power. The interrelatedness of beta and power is based on the

---

alpha: A probability level set by the researcher to determine if the results of the study was due to chance

beta: A probability level that is not set by the research that states that the relationship found in the study is not statistically significant

power: A statistical term in research that determines the extent to which a statistically significant effect can be found

descriptive statistics: Statistical analyses used to provide a summary of the data

inferential statistics: Statistical analyses used to draw conclusions beyond the data by testing hypotheses or research questions

---

Type I error: Related to alpha. An error where the results of the study state that the cause and effect covary when they do not.

formula to derive power, which is 1 – beta(β). The beta level cannot be set by the researcher, but the researcher can influence the beta level through an understanding of the impact that power has on beta. Beta is defined as the probability that there is not a statistically significant effect between the independent and dependent variables. Beta, like alpha, has an error associated with it. This error is referred to as a **Type II error**. A Type II error occurs when the researcher states that the cause and effect do not covary when they actually do. In other words, the researcher determines that there is no cause and effect relationship in the study when a relationship does exist or that the independent variable did not have an effect on the dependent variable when this relationship did exist.

Type II error: Related to beta. An error where the results of the study state that the there is no cause and effect relationship in the study when a relationship exists.

Power

Power, on the other hand, is defined as the extent to which a statistically significant effect can be found. Typically, a power of 0.8 or above is acceptable, and a power analysis should be conducted prior to collecting data. When power is high, there is a greater likelihood that the researcher will find a statistically significant cause and effect relationship in the experiment. Researchers can utilize a power analysis that will determine the minimally acceptable sample size that will yield a specified level of power. Power is important because when the researcher does not have a high enough level of power to detect a statistically significant effect, the likelihood of making an error in the statistical decision increases. As previously discussed, the formula for power is 1 – beta(β). This means that if power is 0.8, beta would be 0.2, which indicates that there is a 20% chance of making a Type II error. Therefore, as power decreases, the chance of making a Type II error increases.

You may be wondering how power is related to the statistical decision if it is related to beta but cannot be set by the researcher. One way to prevent an inflated power is to not oversample. This can be accomplished by conducting a power analysis prior to collecting data. The purpose of conducting a power analysis prior to data collection is to determine an approximate sample size required to obtain a statistical power above 0.8. However, power can be conducted after the data were collected to determine the level of power with the results.

The reason a power analysis is important is because a study with a very large sample size may be more likely to find statistical significance when there may not be any significance or Type I error. Failure to conduct a power analysis or have an appropriate sample may result in an inadequate power to determine statistical significance and ultimately a study that is unable to be published. As previously mentioned, a power level of 0.8 is generally desired. For further review and discussion of statistical power, readers should consult the *Statistical Power Analysis for Behavior Sciences* (2nd ed.) textbook by Cohen (1988).

Avoiding Type I and Type II errors is crucial to determining statistical significance and being able to find results. Whether evaluating or conducting research, you should ensure that the results of the study are valid and reliable. The purpose is not to discuss the nuances of statistically analyzing a research study but rather understand that the relationship between statistics and research is complex. Now that you have an understanding of alpha, beta, Type I error, Type II error, and power, the next step is to understand how these concepts are related to the **null hypothesis** (refer to Chapter 2).

> **null hypothesis:** Opposite of alternative hypothesis. A statement that a study is trying to disprove. States that there is no relationship or effect within the population.

When statistically analyzing a hypothesis, you have two decisions to make. You can either accept the null hypothesis, which may also be known as failing to reject the null hypothesis, or you can reject the null hypothesis. Based on this decision, there can be one of two outcomes: (1) The null hypothesis is true, or (2) the null hypothesis is false. Table 11.1 represents these possible decisions and how they are related to Type I and Type II error. The first option is to accept or fail to reject the null hypothesis when it is true or reject the null hypothesis when it is false. In this case, the correct decision was made. On the other hand, if you accept or fail to reject the null hypothesis when it is false or you reject the null hypothesis when it is true, then you have made an error in your decision. To better understand why this error has occurred, you need to revisit your study design and data collection methods or examine the results section of a study to understand what may have been the reason why. While journals tend to publish studies that are statistically significant, you will notice that not every hypothesis is fully supported in every study. Therefore, you have the ability to critically evaluate the study you are reading on the basis of a potential error in the decision making process.

For example, Sitzmann and Johnson (2012) conducted a study that proposed eight different hypotheses. Upon reviewing the results section of their analyses, not all hypotheses were statistically significant. As we mentioned in Chapter 2, don't be discouraged if a hypothesis is not supported. In this example, the study was a 2×3 between subjects experimental longitudinal design that began with 488 participants and concluded with a final sample of 147 participants who completed all four intended modules required for the study completion. Since participants dropped out of the study during various modules, different sample sizes were included in the analysis of the data. Although statistical power was not reported for the hypotheses that were not significant, you can ask yourself, "Was power adequate enough to detect an effect?"

Table 11.1   Statistical Decisions and Outcomes

	Outcome of the Null Hypothesis	
Decision	**True**	**False**
Accept or fail to reject the null hypothesis	Correct Decision	Type II Error
Reject the null hypothesis	Type I Error	Correct Decision

DESCRIPTIVE AND INFERENTIAL STATISTICS

To begin the transition into the different types of statistical analyses, we provide an intro-duction to descriptive and inferential statistics. Most statistical analyses can be broken down into common terms. The purpose is to introduce you to statistical terms to provide you with the tools and knowledge to discuss or interpret any level of univariate and/or multivariate statistics.

Two main types of statistical concepts you should be familiar with are descriptive and inferential statistics. Descriptive statistics contain terms that help summarize the data set that you are evaluating or analyzing. Inferential statistics are used to test a hypothesis in a population or infer something from the data. You will likely encounter a large data set of numbers. Consider the following examples of published data:

1. A meta-analysis consisting of 78 independent samples from 63 articles with a sample size of 20,014 (Berry, Sackett, & Landers, 2007),

2. An experimental design with a sample size of 251 with survey responses to 35 items assessing six measures and four covariate measures for control (Johnson & Chang, 2008),

3. A quasi-experimental design with a sample size of 101 assessing 40 items comprised of four measures (Banki & Latham, 2011), and

4. A survey design with a sample size of 1,013 assessing 37 items comprised of six measures (Suazo & Stone-Romero, 2011).

In order to analyze this data, you can use either descriptive or inferential statistics to be able to tell a story with the data. Within the realm of descriptive statistics, the methods used to summarize data are referred to as measures of **central tendency**.

Central Tendency

central tendency: Descriptive statistics known as mean, median, and mode that are used to provide a summary of the data

mean: A measure of central tendency that measures the average value in a given distribution

median: A measure of central tendency that measures the middle value in a given distribution

mode: A measure of central tendency that measures the value that appears the most in a distribution

This type of descriptive statistics is used to provide a summary of the data. The most common terms associated with central tendency are **mean**, **median**, and **mode**. Measures of central tendency allow you to describe the distribution of a data set. The most commonly reported measure of central tendency is the mean and is often used in inferential statistics. The other measures of central tendency provide more information about the description of a data set.

The mean or average is a term that is relatively common and is the most widely reported descriptive statistic. Calculating the mean involves adding or summing all the scores found in a data set and then dividing by the total or count of each data point.

The median is found by determining the value or score that falls in the middle of the distribution. The easiest way to figure out what the median is would be to arrange all scores in a data set from lowest to highest or highest to lowest. The decision is up to you how to arrange the data, but it is easier to find the median when all values are arranged numerically. Once the data is arranged in a numerical order, the median can be found by simply counting the number of data points and determine what value is in the middle. This is relatively easy when there are an odd number of values or scores in a data set. However, in the event that the data set has an even number of values or scores, then the median is calculated by taking the average of the middle two numbers. For example, if there were 20 data points in a data set and the middle two numbers were 30 and 31, then the median would be 30.5.

The mode is defined as the value that appears in the data set the most. Similar to determining the median, the mode is easier to find when the data is arranged numerically. After arranging the data set in numerical order, determine how many times each value appears in the data set. If there is only one data point that appears multiple times, then this is the mode. If there are two data points that appear multiple times, then this is okay too! It simply means that you have a **bimodal** distribution. Lastly, it is also possible to have a **multimodal** distribution. This simply means that the data set has more than two values that appear the same number of times. The measure of central tendency that provides the most information about a data set depends on the type of data you are examining. Consider the following example of two data sets presented in Table 11.2.

In the first data set, the first thing you will notice is that the values are relatively close together. When there is little variability between values in a dataset, the mean, median, and mode are typically close together. This is essentially what commonly occurs in a **normal distribution**. In the second data set, you will notice that 100 is one number that sticks out compared to the rest. This number that *sticks out* is what is referred to as an **outlier**. Outliers are values in a data set that can be either extremely high or extremely low, which has an impact on the calculation of the mean or the distribution of the data.

> **bimodal:** A measure of central tendency where two values in a distribution appear the same number of times in a distribution.
>
> **multimodal:** A measure of central tendency where more than two values in a distribution appear the same number of times in a distribution
>
> **normal distribution:** A symmetrical probability distribution
>
> **outlier:** An extremely high or low value that is in a dataset

Variability

Within the aforementioned discussion of measures of central tendency, it is important to recognize variability within the data. This can occur with the presence of outliers that

Table 11.2   How Data Influence Measures of Central Tendency

Data set	Mean	Median	Mode
20, 25, 25, 30, 35	27	25	25
10, 15, 20, 20, 100	33	20	20

range: A measure of variability of a data set calculated by the difference between the highest and lowest value

standard deviation: A measure of variability or spread of a data set around the mean that is measured in the same units as the calculated measure. It is calculated by the square root of the variance.

variance: A measure of variability or spread of a data set around the mean that is not in the same units as the calculated measure

can impact the mean and distribution of the data. When central tendency measures, such as the mean, are reported, it is helpful to also include measures of variability. Variability within a distribution is defined as how spread out your data set is. To better understand this variability, there are statistical terms referred to as the **range, standard deviation**, and **variance**.

The range is the difference between the highest and lowest value in a data set. Similar to mode and median, it is easier to determine the highest and lowest value in a data set when the data are organized numerically. Since the range ignores any value other than the highest and lowest, it is a simplistic measure of variability within a data set.

The standard deviation and variance are other measures of variability that involve more complex calculations. Standard deviation is simply the square root of the variance. Although the term *simply* makes standard deviation sound easy, the formula is fairly complex. The process involves first calculating the mean score for the data set. Then every data point (x_i) is subtracted from the mean score ($\bar{x}$). Since some of the values will result in a negative value, each one of these products are squared. Once this happens, then all of these values are added together and then divided by the sample size minus 1 ($n - 1$). After all this is done, then the last step is to take the square root of the entire result to determine the standard deviation.

$$\text{Standard Deviation} = \frac{[\text{sqrt } \Sigma (x_i - \bar{x})^2]}{n - 1}$$

To calculate the standard deviation with less than 10 values may not be too time consuming. Calculating the standard deviation of 500 values wouldn't be an efficient use of time. Thankfully, statistical software programs can provide this value in seconds. The standard deviation is useful for distributions because it is in the same level of units as the dataset. This implies that when describing a data set of hours worked, the values speak the same language. If a mean of a data set is 38.6 hours with a standard deviation of 7.1, then this 7.1 can be referred to as 7.1 hours. Why is this important? This is because the next term *variance* is not in the same level of units.

Variance is a measure of dispersion around the mean. Variance is calculated by the sum of the squared value of the difference between the raw score (x_i) and the average value ($\bar{x}$) divided by the sample size minus 1 ($n - 1$). Since words may be complicated to process, here is a graphic representation of variance.

$$\text{Variance} = \frac{\Sigma (x_i - \bar{x})^2}{n - 1}$$

As mentioned above, variance is not in the same units as the data set. To go back to the 38.6 mean hours and 7.1 standard deviation hours, the variance would be 50.41. Clearly, this 50.41 value is higher than the mean. The term *variance* can be confusing because the resulting value can be extremely large in comparison to the data set. When given statistical concepts with a resulting value that doesn't seem to make sense, we sometimes use definitions that we are familiar with or try to make sense out of something. Remember variance can have multiple interpretations and definitions. In business, variance is the difference between an observed and expected score. In statistics, variance is a measure of dispersion around the mean. The question that often comes up is, why can't we just call this term something else because it's confusing? Well, the English language is quite confusing when you break it down. How about the word *bow* and the multiple meanings?

1. A ribbon tied onto a present or package

2. Using the body to greet or acknowledge someone

3. A weapon that is used to shoot arrows

4. The front part of a boat or ship

5. Used to play a violin

There may be more definitions to the word *bow* but you get the idea. The reason for writing that was to demonstrate that one word may have multiple connotations depending on how it is written in context or what setting is used. Statistics is no different. There are other words in statistics that mean something else in relation to how it is used. For example, the word *mean* can be used to indicate:

1. In statistics, an average value

2. In describing a mood or state of a person, this person is not nice

3. Describe or represent something

The list of statistical terms and their meanings in different contexts can go on, but then this research methods textbook would turn into an English textbook, which is not the intention.

To better understand measures of variability, Table 11.3 contains the same data set used for the measures of central tendency. As a general rule of thumb, the higher the value in any variability, the higher the variation within the data set. The lower the value of variability, the closer the values in the data set are. In the first data set, you will notice that the values in the data set are close to each other. This means there is little variation within the data. On the other hand, you will notice that in the second data set the range and variance are large values. This highlights the fact that the range is a simplistic calculation of variability and variance is relatively uninterpretable. The only interpretation you can get out of these values is that there is a lot of variability within the data set (Table 11.3).

Table 11.3 How Data Influence Measures of Variability

Data set	Range	Standard Deviation	Variance
20, 25, 25, 30, 35	15	5.70	32.5
10, 15, 20, 20, 100	90	37.68	1,420

CLOSING THOUGHTS ON STATISTICAL TERMINOLOGY

Much of the terminology learned throughout this textbook in relation to validity, research designs, and statistical concepts are all interrelated. Understanding and conducting research is a science that requires time and precision to conduct and evaluate. It is not possible to discuss validity and reliability without integrating statistical concepts. It is also not possible to avoid learning statistical concepts by saying, "I'll just read the abstract, introduction, and discussion section and agree with what the researchers said." This is flawed logic because there are additional insights and information that can be learned through utilizing a critical eye when evaluating research. While this may not happen often, it demonstrates the importance of critically evaluating research and not taking what the researchers state for granted. In the *Journal of Applied Psychology*, Aryee, Walumbwa, Seidu, and Otaye (2012) published a study examining the impact of high-performance work systems in which incorrect confidence intervals were reported. Whether the incorrect presentation of the results was overlooked, an honest mistake, or a mistyped error, with human interaction, a possibility exists that errors can occur. This chapter was designed to provide an introduction to the integration of the relationship between statistical terms and validity. In the next chapter, we further integrate statistical analyses with the scales of measurement to provide a link with these concepts.

STATISTICAL ANALYSIS AND SCALES OF MEASUREMENT

With all this discussion of alpha, power, Type I error, Type II error, decision making, central tendency, and variability, we can begin the transition of these statistical concepts into examining how to statistically analyze or evaluate the results of a study. This can apply to helping you make an appropriate decision with regards to statistically analyzing data or help evaluate a results section in a journal article.

To begin the integration of statistical analysis, reflect back on the scales of measurement discussed in Chapter 2. The reason this is important is because the scale of measurement used dictates the type of statistical analysis that you can conduct. Recall the four different scales of measurement. Nominal and ordinal scales are referred to as qualitative scales of measurement, and interval and ratio scales are referred to as quantitative scales of measurement.

Prior to discussing various statistical analyses or evaluating a results section, it is important to recognize that all statistical tests require assumptions in order to utilize them. All assumptions for a statistical test must be met; otherwise, a threat of violated assumptions of tests is plausible. The goal of the last few sections is to provide a road map for selecting or choosing the most appropriate statistical analysis. This will help guide the decision making process to make it easier, or at least we think it's easier, when consulting a statistical textbook on how to utilize the statistical test. We are by no means undermining the complexity of statistics but rather trying to get out of the minute details to see the light at the end of the tunnel. We leave all the statistical complexities and formulas for the statistics textbooks.

Parametric and Nonparametric Statistics

Before proceeding, stop what you're doing and pause for a minute or 5. Stand up and stretch and think big picture while reading! For starters, all statistics can be broken down into two main categories: **parametric statistics** or **nonparametric statistics**. Within these categories of statistics, they can be broken into qualitative and quantitative analyses. Some statisticians may argue that the first step is determining qualitative or quantitative statistics. Whatever methodology you choose, the end result is the same—there are still *only* two categories. These two major categories of statistics is the first question to begin the process of narrowing down the enormous amount of statistical tests available for analysis.

Going back to the logic of the two main categories being parametric and nonparametric, Table 11.4 contains a list of assumptions for these two categories. The main assumption for all parametric statistics is that the data is normally distributed. When a data set is not normally distributed or the distribution is unknown, then nonparametric statistics may be used. Well now that seems particularly easy! Sorry to disappoint, but it's much more complicated than that.

> **parametric statistics:** Statistical analyses where the data distribution is considered a normal distribution
>
> **nonparametric statistics:** Statistical analyses where the data distribution is not a normal distribution

Table 11.4   Characteristics of Parametric and Nonparametric Statistics

Category	Parametric Statistics	Nonparametric Statistics
Distribution of Data	Normal	Not Normal or Unknown
Scales of Measurement	Interval or Ratio	Nominal or Ordinal
Observations	Independent	Independent or Dependent
Variance	Homogenous	Homogenous or Heterogeneous

Steps to Statistical Analysis

Now here comes the fun part with statistics! We use the term *fun* as in being facetious because the thought of having *fun* and *statistics* in the same sentence is less than humorous for most. After the pleasure of having two different statistics professors at both extremes, we believe this has helped us tremendously understand certain statistical analyses in grave detail (yes, to the point of us wanting to find the nearest beverage for consumption) and the other professor introducing us to multiple statistical tests on an hourly basis (yes, for us still wanting to find the nearest beverage). Statistics is in the eye of the beholder (i.e., you trying to determine a test or your professor teaching your class). We, with a particularly advanced understanding of statistics, have taken the middle ground with the feeling that too much detail or too many statistical tests is enough to drive you crazy. Fortunately, or unfortunately for us, this can be a short drive!

After all that babbling, it's probably important to get back to the purpose of what we're doing. Although tangents are a fun way to take a break with what you're doing to realize that two humans did in fact write this book! Prior to conducting or evaluating a statistical analysis section, there are a series of steps that can be followed to determine what the appropriate analysis is or could be. The following tables are designed to begin the process of narrowing down the various types of statistical analyses into a series of questions. To integrate statistical decision making with research methodology, we framed the questions around research methodology concepts found within this textbook. The figures are not intended to provide an exhaustive list of all possible statistical tests available (remember, no statistical whirlwind) but rather the more common statistical tests conducted. Nonparametric statistical tests are the boxes highlighted in gray. All other boxes are considered parametric statistical tests. Numbered boxes are the questions that need to be answered:

> **covariate:** A variable that is known to interact with the independent and dependent variable and is measured in the study

- Is the analysis a comparison of relationships between variables (Figure 11.4) or means between groups (Figures 11.5, 11.6, and 11.7)?

- Is the number of comparisons between one group (Figure 11.5), two groups (Figure 11.6), or three or more groups (Figure 11.7)?

- Is the scale of measurement for the dependent variable nominal, ordinal, interval, or ratio?

- Are the comparisons of groups independent (between subjects design) or dependent (within subjects design)?

Rather than go through the figures in detail (i.e., our other extreme statistics professor), we believe that anyone, regardless of statistical expertise, can answer a few simple questions. Each one of the figures starts out with a question that must be answered prior to moving through the flow chart. Then, follow the appropriate path based on the answer to the question outside of the line. Within some of the boxes, multiple analyses may be conducted. The type of analysis is dependent upon two questions:

1. How many independent and dependent variables are there?

2. Are any of the variables **covariates**?

Figure 11.4 Decision Tree for Analyzing Relationships Between Variables

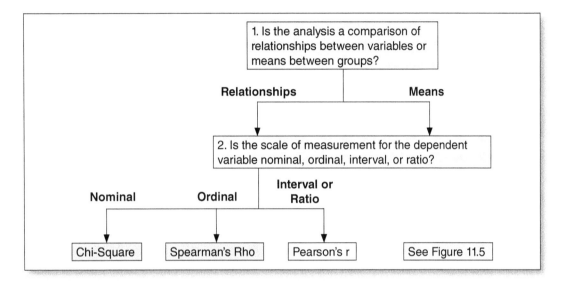

Figure 11.5 Decision Tree to Analyze Means for One Group

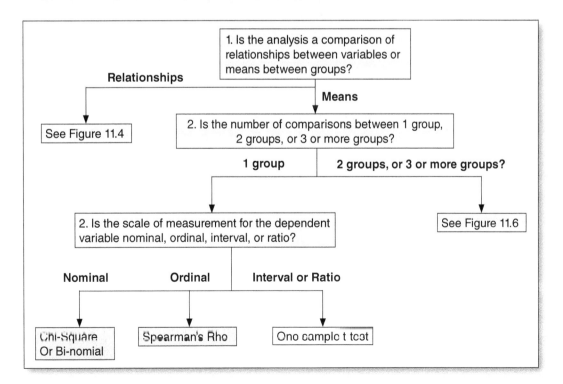

Figure 11.6 Decision Tree to Analyze Means Between Two Groups

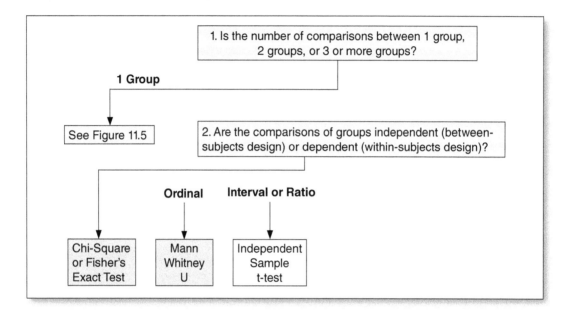

Figure 11.7 Decision Tree to Analyze Means Between Three or More Groups

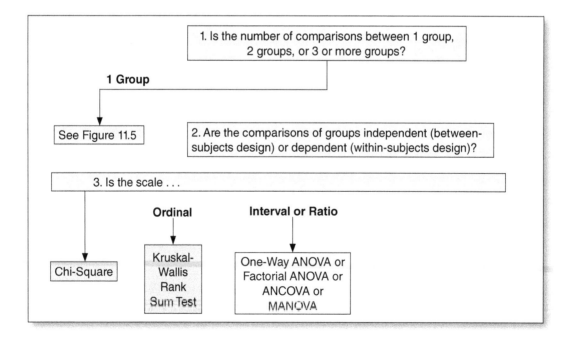

Prediction Analysis

In the aforementioned statistical tests, the purpose of analyzing the variables was for testing the relationship or comparing means between groups. This may not always be the primary focus of conducting a statistical analysis. There may be situations where the intention is to predict a criterion of interest. If this is the purpose, then the statistical analysis will likely be a form of regression. Within the realm of regression, the methodology behind this type of analysis is to use one or multiple independent or predictor variables to estimate one dependent or criterion variable. The main determination between different regression analyses is if the criterion or predictor variable is continuous or dichotomous. A **continuous variable** is generally a quantitative variable that is often measured on an interval or ratio scale of measurement. A **dichotomous variable** is a variable that has only two levels typically identified as 0 and 1. A dichotomous variable can be a result of either a nominal, ordinal, interval or ratio scale because any one of these scales can be converted to two groups if necessary.

> **continuous variable:** A variable that is generally quantitative in nature. These variables often utilize an interval or ratio scale of measurement.
>
> **dichotomous variable:** A variable that has two levels often denoted as a 1 and 0

Statistical Analysis Interpretation

Now comes the challenging part of being able to condense all these statistical tests into a cohesive discussion on interpretation. We leave all the assumptions to statistical tests, formulas, and computations for the statistics textbooks (otherwise this chapter would be a few hundred more pages, and quite frankly, it wouldn't keep our attention for that long). First and foremost, the most important aspect of conducting any statistical analysis is to examine the statistics from a higher level and get out of the details and nuances of each individual statistical analysis.

Regardless of what statistical test is being conducted to analyze a data set, it all comes down to the significance level or alpha level. If a statistical test does not result in an alpha level or significance level of less than 0.05, 0.01, or 0.001, then there is no statistically significant effect being found with the results. This is the first and, in our opinion, the

Table 11.5   Statistical Analysis of Continuous and Dichotomous Variables

Criterion Variable	Predictor Variables	
	All Continuous	**Combination of Continuous and Dichotomous or All Dichotomous**
Continuous	Multiple Regression	Multiple Regression
Dichotomous	Discriminant Analysis	Logistic Regression

most important step or question of any statistical analysis. Figure 11.8 provides the next steps for interpreting the means after answering the question, "Is the alpha level statistically significant?"

When alpha is not statistically significant, this could mean there are threats to validity that may not have been addressed. It is important to critically think about why the results were not statistically significant and if there is a way to enhance the research design. When alpha is statistically significant and there are one or two groups, then it is appropriate to begin to interpret what the means are. However, when there are three or more groups, then the statistical analyses needs to be further drilled down to determine what groups significantly differ. This can be done through a variety of post hoc tests to determine where the statistical significance is within the groups.

Figure 11.8   What to Do When Alpha Is . . .

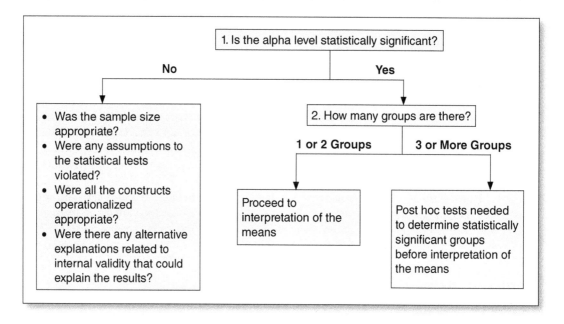

CLOSING THOUGHTS ON STATISTICS

In general, it is our experience that there are some people (i.e., professors, statisticians, or mathematicians) that are so intelligent that they enjoy one of two things: (1) making things more complicated than they really are or (2) not understanding why everyone doesn't already know what they are talking about. The purpose of this chapter was to provide a foundational understanding of selecting an appropriate statistical test and evaluating statistical options within research. Research methodology and statistics go hand in hand because there can't be one without the other. They are both interdependent, and it is critical to have an understanding of how they fit together so that the correct statistical test can be selected.

CHAPTER SUMMARY

- Construct validity is important in regards to understanding the composition of a variable. From the criterion variable perspective, there are three possibilities for measurement: (1) criterion deficiency, (2) criterion relevance, and (3) criterion contamination. Additionally, from the perspective of the predictor variable perspective, there can also be three possibilities of measurements: (1) unexplained variance, (2) uniquely explained variance, and (3) common explained variance.

- Statistical conclusion validity interacts with statistical terminology by having an impact on the research design. Alpha, beta, and power are important statistical terms that can influence the research design that must be considered. Not understanding the relationship between these concepts may result in a Type I or Type II error when making a decision whether to fail to reject or reject the null hypothesis.

- Descriptive and inferential statistics are two types of statistics that serve different purposes. Descriptive statistics are used to describe the distribution of the data through measures of central tendency. Inferential statistics are used to infer or test some phenomenon in a population.

- There are three measures of central tendency. The mean, or average, is the most commonly reported measure. The median, or value in the middle of the distribution, and mode, or the value that appears the most often, are other measures of central tendency.

- In addition to measures of central tendency, measures of variability allow for an understanding of the distribution of the data. The three measures of variability are range, standard deviation, and variance.

- Scales of measurement are important components to understanding the type of statistical analysis. These scales—nominal, ordinal, interval, and ratio—will dictate the type of statistical analysis that can be conducted with the given data set.

- Within the realm of statistics, there are generally two main categories: parametric or nonparametric statistics. Statisticians may also state that the two main categories are qualitative or quantitative statistics. We leave this argument and discussion to the statisticians.

- Parametric statistics are performed when the data distribution is normally distributed. Nonparametric statistics are used when the data distribution is not normal or unknown.

- Determining the most appropriate statistical test for a data set is contingent upon asking a few questions: (1) Is the analysis a comparison of relationships between variables or means between groups? (2) Is the number of comparisons between one group, two groups, or three or more groups? (3) Is the scale of measurement nominal, ordinal, interval, or ratio? and (4) Are the comparisons of groups independent (between subjects) or dependent (within subjects)?

- In addition to those questions, another potential question leading down a different path of analyses is if the purpose of the analysis is to predict a phenomenon. These types of analyses involve a regression analysis.

DISCUSSION QUESTIONS

- How would you integrate the concepts of criterion deficiency, relevance, and contamination with unexplained, uniquely explained, and common explained variance to understand the impact that these concepts have on the measurement of variables in a study design?

- What would you do if you are analyzing a study that resulted in a Type I or Type II error? How would you recommend enhancements to the study design to reduce the plausibility of a Type I or Type II error?

- What would the impact be if you conducted the wrong statistical test when analyzing your data? How would you know you conducted the wrong test?

CHAPTER KEY TERMS

Alpha	Mode	Type II Error
Beta	Multimodal	Unexplained Variance
Bimodal	Nominal Scale	Uniquely Explained
Central Tendency	Nonparametric Statistics	Variance
Classical Test Theory	Normal Distribution	Validity
Common Explained Variance	Ordinal Scale	Validity, Construct
Criterion Contamination	Outlier	Validity, Statistical
Criterion Deficiency	Parametric Statistics	Conclusion
Criterion Relevance	Power	Variable, Continuous
Descriptive Statistics	Range	Variable, Covariate
Hypothesis, Null	Ratio Scale	Variable, Criterion
Inferential Statistics	Reliability	Variable, Dichotomous
Interval Scale	Standard Deviation	Variable, Predictor
Mean	True Score Theory	Variance
Median	Type I Error	

CHAPTER 12

Generalization of Results to Field Settings

As we have discussed throughout this textbook, the most critical element necessary to all research of an applied nature is the ability to take data findings and interpret them accurately to provide insight and value to a targeted need in one or more field settings. Without this application, the research we conduct is meaningless to practitioners and may contribute to the issue commonly referred to as the *science-practice gap*, which we will discuss in the next chapter. Practitioners, whether in a school system, company, hospital, or any other field setting, typically do not examine peer-reviewed research studies published in journals for findings that may support their needs (e.g., the impact that discussion and consensus may have on improving the accuracy of an employee's performance ratings provided by multiple evaluators). Why don't practitioners take advantage of the valuable research findings published in journals and use them to solve problems and make improvements in their respective fields? Some practitioners do, and it often depends on their background and research experience and also the constraints within the field setting in which they work. However, many practitioners do not use research findings directly from the Results sections of published studies.

The reality is that many practitioners may not have access to research journals, and even if they did, they often do not have the time to perform searches, locate relevant articles, and fully understand the results of the studies they selected. The other reality that we have encountered over the years as practitioners in various roles is that many practitioners do not care (gasp!) about understanding the results published in journal articles. We often explain to our graduate students that most practitioners they will work with will probably not understand or ever care to understand the importance of criterion validity or effect size. These, and all the other research methodology concepts and calculations, are for us as applied researchers to understand and translate for practitioners *to run with* to actually use in an effective manner, perhaps to support a new policy or protocol, provide strategic direction for a new program or intervention, allocate resources, conduct a program evaluation, or make improvements to a process in which issues exist. In this chapter, we will discuss this responsibility of *translation and generalization* and the practical considerations associated with obtaining findings from the research we both review and conduct and transform them into relevant and actionable information to use in field settings.

TRANSLATING RESULTS INTO MEANINGFUL INFORMATION

As we proceed through all the steps in conducting a research study, it is important to stay on task. It is quite easy to get derailed while reading the fascinating research ideas and findings presented in journal articles, and though they may be relevant to include in your own research, they should never overtake your research question or methodology. As professors, we have read many research reports that started out with an excellent research question and compelling hypothesis, but then the research design that was developed was not appropriate methodology to attempt to answer the question. When that happens, we know that the rest of the report—the Results and Discussion—will be rather meaningless because the data obtained and analyzed are likely irrelevant to the original research question. The research question pertained to apples, but oranges were measured, and when that occurs, even the most statistically significant findings cannot be translated into usable information for field settings.

Elements of Generalization

Research studies used to gather supporting evidence should represent the *UTOS* in applied field setting as closely as possible. What is *UTOS*, you ask? This is an acronym that stands for Units – Treatments – Outcomes – Settings, developed by Cronbach (1982) to define and organize the elements of a study in an effort to understand the extent to which each may contribute to generalization. Though no one study will yield sufficient data to make generalizations for all four elements, the ability to generalize study findings across as many of these elements as possible is important for increasing the external validity of a study.

Units

In research studies, units can be individuals, animals, special interest groups, and institutions. The units are the element in the study pertaining to the participants that are either assigned to the different conditions or levels of the independent variable(s) or are being examined in the presence of a specified variable or context. In applied research, units are typically individuals such as employees, military personnel, clients, consumers of specific products or services, schoolchildren, and patients. They may also be institutions such as schools, businesses, hospitals, and specific groups such as company departments, neighborhoods, school districts, and labor unions.

The main objective for selection of units for a study is to ensure they are relevant to the population of interest. In addition, the assignment of units to the different conditions should be randomized to ensure each participant has an equal chance to be assigned to any of the conditions. Yes, the latter is an internal validity consideration—reducing the threat of selection—but it can also be an external validity consideration.

Achieving these objectives often poses a challenge in the generalization of applied research. Let's consider each objective. It is pretty obvious why researchers would want to obtain units that are as close to the individuals in the population of interest as possible. For example, if a researcher is interested in examining the effect of break time length on employee productivity, the ideal units to include would be individual employees in an organizational context, not students or children or retired senior citizens. It would make no sense to include any other type of units other than employees to examine this research question because we wouldn't really be measuring job productivity (which is an internal valid-ity problem) and would be unable to generalize to the broader workforce population, which is an external validity problem.

The other challenge concerns the random assign-ment of units to conditions and will segue nicely into the next element, treatments. Even with the most rel-evant units included in the study, generalization may be difficult if the units cannot be randomly assigned to levels of the independent variable(s). In applied research, randomization is not typically included in a study's design most often because of logistics and tim-ing. As applied researchers, we have to account for work shifts and schedules, prior commitments, absences, holidays, and access to individuals at spe-cific times. If we refer to our previous example, a researcher may have obtained employees as units for the break time length study but may not be able to randomize units into the conditions comprised of (1) a 30-minute break group, (2) a 15-minute break group, and (3) a 10-minute break group. The only logistical option may be to assign employees to a condition based on three designated work shifts (morning, afternoon, evening). Perhaps the majority of women employees ages 20 to 45 work the morning shift so they can be home for their children once they return from school, and they are assigned to the 30-min-ute break group. Findings obtained from this condition would be difficult to generalize to other units, including men in any age classification and women under 20 or over 45 years of age.

> **units:** The element in the study pertaining to the participants that are either assigned to the different conditions or levels of the independent variable(s) or are being examined in the presence of a specified variable or context
>
> **treatments:** The element in the study pertaining to the independent variable(s) and their respective levels selected to manipulate; they must be relevant to the research question and the field settings in which findings will be applied

While as applied researchers we strive to ensure that the units are the appropriate fit to the research question, we must deal with the reality that our sample may have to be stu-dents even though the research question concerns employees and that our conditions may lack equivalent units because we have to assign them to conditions based on logistical parameters or convenience. While these situations are sometimes frustrating, we can still make reasonable generalizations through replication with different units and comparisons of study findings to relevant archival data from more appropriate units.

Treatments

The treatments consideration has to do with the independent variable(s) and their respective levels selected to manipulate in the study. Even though a wide variety of variables may be rel-evant to a construct (e.g., the impact that time elapsed, or note taking, or verbal rehearsal has on memory), they will not all be relevant to the research question or the field settings in which findings are to be applied. The conditions developed must be reasonably similar to potential circumstances or situations that could occur in the settings of interest.

Going back to the memory example, let's say we are interested in improving the memory of college students in an effort to implement an effective study tools program that would be offered to students throughout the academic year. The goal would be that such a pro-gram would improve student retention and outcomes such as graduation rate and accep-tances to graduate school and enhance the reputation and competitiveness of the college.

As part of our research process, we interview professors and find that test grade averages are lowest in classes in which the professors provide electronic lecture slides for download. This could indicate that passive students who simply read the lecture slides provided are more likely to have trouble remembering information compared to students who have to take notes because the professors either do not provide lecture slides at all or display them during class but do not provide them for download. Based on this knowledge, a treatment that involves levels of note taking (e.g., all note-taking/no lecture slides, some note-taking/ lecture slides no download, minimal note-taking/lecture slides with download) with a measure of information recall would be the most reasonable condition to implement in a study because this situation is actually present in the setting of interest. If we chose to implement, for example, different levels of verbal rehearsal as the treatment in the study, that would also be relevant to the construct of memory but not generalizable to the unique contextual factors in the field setting of interest.

This is a good example of the "That's nice, but so what?" phenomenon in applied research. It is not enough for us to examine treatments that are broadly relevant to the construct of interest; we must pinpoint the treatment that is important based on what we know about the setting context and its outcome needs. In field settings ranging from global Fortune 500 companies to small nonprofit agencies, resources such as money, time, and people are precious and cannot be expended on treatment efforts that are simply interesting. Treatments must be specifically targeted to potentially be implemented to meet the goals of the setting based on the study findings obtained. This is the "So what?" factor and is critical to address in applied research and the perfect segue to our next elements.

Outcomes

The outcomes consideration pertains to the effects demonstrated through the data collected in the study. A goal for all researchers regardless of discipline is to yield data findings in support of the predicted correlations or causal relationships as stated in the hypothesis(es). For every study in which a researcher is able to demonstrate support for a theory through the effects obtained about the phenomenon of interest, the more confidence that can be placed in the outcome recurring with continued replication.

In applied settings, efficiency in conducting research is always a priority because time and resources are typically limited. As researchers investigating a specific theory, our objective is to yield the same outcome (or as closely similar as possible) from one study to the next because this will enable us to *make our case* for the strength or efficacy of the treatment. Even if the hypotheses among the studies differ somewhat based on the sample (units) or the setting (which we will discuss next), the goal continues to be to obtain consistency in outcomes that support the desired effects. The reality in field settings is that, without this body of outcome-based evidence, treatments such as training and education, counseling, and different types of programs may not receive support and funding from stakeholders to implement. We will explore the importance of outcomes through the concept referred to as *evidence-based practice* a little later on in this chapter.

> **outcomes:** The element in the study pertaining to the effects demonstrated through the data that were collected
>
> **settings:** The element in the study pertaining to the specific environment or context in which the findings from the study will be applied

Settings

The settings consideration is critical in applied research because there are a great deal of behavioral phenomena, such as task performance, group norms, and ethical decision making, that occur in many different environments such as in educational settings, businesses, health care institutions, and so on. As researchers and practitioners examine research to meet specific objectives, research findings that can be applied across myriad settings is quite beneficial on both sides of the coin. For the researcher, this degree of generalizability not only helps to support the external validity of the research study but also ensures utility for a variety of applied field settings—that stakeholders in as many field settings as possible will be able to confidently utilize the findings obtained. For the practitioner, having an understanding that findings relevant to their organizational needs have been demonstrated in many real-world environments may be reasonable evidence to pursue a strategy or intervention plan that clearly has been supported and successful across settings. In other words, if findings obtained from a study supported a particular intervention, say to develop effective team communication, needed in a school system, hotel chain, technology firm, and hospital, it is likely the findings will also be useful in another field setting such as a retail store.

Evidence-Based Practice

While the concept of evidence-based practice has been predominantly used in clinical and medical fields, its implementation is rapidly becoming apparent across a variety of applied needs in field settings. What exactly is evidence-based practice? In early clinical-based research by Sackett, Rosenberg, Gray, Haynes, and Richardson (1996), evidence-based practice is defined as an "explicit and judicious use of current best evidence in making decisions about the care of individual patients" (p. 71). It is a systematic approach for synthesizing and generalizing relevant data findings from research studies to be incorporated into one composite body of evidence that provides not only support for the causal impact of a treatment on an outcome but also support for the application of the evidence to meet a specific intervention need.

Through this approach, researchers are able to use this evidence as a guide in the development of an intervention. With adequate evidence that carries strength in both validity and reliability, researchers and practitioners can use evidence-based practice in the development, implementation, and evaluation of new and existing programs and services. In applied settings, these may include employee training and development, management coaching, health and wellness initiatives, youth after-school programs, support groups, counseling programs, and community programs such as recycling and small business development.

When conducting an evidence-based approach, the focus must be on the strength of the evidence provided in the research studies being integrated. As we discussed with meta-analysis, the approach is only as good as the data that are selected and incorporated into the final product. Poor data findings selection that includes irrelevant, missing, and/or contaminated data will cause the quality of the interpretations made and support for the outcome to suffer. The same holds true for evidence-based practice. What makes this so potentially detrimental for evidence-based approaches is that decisions regarding program interventions may be made based on research support that lacks validity or is inappropriate to the need/issue in question. It's very simple—stronger levels of evidence are more likely to have strong internal validity, and without internal validity, confidence in the findings is virtually nonexistent and generalization across *UTOS* is futile.

In an effort to put a degree of structure or standardization around a process used to determine evidence strength, researchers in a variety of disciplines (Law, 2002; Melnyk & Fineout-Overholt, 2005) have developed classification systems to weight each piece of evidence and categorize it at a certain level on a hierarchy. While the hierarchy of levels may vary slightly in terms of semantics from one researcher to another, they all follow similar classification levels. For researchers and practitioners using an evidence-based approach in their applied decision making and strategic planning, the objective is to integrate as many higher level pieces of evidence as possible into the composite body of evidence.

Levels of Evidence

When following an evidence-based practice approach, it is important to recognize that different pieces of evidence carry different weights. The quality of the decisions made is dependent on the strength and relevance of the various sources of evidence selected. Having confidence in decision quality is critical to stakeholders in real-world settings, whether it is pertaining to a counseling treatment option for a substance abuse rehabilitation program, a corporate mentoring program implementation for junior-level employees, or a reentry training and support intervention for expatriates returning to their home countries after a work assignment abroad. Why do you think this is so important? Programs such as these are considered *high stakes* because they often carry a substantial amount of risk in implementing. There is the risk of wasting the time and effort of all those involved, risk of losing money or misallocating precious budgetary resources, and risk to the well-being of the target population for whom the program is being considered. So, when stakeholders are assessing their options for the most effective program intervention relevant to meeting their objectives, do you think they would want to weigh all the available and validated evidence they can for making as sound and low risk a decision as possible? Absolutely!

> **Evidence-based practice:** A systematic approach for synthesizing and generalizing relevant data findings from research studies to be incorporated into one composite body of evidence that provides support for the causal impact of a treatment on an outcome and support for the application of the evidence to meet a specific intervention need

Working Through Process Steps of Evidence-Based Practice

For applied researchers and field practitioners, the steps involved in an evidence-based practice approach will probably look familiar because the process consists of components similar to the scientific method as well as organizational development process models. Remember, evidence-based practice is a systematic approach that, if conducted appropriately, will ensure consistency and quality, which translates into a thorough process for the researchers involved with an effective outcome for the practitioners and stakeholders involved.

The process begins with a needs assessment to formulate a research question and determine the specific information needed to answer the question. Next, relevant research findings are identified as pieces of evidence and each is weighted and categorized using the levels of evidence hierarchy. The pieces of evidence are integrated together as one composite body of evidence in order to identify possible weak points and gaps in the evidence and to make generalizations. The generalizations made are

Figure 12.1   Process Model for Evidence-Based Practice

Needs Assessment and Determination of Research Question
↓
Identification and Weighting of Research Findings as Evidence
↓
Integration and Generalization of Findings Into Body of Evidence
↓
Alignment of Evidence With Determined Need/Question
↓
Support for Application of Evidence for Program Intervention

evaluated against the determined research question developed in the needs assessment phase to ensure alignment and relevance. Lastly, the evidence is applied in support of a program intervention that will meet the identified needs of the stakeholders and other key constituents.

A FINAL NOTE

As researchers, we believe that every phase in the research method process is of equal importance and deserves no more or less focus and priority than any other phase. That said, we are also practitioners and have worked in diverse organizational and field settings and have an appreciation for the needs, priorities, and expectations of the clients, employees, executives, board members, and other key stakeholders interested in our research findings. The bottom line is that in a real-world context, the phase of the research process we have discussed in this chapter is perhaps the most relevant and critical to applied field practitioners. A good applied researcher must be able to make generalizations of key findings to identify field setting needs. We cannot assume or expect that the practitioners we may work with on projects and initiatives will be able to do this, whether the issue is lack of time, understanding, or interest. Even the most sound, well-validated research studies published will be useless if the findings obtained cannot be interpreted in a meaningful way for application in a real-world context. This is how we as applied researchers *bridge the gap* for the constituents we serve and continue to meet their needs with valuable insights and recommendations.

Table 12.1   Levels of Evidence

	Type of Evidence	Level
Strongest	Evidence from a systematic review or meta-analysis of all relevant randomized experimental studies	I
↑	Evidence from a minimum of one randomized experimental study with a large effect size	II
	Evidence from a systematic review of both randomized experimental and quasi-experimental studies	III
	Evidence from a minimum of one quasi-experimental study with a large effect size	IV
	Evidence from a systematic review of both quasi and nonexperimental studies	V
↓	Evidence from a single descriptive or qualitative case study, or nonexperimental study	VI
Weakest	Evidence from the opinion of authorities and/or reports of expert committees	VII

CHAPTER SUMMARY

- A critical element necessary to all research of an applied nature is the ability to take data findings and interpret them accurately to provide insight and value to a targeted need in one or more field settings. Without this application, the research we conduct is meaningless to practitioners and may contribute to the issue commonly referred to as the *science-practice gap*. Because practitioners in field settings do not typically review and integrate findings from research studies into their day-to-day responsibilities due to time and other constraints, it is important for applied researchers to accommodate this need to provide valuable insight and actionable recommendations.

- Research studies used to gather supporting evidence should represent the *UTOS* in applied field setting as closely as possible. The acronym *UTOS* stands for Units, Treatments, Outcomes, and Settings and is used to define and organize the elements of a study in an effort to understand the extent to which each may contribute to generalization.

- Units can be individuals, animals, special interest groups, and institutions. The units are the element in the study assigned to the different conditions, or levels of the independent variable(s). The treatments element is relevant to the independent variable(s) and their respective levels selected to manipulate in the study. The outcomes element pertains to the effects demonstrated through the data collected in the study. The settings consideration is critical in making generalizations across a variety of different field environments such as educational settings, businesses, and health care institutions.

- Evidence-based practice is a systematic approach for synthesizing and generalizing relevant data findings from research studies to be incorporated into one composite body of evidence that provides not only support for the causal impact of a treatment on an outcome but also support for the application of the evidence to meet a specific intervention need. While this approach has been predominantly used in clinical and medical fields, its implementation is rapidly becoming apparent across a variety of applied needs in field settings.

- When conducting an evidence-based approach, the focus must be on the strength of the evidence provided in the research studies being integrated. Classification systems have been developed to weight each piece of evidence and categorize it at a certain level on a hierarchy. For researchers and practitioners using an evidence-based approach in their applied decision making and strategic planning, the objective is to integrate as many higher level pieces of evidence as possible into the composite body of evidence.

- The process model for evidence-based practice consists of the following steps: (1) a needs assessment to determine an appropriate research question, (2) the identification and weighting of research findings to use as evidence, (3) the integration and generalization of findings into a composite body of evidence, (4) the alignment of evidence with the predetermined need/question, and (5) support for the application of evidence for program intervention.

DISCUSSION QUESTIONS

- Why did Cronbach develop the UTOS model—what is its purpose? What is the goal of UTOS in the application of research findings?

- How is each UTOS element defined, and what is the unique contribution each element provides to a researcher?

- What is evidence-based practice, and what should the focus be for researchers when using this approach? Why is this focus so important?

- Describe the hierarchical levels used with an evidence-based practice approach. How might an applied researcher or field practitioner incorporate data from a combination of these levels to derive a strong body of evidence pertaining to a research question or program decision to be made?

- Consider the following scenario:

    You are a Principal Investigator (PI) examining the impact of a recently implemented nutrition program, *Eating Healthy Rocks!*, in an urban K–12 public school district, which involves the adoption of healthier lunch menu options provided in the cafeterias as well as snacks and beverages offered in the vending machines. This is a fairly new program—to date only one other public school district in the region implemented this program in the past 2 years. This school district has received a 2-year funding grant to demonstrate effectiveness. Future funding is contingent on the extent to which goals are met during the first 2 years, which are (1) a 25% reduction of students with above-average body mass index (BMI) to within a normal BMI range and (2) a 25% increase in physical fitness capabilities as measured by the annual President's Physical Fitness Assessment.

You have been asked by the Board of Education and other local stakeholders, including a youth health advocacy group and the PTA, to compile data and analyze findings over these next 2 years. The groups have asked for baseline data now, followed by data findings in 6-month intervals. You decide the best course of action is to use an evidence-based strategy to deliver your findings and recommendations for how the program should proceed and possibly be modified at each interval.

Design an evidence-based approach that you believe is the most appropriate to this situation. Use the Process Model as a framework, and integrate examples of relevant evidence from the various hierarchical levels as support throughout your examination.

CHAPTER KEY TERMS

Evidence-Based Practice	Levels of Evidence	Treatments
External Validity	Outcomes	Units
Generalization	Settings	Weighting

CHAPTER 13

Bridging the
Science–Practice Gap

As you proceed further along through this textbook, you may be wondering why and how all this information fits together. You may even be thinking about how to incorporate research into everyday life or which design will be the most effective within your organization. The answer to that is "it depends." There are a variety of factors that impact which research design to choose from. Our main goal was to provide you with the tools and knowledge you need in order to select the most appropriate research design to solve the problem you are interested in. There is no one correct way to solve a problem. In fact, research as well as life is filled with unexpected turns that throw us off course, but eventually, we are able to find our way back. Throughout the journey of research (or life!), one of the many challenges you will encounter is how to bridge the gap between science and practice to create applied research that is relevant for both practice and academia.

EVOLUTION OF APPLIED RESEARCH: FROM THE LAB TO THE FIELD

Applied research is based on a body of theories and findings that comprise decades of behavioral research studies examining core constructs and variables (Cozby, 2001). Some of these core constructs are personality, perception, cognition, motivation, and intelligence, and common core variables have typically included demographic and contextual variables unique to a setting of interest. As researchers discovered causal relationships between these and other constructs with different variables, it became apparent that a natural follow-up would be to examine these relationships in the context of various settings. Now, you may be thinking that this idea sounds very much like examining generalizability, and you would be correct. Researchers do wish to determine the extent to which relationships, causal or correlational, and various behavioral phenomena appear across different populations and settings. Applied research is quite similar in that researchers wish to examine the extent to which established findings in behavioral research studies are relevant and apply in specified contexts. This distinction was introduced in the first chapter and revisited in the previous chapter but certainly bears repeating once more in our conclusion as we come full circle in this textbook.

We see a great deal of evidence of this crossover from research in social psychology, developmental psychology, organizational behavior, and marketing to applied research. For example, the concept of social loafing (i.e., the free-rider effect) has been examined in the context of social psychology and group dynamics for years. Findings demonstrate support for an increase in likelihood in social loafing among group members as the size of a group increases, and this phenomenon has been shown to appear in a variety of populations, settings, and situations. Applied researchers may wish to examine this phenomenon in the context of an organizational setting to determine (a) if social loafing appears among employees in a workplace and (b) how this affects performance of a group, such as a department or a project team. The same example can be examined in the context of an educational setting rather than an organization. Applied researchers may wish to determine the extent to which the phenomenon of social loafing occurs in an educational setting, for example, with interactive team-based classroom activities among students, and how addressing student team size prior to implementing a new classroom program will be an important consideration to program performance and success.

In a study that focused on the phenomenon of social loafing in an increasingly common type of field scenario, researchers examined the extent to which such variables as diffusion of responsibility, attribution of blame, and dehumanization mediate the effects of team size and dispersion on social loafing in technology-supported (i.e., virtual) teams (Alnuaimi, Robert, & Maruping, 2010). They conducted a study in which participants (n = 140) were assigned to teams and instructed to perform a brainstorming task using group systems software. Findings demonstrated that dehumanization fully mediated the effects of dispersion on social loafing and diffusion of responsibility, attribution of blame, and dehumanization partially mediated the effects of team size on social loafing (Alnuaimi et al., 2010). This study is an excellent example of the application of a foundational psychological concept, social loafing, in a relevant real-world setting. Teams that work together virtually, through the assistance of technology support and systems, are becoming more common across organizations as a result of such trends as globalization, mergers, and outsourcing and will continue to increase as technology resources become more sophisticated and user-friendly. With that said, such teams must be structured with specific considerations in mind such as team size, geographic dispersion (i.e., time zones), personality traits of the members, team tasks and responsibilities, and the extent to which the technology modalities used provide a richness of communication (i.e., the human element) as this study clearly integrates to examine social loafing effects.

With such examples in mind, is it clear how applied research is used and how it differs from simply replicating a study in a different setting? The word "applied" is the key: We wish to go beyond replicating findings; the goal is to apply findings to address real-world issues and questions to solve problems, meet needs, and make improvements. For applied researchers it is not enough to simply acknowledge a causal or correlational relationship by itself; the next step of examining how this impacts a certain field setting and its implications is critical.

With that said, we absolutely do not want to discount the importance of the findings obtained from nonapplied research studies! Without the developments derived from the vast empirical research of a more scientific nature in areas such as cognition and perception, applied research would have no foundation from which to proceed in different field settings, circumstances, and in the presence of various contextual factors. For example, Weber's Law is a main focal point in the study of stimulus perception and states that an increment in stimulus intensity that is required to produce a *just noticeable difference* is directly proportional to the stimulus itself. While the study of perception is quite scientifically oriented in much of the existing research, the phenomenon of the just noticeable difference, or JND, has been studied in the applied context of marketing and consumer behavior for decades in examining consumer reactions to changes (barely noticeable to subtle to significant) in products and services such as packaging, size, and quite commonly, price (Kamen & Toman, 1971). The foundational, as well as continuing, findings of pure behavioral research and the functional aspects of applied research go hand in hand.

We have been discussing research design and methodology in great detail throughout this textbook, and now we wish to address the *applied* element in more detail in this chapter. As applied researchers and practitioners evaluating research, we must strive to examine constructs of interest and relevance to our respective professional fields and publish findings that can be readily used by practitioners. We as researchers need to be a step ahead in terms of real-world issues and *the next big thing* because research findings must also be timely. A researcher may derive the most impressively valid and important research findings to a particular area, say improving virtual team communication, in the opinion of the research and practitioner communities, but those findings will be meaningless if the research is published years after practitioners actually needed this information to solve a problem or make an improvement. This is one of the challenges in conducting applied research and implementing findings as we will discuss next.

THE CHALLENGES OF APPLIED RESEARCH

Challenge #1: Prioritizing Needs and Handling Constraints

In all areas of research, whether one is conducting a lab experiment, a field quasi-experiment, or a meta-analysis, no method or design will be flawless—ever. There will always be constraints and various contextual elements that may introduce confounds impacting the degree to which we can obtain findings in support of a causal or correlational relationship. In particular, researching behavioral phenomena opens the door to the potential for sometimes unpredictable extraneous variables to impact the study. Variations in data collection settings (such as room temperature or time of day), minor or major distractions (such as noise), and individual participant differences that may affect mood and focus can all alter the type of data collected at a given point.

In addition, researchers are faced with constraints concerning resources and logistics. For example, it may be difficult at times to obtain the ideal sample from a population of interest, due to logistical issues such as time of year or challenges with outreach and making contact, and our sample size is reasonable but perhaps not as representative as we envisioned. Sometimes we obtain a representative sample, but it is quite small, necessitating more of a longitudinal design with multiple data collection points . . . and we cross our fingers and hope no participants drop out during the study. Sometimes (actually most of the time!) budget and time constraints exist, and it may be difficult to determine actual changes across conditions that are due to the treatment or intervention of interest, not due to random fluctuations or other explanations. In any event, we as researchers may have to go back to the drawing board in terms of research design when faced with one or more of these challenges.

Clearly, the more control researchers have while conducting a study, the more likely the data collected will be precise and less likely impacted by extraneous variables—but there is no such thing as having complete control. For this main reason, research is and will continue to be an iterative process. We as researchers must seek to refine and improve upon studies by identifying flaws and gaps in existing studies and conducting follow-up studies for the purpose of continuous improvement, replication, and moving a body of research in a relevant and rigorous direction.

The Trade-Off Issue

In applied research, we are faced with the ever-present *trade-off* issue. Because we as applied researchers are typically conducting studies using quasi-experimental or nonexperimental methods (or a combination of the two), we are faced with the potential for any number of threats to internal validity to emerge. One of our respected doctoral program professors would always remind us that "there will be pain" in our type of research. In class discussions, we would be presented with a research question commonly examined in organizational settings: for example, the impact of posttraining feedback on learning transfer and job performance. We would excitedly design a study to examine such a phenomenon, perhaps recommending a repeated measures design with measures at 1-, 3-, and 5-month intervals after a training program is conducted, with different conditions representing different levels of feedback (but no control group representing a *no feedback* condition because that would be unethical to include with actual employees as participants) and using archival performance data from personnel files for a baseline measure in the place of a pretest. Voila—the *perfect* design! Our respected professor would then challenge us, "What about the threats to internal validity? You must deal with the threat of selection because you cannot implement random assignment. The threat of testing may occur because of the multiple posttest measures, and the threat of attrition may impact findings due to the length of time required to collect data at interval points. There is no perfect design, there will always be pain!" Deflated, but challenged, we came to accept this reality in applied research and learned how applied researchers must be especially creative and strategic when designing studies for use in real-world field settings.

trade-off issue: The challenge researchers face when including a certain design element to reduce the likelihood of one threat to validity introduces the possibility for another threat or design issue to emerge

Now, you may be wondering if applied researchers can bypass all this pain and trade-off and just conduct research in controlled lab settings. Sure, but the study will probably lack the external validity so critical for the field settings we work in, and there will still be some internal validity issues—there always are, even in the most precise and rigorously controlled experiment. In fact, Brutus, Gill, and Duniewicz (2010) reviewed 2,402 literature articles and found that 41.1 % of articles reported at least one threat to internal validity. This challenge is well understood by the applied research community, and it is expected that trade-off issues will be explained thoroughly in the context of strengths and limitations in the Discussion section of research reports and journal articles. The bottom line is that researchers should try to handle identifiable constraints and control for as many extraneous variables as possible before conducting the research and be prepared to explain their emergence and impact on the findings as they appear.

Challenge #2: Maintaining Scientific Rigor Behind the Scenes

As applied researchers and also professors, we often have the discussion with our students about our responsibilities to both the research community and the field settings in which we collaborate with practitioners. We explain that, in an effort to maintain science-practice balance, we must not only have expertise on both sides of the coin but we must also be able to synthesize key research findings and clearly and succinctly translate this information to the practitioner in a meaningful way. This means that, even though the organizational stakeholders we are working with on a program intervention do not know what construct validity is or how it's impacted by the selection of appropriate measures, we must understand this and be able to translate it in a way that makes sense in the context of their objectives.

Without the *scientific* aspect of the research translated appropriately, it will be difficult to gain support and resources for our applied research because stakeholders will not be able to make the connection between the research requirements and the expected application and outcomes—this is something we call the "so what?" factor. If we were working with a consulting client to develop a competency model for their sales force performance measurement and we had to explain the importance of aligning competencies with job responsibilities and performance outcomes to ensure construct validity, we would probably (a) get blank stares from the client and (b) not receive support for the process we recommend because we have not provided an effective translation for the client. Does this mean that we scrap our efforts to ensure construct validity for this type of project because the client doesn't care about it? Absolutely not. But it does mean that we have to explain why we need the resources to conduct a validation effort by describing what this may impact. In this example, the process of ensuring construct validity will mean that the competencies we develop will align with the client's definition of the job and the expected performance outcomes and organizational goals will be met (perhaps even exceeded). The bottom line is that everything will be *on the same page*. Is this a rather rudimentary way to break down construct validity? Yes, but be prepared to make this type of translation effort across myriad field settings. This is how we maintain scientific rigor while receiving stakeholder support and resources to accomplish our projects and objectives.

Quality of Measures and Data Analytics

The most valid and reliable measures available to us must be used to answer research questions and examine variables of interest. Altering quality, validated measures or using inappropriate measures may result in errors in data collection and ultimately in making incorrect causal inferences and poor decisions. Think Type I and Type II errors! Organizational resource constraints, such as the lack of adequate budget, time, or support, may sometimes hinder our efforts to conduct a proper needs assessment and determine the most valid measure given a specific objective or research question. We also use survey research measures such as questionnaires in applied settings quite often, which isn't necessarily a problem, but since respondents may not answer honestly all the time or have issues with accurate recall of information, we shouldn't rely exclusively on these and other self-report measures.

This is the reality in applied field settings, which again requires us to pragmatically consider all the research designs we have knowledge of quickly and creatively, balancing scientific rigor with the parameters of often unpredictable "we need this done as soon as possible with limited budget and assistance" real-world situations.

The more familiar we are with the various tools, instruments, assessments, and other measures that may be relevant to the populations we serve and the environments we work in, the better equipped we will be to respond with confidence to ad hoc requests and needs (and trust us, many of the needs and requests you will encounter will be ad hoc!) by identifying valid measures to implement based on the variables of interest.

Integrity and Diversity of Design Elements and Methodology

In applied disciplines, researchers often rely on quasi-experimental and nonexperimental research designs to answer research questions and address areas of need. Typically, we as researchers turn to correlational designs, various types of survey designs (e.g., questionnaires and interviews), archival data/content analysis, and observation. While these are all sound research methods if conducted properly, we as researchers have a responsibility to examine a construct or phenomenon using multiple methodologies. It may be determined that a nonexperimental design such as archival data collection and analysis may yield important historical information, correlations, and baseline findings to develop a hypothesis and begin a research project followed by an experiment in a lab or controlled setting to ensure validity of measures and a sound methodology. Following a controlled experiment, conducting a quasi-experiment in the appropriate field setting will be a valuable effort in order to replicate the study, originally conducted in a lab or academic setting, in the setting and with a sample that is more relevant to the research question and phenomenon of interest (remember the importance of *UTOS* generalization and evidence-based practice from our previous chapter!).

> **triangulation:** The practice of studying a construct and research question of interest across a series of studies using a variety of different research design elements or methodologies

This practice of studying a construct and research question of interest across a series of studies using a variety of different research design elements or methodologies is referred to as *triangulation*. Why is triangulation necessary? The use of diverse methodologies across studies in a research program helps to ensure we are making an appropriate causal inference, reduces the likelihood of various threats to internal validity, and allows us to determine the extent to which we can make generalizations from the findings and improve external validity.

Triangulation can provide researchers with a more comprehensive depiction of a targeted research question as it is examined in different ways with data collected using different research designs or methodologies. With that said, the selection of design elements must satisfy methodological precision as well as contextual needs and requirements. A major benefit of triangulation for applied researchers is that any design element that may need to be sacrificed in a field setting (e.g., no control group, no randomization, lack of baseline/pretest measure) can be included in another methodology. While time consuming, findings obtained through diverse methodologies can be more greatly substantiated for support and application in real-world situations such as program implementation and change management intervention.

Participant Burnout/Overuse

Researchers continually contend with the issue of participant burnout, or overuse of the same sample for multiple research studies over time (Rogelberg, 2004). It is our responsibility as researchers to be mindful of not over soliciting individuals to serve as participants, which can result in annoyance and a lack of motivation or interest in future participation. This is a common occurrence in academia in which students are called upon to serve as participants for various studies and incented with extra credit, monetary rewards, and small tokens such as raffle tickets and food. It can also occur in other settings in which there is a very specific target sample (e.g., a certain demographic) needed for a series of studies and a limited number of individuals from which to choose. A good example of this can be seen in the field of consumer psychology and market research when researchers are working for clients, perhaps a beverage company, a car manufacturer, and cosmetic company, and all the clients wish to collect data from a certain demographic: for example, 25- to 34-year-old single women in a specific geographic location. Certainly, the researchers cannot request participation from the same individuals across every study, even though they fit the demographic requirements.

Participant burnout can also occur when researchers must tap into the same sample for data collection due to contextual factors, such as limited time and financial resources. The convenience factor becomes the driver for determining the participant sample. An example of this can be seen with the use of social networking sites, such as Facebook and LinkedIn, for data collection. While social networking sites are a valuable and effective means for discussion, sharing of ideas and resources, and outreach, they are increasingly used by researchers and graduate students as a source of research data. A link to an online questionnaire can be distributed to a large pool of potential participants quickly and rather effortlessly. While the convenience factor is obvious and the time and cost requirements are small, it is impossible to determine if the same individuals are participating in every study a researcher posts online through these channels. Even though a researcher may be posting web links for different studies to a professional interest group or one's contact list and those groups may tally in the hundreds (or thousands), the same core of individuals may actually be providing data across every study.

Needless to say, the data collected can be compromised in several ways as a result of participant overuse and burnout.

1. Attrition and Response Rate. Individuals can become annoyed or tired of incessant requests for participation and drop out midstudy or not participate at all.

2. Data Integrity: Individuals can make up responses just to get through the study quickly or, perhaps, because they are only interested in the participation reward.

3. Impression Management: Individuals can provide less than honest responses because they think they know how they *should* respond after participating so often.

Challenge #3: Ensuring Value for Applied Settings

As applied researchers who have also worked in a variety of field settings as practitioners; we have experience working with many stakeholders with diverse needs, such as Human Resources professionals, chief executives, mid to senior-level managers, consulting clients, medical professionals, educators, and board members. Even though many of the challenges they faced were similar, such as retaining talented employees, implementing new programs or evaluating existing programs, and complying with legal and industry regulations, the specific parameters and context were different. As we worked with these stakeholders and their unique needs and objectives, our priority was to provide them with deliverables that were high quality and relevant that could be understood and implemented with ease. These are important outcomes for us to achieve in applied settings: quality, relevance, and clarity.

The quality aspect concerns both quality of the service or outcome we provided to the stakeholders as well as the quality of the research design and methodology used to collect and analyze the data and interpret the findings appropriately. Although stakeholders may not perceive research quality as *their* main focus given the scope of their own professional responsibilities and priorities, they do base their perception of our work as applied researchers on *our* focus and prioritization on the scientific rigor of the research we conduct for them. In other words, conducting quality research may not be on their day-to-day radar, but they want to ensure (and rightfully so!) that it's on our radar!

The relevance and clarity aspects, like research quality, are also key indicators of our perceived value in field settings. As we have mentioned, stakeholder perception of relevance is critical to applied researchers for attaining support and buy-in for our recommendations and obtaining resources to make progress and demonstrate our value. The key to ensuring relevance and clarity is communication and involves the following:

- listening to stakeholder needs and concerns

- synthesizing and capturing this information in terms of actionable next steps

- presenting findings and information from existing research studies that are meaningful to a practitioner audience

- explaining the need to conduct research to achieve their specific objectives

Remember, an excellent tool in our applied researcher toolbox is the "WIIFM" model and our understanding of the "what's in it for me?" question on the minds of all stakeholders. By using our knowledge of stakeholder WIIFM, we are able to successfully articulate that research has value and utility to practitioners by tapping into the needs of the field setting and connecting them to the expected outcome of a targeted research design. This connection will enable us to clearly demonstrate the benefits of research and exactly how findings can be applied to meet those needs.

Looking to the Future

Societal, economic, and organizational shifts will continue to move at an increasingly rapid pace due to technology advancements, globalization and foreign relations, and various other trends. As researchers striving to provide value in myriad applied settings, we must always maintain a focus on conducting research to provide applied settings with timely key findings and insights.

Even though the core constructs we often examine such as ethics, performance, or team dynamics remain relevant, the research questions we examine continue to become more complex and evolve based on the needs in field settings. We must keep current on the topics, challenges, and questions of interest in the field settings we find ourselves in and even try to stay a few steps ahead if possible so that we can forecast trends to be proactive and adaptable. Advanced statistical techniques such as structural equation modeling, or SEM, or hierarchical linear regression modeling are becoming a more frequently used approach for deriving data models for forecasting trends and needs as are data collection via social media modalities and content analysis through credible Internet-based sources of validated public information. For an organization, this may translate into greater innovation, smoother transitions during times of change and instability, cost savings, and agility and competitiveness in an often turbulent market. As applied researchers, we should pursue mutually beneficial collaborative opportunities and partnerships with organizations that may facilitate field data collection across applied settings, thus ensuring balance and alignment between the research and practitioner communities.

A Multidisciplinary Approach

Applied research has utility and relevance in diverse disciplines that often overlap in some way. Having a focus on researching human behavioral phenomena in applied settings means that we may be examining research questions that are pertinent to fields such as business, human resource management, psychology, sociology, anthropology, political science, economics, criminal justice, marketing, communications, public relations, counseling, education, and urban studies. In addition, a researcher may be interested in a question or need in a specific field setting that can be examined using data from other fields and possibly benefit tremendously from relevant findings in different disciplines.

We can refer to a rather well-known example of how research data from multiple disciplines has been used in an applied manner through organizational response to employee work-life balance needs as a result of economic conditions and shifting workforce demographics. An unpredictable and tumultuous economy over the past few decades resulted in a financial need for two full-time incomes in many U.S. households. With increasing numbers of women entering in the workplace at the time, organizations were faced with having to accommodate different worker needs, specifically child care responsibilities necessitating flexible work hours and schedules. Over time, we saw the emergence of such employer benefit options as onsite child care, flextime, and telecommuting. However, not every type of job is suitable for telecommuting—have you ever heard of a nurse or retail salesperson working from home? This disparity of benefits offered to some jobs but not others created equity and motivation issues for employers to contend with, requiring a renewed focus on job data collection and analysis to ensure the expectations and responsibilities of every job are accurate and clearly communicated to job candidates and employees and also attention to developing and implementing a variety of meaningful benefits and incentives to accommodate work-life balance for all employees. The reality is that a retail salesperson or nurse cannot work from home, but perhaps they can work flexible shifts (e.g., four 10-hour shifts with 3 days off) or accrue comp time to take at an approved later date.

Many of you may be familiar with this issue and its evolution or have even personally experienced it. However, it may not have occurred to you that this identification of a real-world issue and implementation of organizational programs in an effort to improve work-life balance for employees were the result of the integration of data and findings from several key disciplines. Economists continue to track these and other trends, such as globalization, unemployment fluctuation, industry regulation, mergers, and outsourcing. Organizational stakeholders will leverage their findings and forecasts to better understand how such trends will impact the workforce and develop strategies to manage change effectively and deal with any challenges while maintaining a competitive market position.

A more recent example of a fascinating multidisciplinary focus in applied research is in the use of anthropological concepts and methodologies in marketing and consumer research applications. Ethnographic market research integrates the use of ethnography, which is the anthropological study of cultural norms and beliefs, traditions, trends, and lifestyle of people in their actual living situations and settings rather than hypothetical situations or artificial lab-based settings (McFarland, 2001). Market researchers may place video and audio recording devices in the homes of volunteers to collect observational data about how a product fits into consumers' lives. A packaged foods company may be interested in data depicting volunteer participants consuming a snack food such as microwave popcorn in the context of *family movie night* that involves the ritual of several family members gathering to watch a movie together on a certain night of the week, with each family member consuming the product in their own personal popcorn bowl. Perhaps different family members even consume different popcorn varieties; one family member may select the extra-buttery style popcorn to enjoy during movie night, while another may prefer the kettle corn flavor. This type of ethnographic research may give marketers valuable insight regarding how to package the popcorn (e.g., number of servings per pouch, number of pouches per bag, a variety pack offering) based on how the product's use actually fits into the consumer lifestyle, rather than solely relying on gathering information from respondents recollecting their product use through interviews and self-report questionnaires.

> **ethnography:** An anthropological study of cultural norms and beliefs, traditions, trends, and lifestyle of people in their actual living situations and settings rather than hypothetical situations or artificial lab-based settings

Researchers should strive to engage and encompass other disciplines in approach and findings—without compromising validity or relevance. As applied researchers, we should review research and trends across a variety of disciplines, identify studies that may be valuable to our own niche area or research agenda in some meaningful way, and use key data to garner support for our research questions and to apply findings to achieve our field-specific objectives.

Box 13.1	Practitioner Spotlight: A Case Study From the Organizational Development Department

Organizational Development

Bridging the gap between science and practice is a balancing act at an international consumer packaged goods organization. While the company does an excellent job of supporting industrial/organizational psychology (I/O) (in fact, HR has an entire subfunction dedicated to it), we are still tasked with delivering results in a fast-paced, competitive corporate environment. Therefore, we are not often able to bring science to practice in the straightforward way textbooks and research articles often like to suppose.

The first step in bridging the gap for most practitioners is not about the tools of science but rather maintaining a scientific mindset. Remember, science at its core is a way of thinking—the statistics, theory, and tools of I/O psychology come from the scientific method. While I/O practitioners deliver unique insight into the science of human behavior, the key is maintaining a mindset which keeps you open to opportunities to provide that advantage without forcing science into places it doesn't fit.

This is a very important distinction because when you stop thinking about science as a toolkit and start thinking about it as a disposition, it fundamentally changes your approach. The former implies conscious and deliberate application. The latter expects a foundational, day-to-day mindset and conscientious approach to your role. In the following examples, you will see the most effective way to bridge the gap is not initially by applying some sort of theory or test but rather by being an observant and creative business partner on the lookout for appropriate places to leverage and infuse I/O into the business.

Effective Communication

In 2010, an international consumer packaged goods organization launched an employee engagement program designed to get our Research & Development (R&D) employees around the world to share their efforts with the organization. In essence, we wanted to increase awareness of local activity at a global level and facilitate interaction across geographies and business units. Associates created short video blogs about what they are doing in their locations, and then we posted them online for all associates to see. During a 2-week viewing window, we encouraged employees to go online, watch the videos, and rate the ones they liked the most. The best videos were then selected and their teams given a monetary sum to donate to a local charity of their choice.

The results for this program in its first 2 years have been outstanding. Both occurrences enjoyed participants from every geographical sector at the organization, and the winners to date have supported domestic and international causes ranging from hunger relief to cancer research to fighting domestic violence.

However, in a company with over 250,000 employees, facilitating participation in initiatives like this is not easy—we must communicate to associates across six major sectors in every time zone on the planet. Therefore, a critical piece of this program was communication strategy.

(Continued)

(Continued)

The challenge with communication in general is understanding the most effective practices. Historically, experience informs the process—more experienced practitioners guide strategy since they have insight based on past projects. However, a scientific mindset allowed us to better understand communications during this program because we saw an opportunity that we don't usually get in the business world: a true dependent variable.

As stated earlier, we wanted our users to watch and rate the video blogs online. By simply counting the number of views as a measure and comparing it to when and how we sent communications, we were able to objectively judge the efficacy of our different communication styles.

The data showed interesting results. Of the three ways we communicated, only one method significantly increased viewership. This is very important because we spent a lot of time and effort developing the other two. Imagine you were advertising the sale of a product through TV commercials, billboards, and the Internet. If you discovered that TV commercials increased sales 2%, billboards increased them 1%, and Internet advertising increased them 25%, which method would you focus on?

This Insight provided immediate advantage to the business. By collecting and analyzing these data, we were able to quantify the effectiveness of our communications and easily adapt our strategy to take advantage of the new knowledge.

Building a Business Case

This international consumer packaged goods organization in the United States currently has a partnership with a large university to provide graduate-level degrees to its employees. In accordance with an accredited distance learning program, their associates can attend college courses on an R&D campus and receive a MS or PhD in Food Science over the course of several years. This is a great advantage to associates since they can pursue higher education without leaving their place of work and a great advantage to their organization because it helps us build the talent and capability of our people.

This program was chartered in 1999 and has enjoyed success during the last decade. Over the years, however, the program has aged and the processes needed updating. In addition, many of the original regulators of the program had moved on to different roles or different companies, so most of the tacit knowledge of the program had left our team.

By 2011, these circumstances warranted substantial changes to the program. However, due to the size and the visibility across R&D, it would not be prudent to simply cut the program or change it without investigating potential implications. We needed a business case.

Basically, a business case is an objective story explaining why you want or need to do something. They are especially important in circumstances like this when many budgets, associates, and executives stand to be impacted by a change. Again we saw an opportunity for I/O. After 12 years of operation, the program had a large amount of data about everything from graduation rates to financial expenditure. Using basic statistics, we were able to uncover some clear patterns and see what was really happening.

One of the major things we saw was that students moved along quickly in the beginning of the program but slowed down the closer they got to graduation. In the first 4 years, students completed approximately three credits per semester, but for the next 3 years, that rate dropped to about 1.5 credits a semester. Whereas in the last case study, the data answered the question (which communication methods work best?), in this case, the data *raised* the question: Why were credits per semester slowing down? This time the theory helped us—we found two major reasons.

The first was a basic learning and conditioning principal called *avoidance*. Basically, people will avoid aversive stimuli. For example, students often avoid studying because they don't like it. This is pretty intuitive. However, bad grades are also aversive, so most students will study to avoid flunking a test. In a way, the aversive stimulus of failing motivates students to engage in the unpleasant activity of studying. This is important because the program had a very aversive stimulus: a huge final project required for graduation. However, unlike our studying example, there was no date requiring students to complete the degree. The result was that students could *avoid* the project with nothing to penalize (i.e., motivate) them.

The second factor was the course selection process. As a distance learning program, we are not able to offer every course the university offers. Therefore, each semester the organization has to choose which courses are offered to the students (typically one or two). The early program design left this decision to popular vote. Some very basic probability theory will tell you that the more courses you take, the fewer that are available you can take to graduate. As such, newer students (the majority) were outvoting older students (the minority), reducing their ability to finish the degree!

These challenges and design flaws were somewhat intuitive, but I/O and statistics helped us clearly understand and articulate the business case. Statistics showed us the challenges (e.g., reduced credits per semester toward the end of the program), and theory (avoidance and probability) helped explain them. By telling the story through this objective lens, we were easily able to illustrate these systematic flaws in the design as well as prescribe simple yet effective solutions based in verified scientific theory.

As an I/O practitioner, it is always important to remember what you bring to your organization: a unique understanding of human behavior that provides strategic and tactical advantage to business process. This skill set is critical but must always be moderated by your sensitivity to the overall needs of the business. As you saw in the previous examples, we never set out to apply I/O theory. Rather, as we supported our clients, we saw opportunities to leverage theory and statistics to add additional value to the project or initiative. Bridging the gap is about being a conscientious business partner who keeps their eyes open for opportunities to bring science to practice. If you're doing it right, they probably won't even notice it's I/O psychology at all.

CHAPTER SUMMARY

- Applied research is based on a body of theories and findings that comprise decades of behavioral research studies examining constructs and variables that are important to field settings in a variety of ways. The goal of applied researchers is to apply findings to address real-world issues and questions to solve problems, meet needs, and make improvements.

- Researchers must seek to refine and improve upon studies by identifying flaws and gaps in existing studies and conducting follow-up studies for the purpose of continuous improvement, replication, and moving a body of research in a relevant and rigorous direction. In an effort to maintain science-practice balance, we must not only have expertise on both sides of the coin but we must also be able to synthesize key research findings and clearly and succinctly translate this information to the practitioner in a meaningful way.

- Because applied researchers are typically conducting studies using quasi-experimental or nonexperimental methods (or a combination of the two), we are faced with the potential for any number of threats to internal validity to emerge. As we address individual threats to validity with certain research design elements, we may be introducing the potential for other threats to emerge, and this is the ever-present *trade-off* issue with which we contend. Researchers must pragmatically consider available research designs quickly and creatively, balancing scientific rigor with the parameters of often unpredictable real-world situations. The more familiar we are with the various tools, instruments, assessments, and other measures that may be relevant to the populations we serve and the environments we work in, the better equipped we will be to respond with confidence to ad hoc requests and needs by identifying valid measures to implement based on the variables of interest.

- While experimental, quasi-experimental, and nonexperimental designs are all sound research methods on their own if conducted properly, researchers have a responsibility to examine a construct or phenomenon using multiple methodologies. This practice of studying a construct and research question of interest across a series of studies using a variety of different research design elements or methodologies is referred to as *triangulation*. The use of diverse methodologies across studies in a research program helps to ensure we are making an appropriate causal inference, reduces the likelihood of various threats to internal validity, and allows us to determine the extent to which we can make generalizations from the findings and improve external validity. Triangulation can provide researchers with a more comprehensive depiction of a targeted research question as it is examined in different ways with data collected using different research designs or methodologies.

- Researchers continually contend with the issue of participant burnout, or overuse of the same sample for multiple research studies over a period of time. It is our responsibility as researchers to be mindful of not over soliciting individuals to serve as participants, which can result in annoyance, lack of honesty in participation behaviors and responses, and lack of motivation or interest in future participation.

- As researchers striving to provide value in myriad applied settings, we must always maintain a focus on conducting research to provide applied settings with timely key findings and insights. We must keep current on the topics, challenges, and questions of interest in the field settings we find ourselves in and even try to stay a few steps ahead if possible so that we can forecast trends to be proactive and adaptable.

- A multidisciplinary approach can be valuable in applied research as a researcher may be interested in a question or need in a specific field setting that can be examined using data from other fields and possibly benefit tremendously from relevant findings in different disciplines. Researchers should strive to engage and encompass other disciplines in approach and findings—without compromising validity or relevance. As applied researchers, we should review research and trends across a variety of disciplines, identify studies that may be valuable to our own niche area or research agenda in some meaningful way, and use key data to garner support for our research questions and to apply findings to achieve our field-specific objectives.

DISCUSSION QUESTIONS

- What is meant by the *trade-off* issue in the context of applied research? How and where does a researcher address such issues when they have been found to occur in a study?

- What are two common constraints in field settings that researchers must be prepared to handle? Provide an example of such a constraint and how it can be dealt with as effectively as possible.

- What is triangulation? Why is this practice necessary, and what benefits can triangulation provide to researchers?

- How can data potentially be compromised due to participant overuse and/or burnout?

- Consider the following scenario:

    You are an external management consultant working on a leadership development program with a global Fortune 500 company. Internal senior management candidates currently in junior management positions have been identified by the company's talent management team, and you have been asked to conduct a needs assessment for the candidates in the areas of decision making, communication, conflict resolution, team building, and goal setting. Following the needs assessment, you will design and facilitate training and development activities and evaluate their effectiveness based on program objectives provided to you by the talent management team.

    As you examine sources of archival data prior to beginning the project, including performance appraisals, job descriptions, and training records, you realize the competency model developed for this junior management role does not include competencies for decision making, conflict resolution, and goal setting. This poses a problem because these junior-level managers have been selected and evaluated based on the existing competency model. It is highly likely that these internal candidates may not be the most suitable choices based on this discrepancy. If this project is to be successful, you need to deal with the competency model issue before proceeding. However, this will add another 1 to 2 months to the project timeline, delaying implementation until the summer when several of the candidates are scheduled to take vacation time.

How do you communicate this issue, the options for remediating the problem, and your recommendations and rationale while continuing to ensure value and relevance to the stakeholders involved? What techniques should you use to explain the situation and obtain their support? How would you handle objections and concerns?

CHAPTER KEY TERMS

Ad Hoc	Ethnography	Structural Equation Modeling
Applied	Multidisciplinary	Trade-Off
Construct Validity	Participant Burnout/Overuse	Triangulation
Contextual Factors	Science-Practice Gap	Utility
Data Integrity	Stakeholder	

CHAPTER 14

Writing a Research Report

This final chapter is all about writing up your research. You have conducted your study and analyzed the data collected, and the next step is to report your findings. The research write-up may vary a bit in terms of length and level of detail depending on the context and scope of its publication and/or presentation. For example, a thesis or dissertation will be very detailed and specific, and there is typically no maximum length, while a research presentation (e.g., a poster presentation) for a conference or a manuscript submitted for journal publication will be much more brief and consist of only the most pertinent points and findings. Though the length and breadth of content will vary, the framework or structure of the research report will always be consistent. The research community adheres to the inclusion of specific sections in a research report and in a particular sequential order. In addition, the progression of the research report will generally follow a typical pattern that begins broadly as you describe the construct of focus and independent/dependent variables and gets more specific as you move closer to your own hypothesis, method, and results. Then, the report will broaden again as you move into the implications of the findings, their value in various contexts and settings, and future directions for this area of research.

We will focus on this research report structure and style in this chapter and provide you with some examples of how an actual research report should look in an academic context because you have already seen the end result for a research manuscript that becomes a journal publication! We will also provide you with a checklist that is comprised of all the requirements for an academic research paper that you should use as a benchmark before submitting your report for review and evaluation.

STRUCTURE OF A RESEARCH REPORT

A research report, whether it is written for the academic purposes (e.g., a course, thesis, dissertation) or for presentation and potential publication to the research community or in the context of one's profession (e.g., business, health care, nonprofit), will be comprised of seven required sections and one optional section. Here are the required sections in the order they appear in the research report: (1) Title Page, (2) Abstract, (3) Introduction, (4) Method, (5) Results, (6) Discussion, and (7) References. A research report may also contain one or more Appendix sections, depending on the needs and presentation requirements of the report and inclusion of ancillary information. In the context of applied research, we follow the format standards and style requirements as published by the American Psychological Association, also referred to as APA format (American Psychological Association, 2010). In this final chapter, we will explore each of these components in detail and conclude with a discussion of leveraging research across both the academic/scholarly and applied practitioner audiences.

Section 1: Title Page

The Title Page (Figure 14. 1) is the first page of the research paper and is formatted as page number 1. This page consists of the following elements:

- The running head designation in the upper left side of the page

- The page number in the upper right corner of the page

- The full title of the paper halfway down the page and centered

- Author name and institutional/organizational affiliation

While the Title Page is relatively straightforward, the running head is often a challenge to create for research writers. It doesn't have to be confusing! The purpose of the running head is to create an abbreviated version of the full title that will appear in all uppercase letters in the upper left corner of every page of the paper, along with the page number, which appears in the upper right corner of every page. Here is an example of a research paper title and an appropriate running head:

Title: The Effect of Group Consensus on Performance Rating Accuracy

Running head: RATING ACCURACY

The title of the research report should be succinct but incorporate the necessary words that will adequately describe the study. The title of a research report should provide an adequate level of detail to describe the focus of the study. Ideally, a research report title should be no more than 12 to 15 words in length. A researcher may choose to break up a longer title by including a colon, for example, "The Effect of Group Consensus on Performance Rating Accuracy: Moderating Effects of Personality Traits." The title's wording is especially important for published journal articles so it will appear in appropriate search results when other

> **running head:** an abbreviated version of the title of a research report that appears in the upper left corner of every page.

researchers and students are looking for relevant journal articles through database keyword searches. In the example we provided, all the necessary keywords are included in the title: *consensus, performance, rating, accuracy, personality*. It is not necessary to include words and phrases that are redundant or serve no value, such as "a study of," "research study," and "reporting results." Researchers often take a backward approach with the development of both the title and abstract (as we will discuss next), and they formulate these components

Figure 14.1 Sample Title Page

Running head: RATING ACCURACY 1

The Effect of Group Consensus on Performance Rating Accuracy

Carrie Picardi

Hofstra University

after writing the rest of the research report to ensure all the most relevant words throughout the report have been considered for inclusion in the title.

Section 2: Abstract

While the Abstract (Figure 14. 2) is the first section of the paper immediately following the Title Page, it is typically the last section of the research paper to be written. The Abstract section is essentially a summary of the entire research report, which is the reason that it is written last. The Abstract section is typically between 100 to 150 words in length and includes the most pertinent information from the entire report. It is comprised of the following elements from each section of the research report:

- From the Introduction section: several statements explaining the construct and variables under examination and the hypothesis statement(s); e.g., "In the present study, the construct of _____ was examined."

- From the Method section: an overview of the methodology with details such as sample size (n), explanation of the IV(s) and DV(s), and a brief summary of key procedural elements

- From the Results section: key findings and whether support for the hypothesis(es) was obtained; e.g., "Data findings supported the hypothesis, which stated . . ."

- From the Discussion section: a concluding statement articulating the importance of the study and implications for future research in the focus area

The Abstract is particularly valuable when searching through dozens of research articles in a journal database to review for possible inclusion in a research study. The Abstract is typically included with the reference information for a research article in the list of displayed search results obtained through a journal database. This is why it's so important to include all the most important keywords in your title and Abstract because most of us conduct database searches by, you guessed it—keywords. If the appropriate keywords are not in the title or Abstract, the research article will not appear on the list of other similar research articles in the search results.

The information provided in the Abstract will help the reader determine the extent to which the research article is relevant to their needs. The content included in the Abstract should be comprehensive and detailed enough to stand out among other, possibly similar, research article results but in a concise format that complies with APA format standards. Even though it's a brief section, the Abstract is often a challenge for many research writers because it can be difficult to condense so much information into a short summary that is clearly articulated and includes all key points. Our advice to you is not to panic! Try writing a first draft version of a brief summary of your research study, examine its length and content, and then gradually whittle it down until it's the proper length for an abstract. Writing a detailed yet concise Abstract section gets easier with practice.

One way to better understand the structure of a well-written Abstract is to conduct a journal database search on a research topic using several keywords you are familiar with and reviewing the Abstracts of all the search results. If the Abstracts are informative, relevant, and cover all the key points of the research study, it is probably a good Abstract to use as a benchmark. If

Box 14.1 Selecting Research Articles Based on Abstracts

Since the sample research report in this chapter deals with performance rating accuracy, let's use this example for an exercise in article selection. Say your hypothesis states that participants will demonstrate greater rating accuracy when required to reach consensus in a group on a collective set of performance ratings than when providing ratings on their own. What keywords would you choose to use to run a journal article search—perhaps *performance, rating, consensus, accuracy, employee*? After entering these keywords, you receive the results below. Which Abstract represents the most relevant article based on your hypothesis, and why?

1. Borman, W. C. , & Hallam, G. L. (1991). Observation accuracy for assessors of work-sample performance: Consistency across task and individual-differences correlates. *Journal of Applied Psychology, 76*(1), 11–18.

Abstract: Consistency and correlates of observation accuracy were examined with videotapes of mechanics performing 2 jet-engine installation tasks. Job experts confirmed errors scripted into selected task steps. Their **consensus** pass/fail evaluations became target scores for evaluating observation accuracy. 79 jet-engine mechanics viewed the videotapes, made pass/fail **ratings** on each task step, and completed cognitive, personality, **rating**-style, and task-effort measures. Hit rate, false-alarm rate, and bias indexes were more consistent across the 2 tasks than in previous research on **performance**-evaluation accuracy. A discrimination index was less stable. The pattern of individual-differences correlates of observation accuracy was for the most part different from the pattern found in research on **performance** evaluation and person perception.

2. Roch, S. G. (2006). Discussion and **consensus** in **rater** groups: Implications for behavioral and rating accuracy. *Human Performance, 19*(2), 91–115.

Abstract: Very little research has explored the importance of discussion and **consensus** among **raters** in determining both behavioral and rating **accuracy**; yet groups of **raters** are routinely used in personnel practices such as assessment centers and panel interviews. Results, based on 225 **raters** in 75 three-person teams, show that not only does the anticipation of group discussion result in initial superior behavioral **accuracy**, but also requiring **raters** to reach **consensus** results in even greater improvements in behavioral **accuracy**. On the other hand, even though behavioral **accuracy** improved in anticipation of group discussion, rating **accuracy** simultaneously decreased. Rating **accuracy**, however, did significantly increase during the process of reaching **consensus** to levels comparable to those groups not anticipating discussion. Overall, group discussion and **consensus** appear to have larger effects on behavioral **accuracy** than rating **accuracy**. Implications, especially for both assessment centers and panel interviews, are discussed.

3. Connelly, B. S. , & Ones, D. S. (2010). Another perspective on personality: Meta-analytic integration of observers' accuracy and predictive validity. *Psychological Bulletin, 136*(6), 1092–1122.

(Continued)

(Continued)

Abstract: The bulk of personality research has been built from self-report measures of personality. However, collecting personality ratings from other-**raters**, such as family, friends, and even strangers, is a dramatically underutilized method that allows better explanation and prediction of personality's role in many domains of psychology. Drawing hypotheses from D. C. Funder's (1995) realistic **accuracy** model about trait and information moderators of **accuracy**, we offer 3 meta-analyses to help researchers and applied psychologists understand and interpret both consistencies and unique insights afforded by other-ratings of personality. These meta-analyses integrate findings based on 44,178 target individuals rated across 263 independent samples. Each meta-analysis assessed the **accuracy** of observer ratings, as indexed by interrater **consensus**/reliability (Study 1), self–other correlations (Study 2), and predictions of behavior (Study 3). The results show that although increased frequency of interacting with targets does improve **accuracy** in rating personality, informants' interpersonal intimacy with the target is necessary for substantial increases in other-rating **accuracy**. Interpersonal intimacy improved **accuracy** especially for traits low in visibility (e.g., Emotional Stability) but only minimally for traits high in evaluativeness (e.g., Agreeableness). In addition, observer ratings were strong predictors of behaviors. When the criterion was academic achievement or job **performance**, other-ratings yielded predictive validities substantially greater than and incremental to self-ratings. These findings indicate that extraordinary value can gained by using other-reports to measure personality, and these findings provide guidelines toward enriching personality theory. Various subfields of psychology in which personality variables are systematically assessed and utilized in research and practice can benefit tremendously from use of others' ratings to measure personality variables.

Figure 14.2 Sample Abstract

RATING ACCURACY   2

ABSTRACT

This study examined the extent that consensus affects performance rating accuracy. Participants (*n* = 96) viewed a video depicting teams working on a problem-solving exercise. The ratees were evaluated on behaviors within three performance dimensions: verbal communication, collaboration, and decision making. Rating accuracy across three conditions (consensus, discussion without consensus, control) was calculated using Cronbach's (1955) accuracy indexes: elevation, differential elevation, stereotype accuracy, and differential accuracy. It was hypothesized that ratings provided by participants in the consensus condition would demonstrate the highest degree of accuracy. Findings in support of this hypothesis provided justification for use of consensus-driven multirater teams for performance evaluation. Moreover, organizations that incorporate a multirater strategy in the performance management process may consider a consensus approach rather than individual ratings submission to enhance accuracy.

after reading an Abstract you still have questions about any aspect of the study or are still unclear about how the constructs were examined, it is probably not a good example of an Abstract. This exercise may be helpful to you for discerning what content to include/not to include and how to pack a lot of meaningful information into a few well-constructed sentences.

Section 3: Introduction

The Introduction (Figures 14.3a and 14.3b) is an important section of the research report because it sets the stage for your research study. The Introduction section of the research report is designed to provide the reader with the information necessary to fully understand the existing body of research in a particular topic area and the rationale for the present study before moving into the Method section. This section begins as a review of the literature and answers pertinent questions about the types of theories that have emerged, how the construct of interest has been defined, what specific questions have been posed and examined by other researchers, and which variables have been included across studies and why. The literature review will gradually narrow in scope to transition the reader from past studies and their findings to your focus for the present study and conclude with your problem statement and hypothesis in order to segue to the Method section. The Introduction section of the research report begins on page 3 and is structured in the following format:

1. An introduction of the construct(s) being examined and the phenomenon, issue, and/or research question developed for investigation

2. A review of the literature in the topic area, incorporating information about similar research studies, validated research methods and findings from published research articles as each construct, variable, and measure used in the present research study is introduced and explained

3. A statement of the problem that identifies the need for the present study based on the gaps, limitations, and unmet needs of the research studies previously discussed

4. A hypothesis statement, or statements, which are the predictions of the outcome(s) for the present study

A review of existing published research articles is valuable because it provides an understanding of the various studies that have been conducted in a particular topic area. Among the different studies, there may be variations of operational definitions of the construct being examined, different types and levels of independent variables, different dependent variables and measures, samples, and so on. Some studies may have been conducted with a simple design, while others may have incorporated a more elaborate design. A review of the literature also enables the identification of consistencies across studies and what elements (e.g., operational definitions, measures) may have been validated and used in several studies in this topic area. Identifying these elements is crucial to ensuring the validity of your own research study design. Say you have an idea about how to operationalize certain variables, in an effort to examine a construct of interest, for example, the impact that personality traits have on organizational citizenship behavior (OCB) and ethical decision making, and your operational definitions of OCB and ethical decision making are nowhere to be found in the existing literature. If this happens, you may have some construct validity issues that need to be addressed.

Remember—various findings in the literature that both support and do not support your hypothesis can and should be included! It is quite reasonable to include contradictory studies to show the full picture of a particular body of research rather than only the positive side. Lastly, a review of the literature may be helpful in the identification of elements that have not yet been addressed in any existing studies, such as a particularly relevant demographic variable or setting, that you may consider examining in your study and may enhance its external validity.

Often students ask us the question, "How long should the Introduction section be?" The answer we give is, "As long as you need it to be in order to introduce and explain all the constructs and variables in your research study in a comprehensive manner!" A research study that involves a $3 \times 3 \times 2$ factorial design will certainly necessitate a lengthier Introduction section compared to a study that consists of one independent variable with two levels and one dependent variable. This review of the literature will be useful as you consider the appropriate elements to incorporate in your research study from existing studies. Remember, for every construct and variable you as the research writer include, you must not only explain these elements, provide operational definitions, and describe measures but you must also offer rationale for your inclusion and definition of each element using information from relevant studies in which the researchers incorporated similar elements for the same reasons. Attention to this level of explanation and rationale is critical for addressing and supporting the construct validity of the study. You will not find every element you need in one research study, organized to perfectly suit your needs and tied neatly with a bow! The elements you wish to include for examination in your research study may be found within many (many!) research studies. You will most likely locate the operational definitions for your chosen variables, for example, in one or two research studies, and the appropriate measure for your dependent variable in another study. The more complex your design in terms of number of independent variables and conditions within each one and number of dependent variables, the more research studies you will likely have to include to provide support for each element. This is the reason why published research articles and academic research reports such as theses and dissertations contain so many references. Each reference entry has probably provided only one or two needed components for that research report.

With that said, it is necessary to examine the length requirement for the type of research report you are writing as there may be circumstances in which a word count maximum is specified to comply with the parameters of a publication such as a journal or trade periodical. This is a good example of why an outline is helpful as the structure of the research report is developed—an outline will help you ensure that all the topics are covered with the appropriate content in the most logical sequence and there is a sufficient amount of information presented per the length parameters of the final report.

The Introduction must be clear and well articulated and the main construct must be defined so that a reader with limited knowledge about your topic of interest will be able to comprehend. All subtopics, such as operational definitions of the independent and dependent variables, should be integrated carefully and with a logical flow from paragraph to paragraph so the content does not appear choppy or disjointed. The content should be presented in a way that clearly and logically connects all the previous research described

Figure 14.3a Sample Introduction—Opening Paragraph

RATING ACCURACY 3

Performance management is acknowledged by many organizations to be a valuable and necessary component in the evaluation of employees and will impact other facets of the employee lifecycle, including training and development, compensation, rewards and incentives, and disciplinary action. The domain of performance management is comprised of several distinct areas: (1) assessment, (2) feedback, and (3) reactions, with each area consisting of specific strategies and processes. A critical goal of organizations is to establish a relationship between employees' assessed behaviors and performance outcomes. An appropriately designed and implemented performance management system in an organization, with adequate attention to key elements such as competency and rating scale development, alignment of performance outcomes to organizational objectives, rating accuracy, feedback, goal setting, and development opportunities, may offer substantial value in terms of a high-performing workforce and successful achievement of organizational objectives (London, Mone, & Scott, 2004).

Figure 14.3b Sample Introduction—Concluding Paragraph

RATING ACCURACY 23

The focus of the present research is on the implications of multirater consensus on performance rating accuracy. The inclusion of multiple raters, such as peers, managers, and/or customers, who may interact with the ratee in a variety of workplace situations, will likely have different perspectives on the ratee's performance based on their unique observations and interactions with the rate in certain contexts. Roch (2006) examined behavioral and rating accuracy in the context of both a discussion-only condition and a discussion with consensus condition in addition to the control condition; similarly the same three conditions will be implemented in the present study which will attempt to provide support for Roch's (2006) findings pertaining to rating accuracy of consensus-driven groups. It is proposed that a consensus requirement for the group, along with appropriate rating accuracy measures, will offer a feasible method for improvement and enhanced value to the performance assessment process. The following hypothesis has been developed:

Hypothesis 1: *Individuals in the consensus rating condition will have greater rating accuracy in their consensus ratings than individuals in the no consensus rating condition or the control condition will have in their individual summary ratings.*

in the review of the literature with the focus and objectives of the present study. A reader should get a sense of a story unfolding as the Introduction section progresses with it concluding by the introduction of the research question and statement of the problem being addressed in your study and an accompanying hypothesis or hypotheses. This will provide a clear and seamless segue into the following Method section.

Section 4: Method

The Method section (Figures 14.4a and 14.4b) of the research report provides the reader with detailed information about how the present study was conducted and includes three main sections entitled Participants, Materials and Measures, and Procedure. If the methodology was particularly complex, a brief overview presented in the beginning of the Method section may be appropriate to reacquaint the reader with the study's scope and key elements. The Method section should be highly detailed and include all the necessary information to

Figure 14.4a   Sample Method—Participants, Materials, Measures

RATING ACCURACY   24

METHOD

Participants

Participants ($n = 102$) were graduate students of a liberal arts college in the Northeast United States and were enrolled in several different psychology master's degree programs.

Materials

A video of a three-person group working together on a problem-solving simulation exercise was shown to participants during the rating sessions. The use of video vignettes is a method initiated in performance rating research by Borman (1978) that gained support (Martell & Borg, 1993; Roch, 2006) for enhancing generalizability of rating accuracy findings to applied settings.

Measures

Independent Variable. The independent variable was the rating consensus requirement, and there were three levels: a consensus condition, a discussion-only condition, and a control condition. Though the participants in the discussion-only and control conditions made their ratings independently, they were also placed in groups of three raters in alignment with the same setting in which the consensus rating condition participants were placed.

Dependent Variables. The study included four dependent variables, using Cronbach's (1955) four accuracy indexes, which are predominantly used by researchers examining performance rating accuracy (Borman, 1977; Murphy & Balzer, 1989; Roch, 2006) and have received significant empirical support as direct measures of the accuracy of subjective performance ratings.

Figure 14.4b Sample Method—Procedure

RATING ACCURACY   25
Procedure
The participants were randomly assigned to groups of three in one of the three experimental conditions. The participants in each session viewed a video that presented a group of three individuals (ratees) working through a problem-solving simulation exercise. The same video was shown to all groups in all three conditions. While viewing the video, the participants provided rating scores for the level of performance of each of the three specified performance dimensions for each ratee. All participants used a 7-point rating scale, with a rating of 1 for inadequate performance and a rating of 7 for excellent performance, for each of the three performance dimensions and each of the three ratees.

Participants in the consensus condition were required to discuss their individual ratings with their fellow group members and reach consensus on one collective second set of ratings. Participants in the discussion with no consensus condition were required to discuss their individual ratings with their fellow group members and, after several minutes of discussion-free individual reflection, independently make a second set of summary rating scores. Participants in the control condition were required to complete a 10-item questionnaire consisting of opinion questions regarding the video presentation and then independently make a second set of summary rating scores. Following the summary rating score completion, the participants were debriefed and adjourned.

---

replicate the study. Imagine you were attempting to bake a pie that someone else baked and you enjoyed and you had to rely on the ingredients list and baking details of an unfamiliar recipe to re-create it. Without knowing all the ingredients and their required amounts and the exact procedure in its sequential order, you would not be able to re-create that pie. The detail and procedure order is just as important in the Method section of a research report. If someone is unable to replicate your study after reading and following the information presented in your Method section, then it doesn't contain all the necessary information.

The sections comprising the Method typically follow a standard structure:

Description of the sample including the number of participants, referred to as n, the population from which they were selected (e.g., school, company, hospital), and a breakdown of all relevant demographic information (e.g., gender, age, occupation, ethnicity, marital status) collected. This description typically contains generic descriptors (e.g., undergraduate students at a private northeastern university, employees in management positions from a global consumer goods retailer).

- Description of all materials and measures used in the study, such as video/audio recordings, questionnaires, checklists, activities and exercises, scenario vignettes, and all measures of the dependent variable(s) such as tests and assessment instruments.

- Procedure for data collection that begins with an explanation of the recruitment and coordination of the participants and continues with explanation of participant assignment to the different conditions, acquiring informed consent, explanation of the manner in which the study was conducted in sequential step-by-step description including manipulation techniques of the independent variables and measurement of the dependent variables, and concludes with participant debriefing and adjournment.

The Method section is the most straightforward part of the research report to write, but it must be very detailed and organized in the correct sequence of events. This is an important requirement because it will enable accurate and consistent interpretation as well as replication of the study by other researchers. It will be a helpful approach to use the published research papers that you have selected to review and include in your project as a guide as you develop the framework for the Method section. You will see that while the papers may vary in their Introduction, Results, and Discussion sections, they all follow a basic structure for the Method section.

Section 5: Results

In the Results section (Figure 14. 5) of a research report, the researcher(s) explain the statistical procedures used to analyze the data collected, key findings, and the extent to which their hypothesis was supported. In studies not yet conducted, such as academic research proposals and proposed studies that have been submitted to an Institutional Review Board (IRB) for review and approval of the study's compliance with the code of ethics (refer to Chapter 3 for details on ethics guidelines and IRB protocol), the Results section is referred to as the Proposed Data Analysis section and is written in the future tense (e.g., "the expected sample size will be 150"). Although it is tempting to discuss the findings here along with the actual data obtained, it is not the appropriate place to do so; this content must be saved for the Discussion section.

The most important element in the Results section is the explanation of the extent to which the findings support the hypothesis. It is common practice to include a brief description of the hypothesis prior to describing the level of support. If there are multiple hypotheses, each should be addressed separately. When discussing each hypothesis, researchers also include the significance level, alpha level, or p value. This value should be included even if the result was not statistically significant (e.g., $p = .313$) and the hypothesis was not supported. If the results are statistically significant, the p value will actually be reported in a slightly different way than the statistical output displays. We don't report that $p = 0.027$, but rather say that $p < 0.05$. Depending on the significance level selected, a researcher can use one of the following three values to indicate the correct level of statistical significance: $p < 0.05, p < 0.01$, or $p < 0.001$.

> **effect size:** A value that describes the strength of the relationship between variables

Another important element in the Results section is the size and direction of the effect. As we discussed in Chapter 11, effect size describes the strength of the relationship between the independent and dependent variables. In statistical output, effect size is represented by d and r values and is expressed in standard deviation units. The d value represents the degree of difference that the levels of the independent variable have on the dependent variable. The *r* value, often referred to as the Pearson correlation coefficient, represents the strength of the association between variables. The reason that effect size data are included in research results is because this information provides us with insight about the relationship between variables that is not always apparent with the data on statistical significance alone. For example, a study with a large sample may yield statistical significance but still depict a weak relationship between variables (i.e., low effect size). Thus, effect size findings are also expected to be reported in the Results section.

Box 14.2 **A Word of Caution About the Word** *Cause*

In everyday communication, we use the word *cause* often, for example, when someone states that the rain causes their arthritis to exacerbate or when an employee believes that focusing more attention on customer service caused improved customer satisfaction feedback. However, in research we must be careful about how the word *cause* is used. Because findings are never absolutely confirmatory, in other words we can never *prove* the existence of a phenomenon in the social sciences based on the findings from a research study, we cannot state that one variable will always cause the same reaction in another variable. This outcome may have occurred in a particular study, but it may not be the case across all studies. In research writing, the preferred terminology is to state that a causal relationship was demonstrated between the variables being examined. Another way to articulate this type of outcome appropriately would be to state that a causal inference can be made based on the findings of the study.

It is imperative that the researcher have a comprehensive understanding of the various statistical calculations and their appropriate use. For example, to apply the incorrect statistical calculation, such as running an analysis of variance (ANOVA) when there is no independent variable being manipulated (in which case a correlation would be the suitable statistical procedure), would be a serious error and compromise the study's findings. Selection of the correct statistical calculations as well as the providing of credible rationale for the selection(s) made are necessary steps in writing the Results section of a research paper. For an academic paper such as a thesis or dissertation, rationale for all the statistical procedures selected must be made as they are explained in this section. It is not enough to simply state, "A MANOVA was run to analyze the data." It is necessary to go further with an explanation, such as "Because the study consisted of multiple independent variables and multiple dependent variables, a MANOVA was run to analyze the data." For journals and other publications, it is typically unnecessary to include the rationale due to publication length requirements and also because it is expected that a manuscript worthy of publication will have included the correct statistical calculations—no need to explain!

The placement of information in the Results section follows a specific format just as with the other sections of the research report. Following an explanation of the support for each hypothesis, the significance level, and the effect size/direction, all other statistical values are provided such as *F* values for any ANOVAs conducted and degrees of freedom. These values, along with descriptive statistics, are typically included in the narrative explanation of the findings as well as in a table. All tables, figures, and graphs are included at the end of the report, in an appendix.

Figure 14.5   Sample Results

RATING ACCURACY   38

RESULTS

The following results demonstrated a significantly greater degree of rating accuracy for the consensus condition than for the discussion-only condition or control condition across all four accuracy indexes, thus providing support for this hypothesis.

Elevation. Results indicated a significant difference between posttest scores across all three experimental conditions, $F(2, 74) = 3.491$, $p < .05$, $\eta^2 = 0.060$, for elevation (E), which is described as the average level of rater accuracy across all ratees and performance dimensions (Table 1).

Table 1.

Analysis of Covariance Summary Table—Elevation

Source	SS	df	MS	F	p	η^2
Between Treatments	13.074	2	6.537	3.491	<.05	.060
Error	150.987	71	2.068			
Total	255.349	74				

Section 6: Discussion

The Discussion section (Figure 14.6) of a research report, similar to the Method section, is fairly straightforward to develop and is typically structured in the following manner:

1. Explanation of key findings and whether or not the hypothesis/hypotheses were supported; extent to which results served the purpose and objective(s) of the study; expected/unexpected findings.

2. Implications of the findings, the extent to which findings may be applied in various contexts

3. Strengths of the research study
   - e.g., large sample size, use of a control group, ability to generalize to a specific field setting

4. Limitations (i.e., flaws, weaknesses) of the research study
   - e.g., lack of random assignment, no availability of a pretest/archival data to identify a baseline prior to implementing a treatment
   - also included here are potential threats to validity and rationale (e.g., history, selection)

5. Future research directions in this topic area

6. Concluding remarks

In the Discussion section, it is important to remember that this section is a discussion of the entire study. The purpose is to wrap all concepts and ideas together by integrating the Introduction and the hypothesis(es) with the Results section. Keep in mind that whenever research is conducted, a possibility exists that you will not find support for a hypothesis that you thought would occur. Don't panic! This may happen and the discussion section is where you explain the current findings.

Within this explanation, you can discuss the strengths of the current study and why you may or may not have found support for your hypothesis(es) and any potential limitations. Recall from our earlier discussion on validity that no design is flawless and there will be some threats to validity. This is where you can state the potential threats to the validity of the results and provide an explanation as to why this may be or why you were willing to accept this threat. For example, the study presented in this chapter dealt with rater accuracy and external validity being a possible threat because the findings conducted in a laboratory setting may not be representative of an applied setting. However, conducting a research study on rater accuracy requires a high level of control, so a laboratory design was

Figure 14.6 Sample Discussion

RATING ACCURACY 43

DISCUSSION

Trends in Research and Practice

Performance management is a multifaceted domain consisting of three distinct areas: assessment, feedback, and reaction/outcomes. Research, regardless of domain focus, should strive to provide support for a common underlying theme: the improvement of an organization's performance management strategy for greater utility and relevance to business objectives.

Explanation of the Results

The findings obtained in the present research demonstrated the superior accuracy in the rating scores provided by participants in the consensus condition compared to the rating scores provided by participants in either the discussion-only or control conditions.

Research Limitations

The present study may possess limitations consistent with related research (Murphy, Garcia, Kerkar, Martin, & Balzer, 1982; Roch, 2006). Researchers attempting to make generalizations to applied settings from findings produced by studies in laboratory settings should do so cautiously, particularly with such organizationally relevant constructs as employee performance ratings.

Future Research Directions

The present study provides support for the integration of multirater judgment in a consensus decision regarding incumbent performance across several dimensions.

preferred to an applied setting to control for extraneous/confounding variables that may be present in an applied setting.

The potential threats to internal or external validity tie well into providing the future research directions section. In the future research directions section, a researcher will describe feasible ideas for research studies that should be conducted in this area. It is often recommended that follow-up studies should be conducted to address identified flaws/limitations in the present study or to examine variables that are important but have not yet been examined in any other similar studies to date.

Finally, a brief concluding paragraph should wrap up the entire report. It is not necessary to start this paragraph with, "In conclusion, . . . " Simply write a few sentences tying everything together so there is an obvious ending to the paper. Do not allow the research paper to just trail off without some sense of finality—it is imperative to reach a clear conclusion to the research report.

Section 7: References

The References section (Figure 14. 7) includes all the sources cited throughout the research report, including books, articles, dissertations, websites, and other media. The References section can become a bit unwieldy in a paper that is lengthy and/or complex and includes dozens of sources. It is recommended that this section be worked on gradually as new references are gathered and integrated in the paper. Every time you include a new reference source in your paper, create a reference entry for it at that time. To *save up* all the references and compile the entire References section as a final task can easily become overwhelming and lead to errors. By keeping up with this section as you write the research report, you will ensure that every citation throughout the paper has a complete and accurate reference entry.

Figure 14.7 Sample References

RATING ACCURACY   50

REFERENCES

Balzer, W. K., & Sulsky, L. M. (1990). Performance appraisal effectiveness. In K. R. Murphy & F. E. Saal (Eds.), *Psychology in organizations: Integrating science and practice* (pp. 133–156). Hillsdale, NJ: Erlbaum.

Barnes-Farrell, J. L., & Lynch, A. M. (2003). Performance appraisal and feedback programs. In J. E. Edwards, J. C. Scott, & N. S. Raju (Eds.), *The human resources program-evaluation handbook* (pp. 155–176). Thousand Oaks, CA: Sage.

Borman, W. C. (1977). Consistency of rating accuracy and rating errors in the judgment of human performance. *Organizational Behavior and Human Performance, 20*, 238–252.

Cronbach, L. J. (1955). Processes affecting scores on understanding of others and assumed "similarity." *Psychological Bulletin, 52*, 177–193.

Guion, R. M. (1965). *Personnel testing*. New York, NY: McGraw-Hill.

Ilgen, D. R., & Favero, J. L. (1985). Limits in generalization from psychological research to performance appraisal processes. *Academy of Management Review, 10*, 311–321.

Section 8: Appendices

The Appendix section (Figure 14. 8) is the last part of the research report and follows the References section. Typically, the Informed Consent form used in the study is presented as Appendix A, though there may be instances in which another item, such as an informational flyer or study recruitment form, is presented as Appendix A and the Informed Consent form becomes Appendix B. The submission of additional appendixes will be relevant to the various assessments, surveys, handouts, and other documents that are part of the Materials and Measures section of the Method section. It is appropriate for researchers to provide a separate appendix for any measure, set of instructions, scale, table, or instrument that is critical to the methodology of the study. Often, research journals will omit appendices from a published article for sake of space in the journal, but the inclusion of all necessary appendices is required for an academic research paper.

Style of a Research Report

If you have ever evaluated research papers for any reason, for example, while serving on a thesis or dissertation committee, or as an instructor for a course, you know that individual writing style varies tremendously! While there is not necessarily one set style of writing

Figure 14.8 Sample Appendix—Informed Consent

RATING ACCURACY   55

APPENDIX A

Informed Consent

May 2009

The following study, about performance management and evaluation processes, is part of a research initiative being conducted by Carrie Picardi. As a participant, you will be asked to complete a 1-hour session in which you will view a video of a group team-building and decision-making activity and provide performance ratings for specified behaviors. For your voluntary participation in this study, you will receive five (5) extra-credit points. You may withdraw from the study at any time, but in order to receive participation credit, you must attend the entire session and complete all requirements.

I appreciate your assistance and am available to answer any questions regarding your participation in the research study. I am happy to share the findings of the study with anyone who is interested in this information. Thank you for your interest and cooperation.

Best regards,

Carrie Picardi

I have read and understand the information provided above and agree to participate in this research study.

Signature: _____ Date: _____

that we all must adhere to, there are certainly important guidelines and recommendations to follow when writing up research. The main goal for a research report should always be to produce a paper that meets all requirements and is audience appropriate. Following this goal, it is also critical to ensure the content of the paper is clear, contains adequate details and definitions, follows a logical flow of topics and subtopics, and is presented in an objective, unemotional, and unbiased manner. Let's examine each of these facets in more detail.

Clarity

Have you ever written a lengthy term paper, perhaps with more than eight or nine references? Was it easy to take all of these published articles, similar in topic but perhaps presented in very different ways, and report on them as a collective in your own original paper? It most likely was a challenging undertaking, especially if the topics and language in the papers were quite new to you. Yet, this is the first style goal for a research report, to create a new body of information that combines past, present, and future—previous studies, your own current research and findings, and future directions—all seamlessly. A reader should not have to look up every other word in your paper, have to do an Internet search to identify industry jargon and acronyms, or have to bounce back and forth throughout your paper to be able to understand your points and *where you're going* with the research paper. A good research writer is able to do the following actions:

1. develop original ideas and articulate a research direction/objective based on existing information and findings from a variety of credible sources,

2. capture and integrate the elements of existing research articles that are the most relevant to the research paper, and

3. present it in a way that captures the reader's attention, follows a logical progression of concepts, answers questions, and contributes a new and valuable perspective to an existing body of research.

This is the importance of clarity in writing a research report. In this section, we will explain the difference between a well-written and a poorly written research report and tips and tools for honing your research writing skills.

Box 14.3   The Importance of an Outline

In our years of teaching research methods courses at the undergraduate and graduate level, we have found the majority of students construct research papers in the same way: They stare at a blank document screen on their computers and start writing about their topic from the beginning. Now, this is the way we all read, but should it be the way we write as well? The answer is simply, no! Writing, especially a lengthy and complex research paper, requires a plan and a framework determined in advance of the actual writing. It is not unlike an Internet search. Have you ever randomly searched for a topic on the Internet, only to be derailed by the myriad search results that put you on a completely different search path, sometimes wasting hours of time? This happens to all of us, but when we allow the same winding, rambling pattern to emerge in our writing, the result is a paper that may be the following:

- Choppy and disjointed
- Overly reliant on other research articles to drive your paper
- Lacking a flow and logical transition of topics/subtopics
- Missing pertinent information, such as answers to previously posed questions and conclusions
- Redundant and contain repeating information (yes, we were redundant here on purpose!)

The solution to this common writer challenge is simple—create an outline! An outline creates a framework for the paper and is the structure that enables you as the writer to have a plan for exactly what you want to present: the inclusion of topics and subtopics in an appropriate sequential order. With an outline in place, your research paper will stay organized and relevant as you develop multiple drafts and work toward the final version. An outline will also enable you as the writer to identify which sections contain an adequate amount of content and which sections look a bit sparse and may need additional information. Lastly, an outline will help you avoid what we refer to as the "Researchers found . . . " problem, which is the creation of new paragraphs to introduce what other research articles have examined. While the inclusion of existing research findings is a necessary aspect of research writing, remember this is your paper—do not allow other researchers to drive your bus! By creating topic sections in an outline, you will be better equipped to manage the flow from one topic to the next, introduce the next concept in your own voice as a segue from the previous concept, and integrate existing research findings to validate and provide rationale for your assertions.

We have found when students write research papers after developing a relevant and well-organized outline, it makes a world of difference in terms of reading a clearly articulated and seamless body of information versus reading a paper that is presented as a mass of individual pieces of information haphazardly pasted together.

The Active Voice and the Passive Voice

Another aspect of clarity is your *voice* as a writer, specifically the active voice and the passive voice. Here are a few examples of each style:

Active Voice:
Participants completed a 50-item questionnaire.
Researchers determined that a correlation exists between organizational culture and ethical decision making.
I believe consistent and timely feedback will improve work performance.

Passive Voice:

A 50-item questionnaire was completed by participants.

It was determined by researchers that a correlation exists between organizational culture and ethical decision making.

It is the belief of the researcher that consistent and timely feedback will improve work performance.

As a reader, which voice do you prefer? Most of us would likely prefer the active voice as it provides us with a clearer and more direct message than the passive voice, which provides us with the same information but in a more *roundabout* way. However, in research writing, we often rely on the passive voice because we are instructed not to use first-person pronouns (e.g., I, we) in research papers, which are commonly found in the active voice style. As you can see from the examples we presented, it is possible to write in the active voice and also avoid using first-person pronouns. Of the three example sentences for the active voice, two do not include first-person pronouns. Does this mean that you should avoid the passive voice altogether? No, it does not. An ideal writing style incorporates both the active and passive voice. A balance of the two voice styles is essential as too much active voice will come across clipped and dry and too much passive voice will come across as confusing and pedantic. A good rule of thumb is to use a bit more active voice in the Abstract, Method, and Results sections of a paper, which require very concise and direct writing, and to balance active and passive voice in the Introduction and Discussion sections, which benefit from a more engaging narrative style. An articulate writer will know how to balance the two voice styles to create a clear, informative, and interesting research paper.

Quotes

Another element of detail in a research report is the appropriate inclusion of quotes from existing research articles, websites, periodicals, and books. Researchers use quotes from sources such as these quite often but do so prudently. The quality and credibility of quotes are important considerations as well as the number of quotes you decide to include and their location in the body of the paper.

A quote should be included if it provides support for an idea or finding you propose is valuable and relevant to your research study and its potential applications. The author or originator of the quote should be well-respected and perceived as having expertise in the domain because the whole point of including a quote is to provide validation from an influential source that provides a bit of *oomph* to the information you are presenting. With that said, too many quotes are distracting and will confuse the reader in terms of which information is your own original content and which information is someone else's content. As professors, we have read many papers in which a student fills an entire page with quotes, with perhaps two or three sentences of their own original content! This is an easy pitfall because other authors have probably said what you are trying to say and it sounds so well-articulated from them that you may be unsure how to make it sound any better coming from you! As a writer, you must make a clear distinction between your content and the quotes you include, and correct citations will be necessary to avoid being suspected of plagiarism.

> **plagiarism:** the act of copying the writing of another author verbatim and submitting it as your own original work

The last consideration with inclusion of quotes is their placement. A quote will look misplaced and irrelevant if it appears several sentences or a paragraph before or after the content you have written for which the quote is meant to support. A good writer will make sure that the quote being included is directly related to the information it immediately precedes or follows.

Logical Flow of Topics

Organization of ideas can be a challenge for many research writers for lengthy papers and shorter papers alike. Lengthy academic papers, such as theses and dissertations, can become unwieldy quickly, and a writer can easily forget where a point was mentioned and if the same point was mentioned several times. Shorter papers, for journal submissions and industry publications, can also present an organizational challenge as the writer now needs to condense a lot of information into a short and succinct manuscript. The challenge then becomes a question of what content stays or gets cut and also how this type of editing affects and potentially disrupts the flow of ideas.

If you find yourself writing "as previously mentioned, . . . " several times, there is a good chance your flow of topics and content organization could use some work. You should not have to backtrack to previously stated points too often in your paper.

Objectivity

The last writing style topic we will cover is objectivity. As individuals, of course we have certain attitudes, opinions, and topics that elicit strong emotions. This is normal for everyone. However, as researchers we must be careful to eliminate all evidence of personal subjectivity in our writing and strive to be as objective as possible, even (and especially!) when we take a certain position or have a strong opinion with regard to the topic of interest.

Subjectivity in our own writing is often unintentional, and we may not even realize that we are referring to or describing individuals and/or groups inappropriately or offensively. Care should be taken to avoid words that may be perceived as insensitive, biased, or discriminatory when it comes to referring to certain groups or categories of individuals such as gender, race, ethnicity, sexual orientation, and physical or mental disability/illness. A common error is to compare one group, such as individuals diagnosed with ADHD, to a group described as *normal* individuals. The appropriate language would be "individuals diagnosed with ADHD and individuals without ADHD." As biased or emotionally charged wording is identified, neutral words should be substituted and used consistently throughout the paper. Sometimes this requires an outside reader with a fresh perspective to read our work and identify any issues that may be more challenging for us to see in our own writing.

PUTTING IT ALL TOGETHER—FINAL THOUGHTS

As we developed this textbook with both the academic and practitioner audiences in mind, so you should consider this balance in your own research and writing, which is critical to the applied nature of our professional disciplines. As undergraduate students (as we all have been at some point!), we typically view our academic writing and research reporting as transactional—the paper is written and submitted, and a grade is received. As graduate students, we also enter into this advanced degree program with a similar perspective because this is all that we know. But, this perspective will not serve many graduate students well as they prepare to enter their respective fields of interest. As graduate students, you must begin to take ownership of your work, your intellectual property, and see your research and writing efforts as intrinsic to your intended field and not merely a stepping stone to acquiring credits toward your degree. As you explore and conduct research and hone your writing skills, you should clearly see the specific topics areas you are passionate about and how they are applied in a meaningful way in the field you will hopefully enter upon, or even perhaps before, graduation. For many of us, this is an "Ah ha!" moment—when your academic and professional interests align.

As you continue this exploration (as we hope you do beyond graduate school!), you will gain a greater understanding of your topical interest areas in both the research community and practitioner contexts. This will serve you well as you will develop an appreciation for how to conduct sound research studies in the most feasible, yet rigorous, manner and how to translate your findings to a practitioner audience typically comprised of laypersons that may not understand nor care about construct validity or effect size. As you write or present valuable findings to an audience, always keep in mind their WIIFM (What's In It For Me?), whether that audience is comprised of researchers focused on statistical significance and internal validity or field professionals interested in funding and budgets and legal compliance. As applied researchers, *we* are the bridge. It is our responsibility to conduct, interpret, and present research to our stakeholders in the most relevant manner so that they can take that information and actually go use it to make improvements and progress in our respective fields.

Box 14.4 Research Paper Checklist

Before you submit your research paper for review and evaluation, make sure you have all the required elements and have paid attention to every detail!

APA Format

- ☐ Do you have a running head on the Title Page?
- ☐ Does the running head wording on the Title Page match with the wording on the header of every page?
- ☐ Do your page numbers begin on the Title Page and appear in the upper right corner?
- ☐ Is the entire paper double-spaced (including your reference entries)?
- ☐ Is the entire paper formatted in Times New Roman 12-point font?
- ☐ Is the paper layout correct (i.e., section headings and content centered or left justified properly)?
- ☐ Did you include the correct citations in the body of the paper?
- ☐ Do the in-text citations (author names and publication years) match up with the references entries?

Mechanics

☐ Did you run spell check and correct all spelling and grammatical errors?

☐ Did you proofread to ensure any errors not picked up by spell check were identified and corrected (e.g., using *too* instead of *two*)?

☐ Did you use e.g. and i.e. correctly? The former means "for example" and the latter means "in other words."

☐ Did you remove all contractions and replace them with complete words (e.g., *doesn't* to *does not*)?

☐ Did you avoid using first-person pronouns (e.g., *I*, *we*)?

Style

☐ Are your paragraphs written in a logical transition and with flow (i.e., does the ending of a paragraph clearly segue into the beginning of the next paragraph)?

☐ Did you remove any wording redundancies (e.g., "more and more," "a very, very small number")?

☐ Is the tone of the content objective and unemotional? Are there emotional trigger words or phrases (e.g., *devastating*, *useless*, *unappreciated*, *abnormal*, *immoral*) that should be examined for personal subjectivity?

☐ Did you maintain a reasonable limit to the number of quotes you included in the paper from credible sources? Are they cited properly?

CHAPTER SUMMARY

- While the research report may vary a bit in terms of length and level of detail, which depends on the context and scope of its publication and/or presentation, the framework or structure of the research paper will always be consistent. The research community adheres to the inclusion of specific sections in a research report and in a particular sequential order.

- The required sections in the order they appear in the research report are (1) Title Page, (2) Abstract, (3) Introduction, (4) Method, (5) Results, (6) Discussion, and (7) References. A research report may also contain one or more Appendix sections, depending on the needs and presentation requirements of the report and inclusion of ancillary information.

- The progression of the research report will generally follow a typical pattern that begins broadly as you describe the construct of focus and independent/dependent variables and gets more specific as you move closer to your own hypothesis, method, and results. The report will broaden again as you move into the implications of the findings, their value in various contexts and settings, and future directions for this area of research.

- The main goal for a research report should always be to produce a paper that meets all requirements and is audience appropriate. Following this goal, it is also critical to ensure the content of the paper is clear, contains adequate details and definitions, follows a logical flow of topics and subtopics, and is presented in an objective, unemotional, and unbiased manner.

DISCUSSION QUESTIONS

- What are the main components or subsections of each of the main sections of a research report? List and describe the content that should appear in these different sections.

- What is the difference between the active voice and passive voice? How can a researcher balance these two types for an effective writing style that is engaging yet clear and concise?

- How should a researcher explain any issues that may have occurred during the course of the study, such as sampling issues and threats to validity?

- What are some examples of information that would likely appear as an Appendix, and how are the Appendixes ordered within a research report? Why are Appendixes often omitted when studies are published in peer-reviewed journals?

CHAPTER KEY TERMS

Abstract
Active Voice
APA Format
Appendix
Citation
Discussion

Introduction
Manuscript
Method
Passive Voice
Pedantic
Plagiarism

Poster Presentation
References
Results
Running Head

Glossary

Abstract – a summary of the entire research report that is typically between 100–150 words in length and includes the most pertinent information from the entire report

Active Voice – a sentence where the subject performs the action defined by the verb

Ad Hoc – something that is done for a specific purpose or situation

Age Discrimination in Employment Act (ADEA) – signed into effect in 1967, it is a law that prohibits discrimination against individuals age 40 and older

Alpha – a probability level set by the researcher to determine if the results of the study were due to chance

Ambiguous Temporal Precedence – internal validity threat. Cause must precede an effect, but it may not be known whether the cause preceded the effect.

Americans with Disabilities Act (ADA) – signed into effect in 1990, it is a law that prohibits discrimination against a qualified individual with a disability

Analysis of Variance (ANOVA) – also known as ANOVA. A statistical technique utilizing an F ratio to determine if an independent variable has a statistically significant effect on a dependent variable.

Anonymity – the identity of the participants is not known by anyone who is reading or involved in the research, including the researcher

APA Format – a format style used in the social sciences to provide writers with how to structure the introduction, methodology, results, discussion, abstract, references, tables, and figures when writing a research study

Appendix – an addition to a document that often contains supplemental material

Applied – a situation that has a practical purpose

Applied Research – type of research conducted to solve a problem that occurs on an every-day basis

Archival Data – research involves the use of existing data that have been collected and stored for a variety of needs

Attrition – internal validity threat. Loss of participants from the beginning to end of the experiment.

Autonomous Agents – in ethics, each individual subject is physically and mentally capable of making decisions and choices regarding entering and participating in a study and that participation in a study is voluntary

Basic Research – type of research where questions are developed to understand the fundamental process of a phenomenon

Belmont Report – published by the U.S. Public Health Service's National Commission for the Protection of Human Subjects of Biomedical and Behavioral Research (1979) containing three principles: respect for persons, beneficence, and justice

Beneficence – principle in the Belmont Report on ethics that states that researchers should not cause harm to their subjects and that researchers should strive for positive outcomes for the subjects as well as for themselves, the research community, and society. The primary goal should always be maximizing benefits of the research while minimizing the risk of both probability and degree of harm.

Beta – a probability level that is not set by the research that states that the relationship found in the study is not statistically significant

Between Subjects – a research design component where participants are exposed to only one condition in a study

Bias – a tendency or belief that may lead to an inappropriate or incorrect decision

Bimodal – a measure of central tendency where two values in a distribution appear the same number of times in a distribution

Case – may also be referred to as an element and is an individual participant/object in a research study

Case Study – an in-depth exploration of a particular individual, group of individuals, or entity, such as a team, family, organization, special interest group, or neighborhood

Central Tendency – descriptive statistics known as mean, median, and mode that are used to provide a summary of the data

Citation – a technique used to provide credit to authors of a research article being referenced in a research study to avoid plagiarism

Civil Rights Act of 1964 – a landmark civil rights law that prohibits making selection decisions on the basis of race or sex

Classical Test Theory – also referred to as True Score Theory. A measurement error theory derived from the thought that a raw score consists of a true and random component.

Close-Ended Question – a technique in survey design where a question is one in which the respondent must provide an answer from a limited number of responses

Cluster Sampling – a probability technique that involves grouping individuals and then randomly selecting them for participation in a research study

Codebook – a document used to record and keep their coding systems well organized

Coding System – created before qualitative data analysis that is designed to clearly define categories and avoid confusion about where data should be placed in a category

Common Explained Variance – variability that is shared between two predictors that both explain the same variance in the criterion

Compensatory Equalization – construct validity threat. When researchers provide compensation to the participant group not receiving the treatment.

Compensatory Rivalry – construct validity threat. Participants that do not receive the treatment may be motivated to do as well as the treatment group.

Confederate – an individual working with a researcher but pretending to be a participant in the study, acting in a specified role necessary to the procedure

Confidence Interval – a value used to depict the degree of a sample's representativeness to the population from which it was

Confidentiality – the researcher knows the identity of the participants but does not disclose that information to anyone and ensures no identifiers exist anywhere in the research report itself for readers to *figure out* which participants provided which pieces of data

Confirmatory Factor Analysis – a multivariate statistical technique utilized to determine if the constructs or factors are consistent with a researcher's understanding of a variable

Confounding Constructs With Levels of Constructs – construct validity threat. Variables that do not account for all possible levels of a construct may confound the results by not allowing a researcher to generalize results to the entire construct.

Construct Confounding – construct validity threat. Variables are complex and confounding occurs when a researcher does not adequately explain all constructs.

Content Analysis – a computerized technique used by researchers to analyze text to classify variables

Contextual Factors – an attribute that is present in a specific area that has social characteristics

Controlled Observation – an observation that takes place in a simulated lab setting may provide the researcher with a greater degree of control of the environmental parameters

Convenience Sampling – a nonprobability sampling technique where participants are chosen on the basis of being in close proximity to the researcher

Correlational Design – a nonexperiemental design that examines relationships between variables that are not manipulated

Counterbalancing – a process utilized to counter order effects of a within subjects design where conditions to which participants are assigned are systematically varied

Criterion Contamination – the part of the criterion that measures a different predictor

Criterion Deficiency – the part of a predictor that is not measured by the criterion

Criterion Relevance – the part of the predictor that is measured by the criterion

Data Integrity – a process where a researcher ensures the validity or accuracy of the data

Debriefing – takes place after a research study where the researcher explains the study's purpose and procedures in detail to the participants

Deception – a technique used in research studies where the participant is misled about the purpose or procedure

Deduction – using logical reasoning or current knowledge as a way of learning

Degrees of Freedom – the number of values in a statistical test that are free to vary

Descriptive Statistics – Statistical analyses used to provide a summary of the data

Discrimination – when an individual is treated differently on the basis of their membership to a specific group

Discussion – the last section when writing a research study that includes a nonstatistical discussion of the results, limitations, and suggestions for future research

Double-Barreled Question – a question in survey research that includes two questions or is comprised of two topics in one question

Effect Size – a value that describes the strength of the relationship between variables

Element – may also be referred to as a case and is an individual participant/object in a research study

Ethics – examines how individuals act; the individual, group, and societal judgments about these actions (good or bad, right or wrong); and rules for categorizing these actions

Ethnography – anthropological study of cultural norms and beliefs, traditions, trends, and lifestyle of people in their actual living situations and settings rather than hypothetical situations or artificial lab-based settings

Evidence-Based Practice – a systematic approach for synthesizing and generalizing relevant data findings from research studies to be incorporated into one composite body of evidence that provides not only support for the causal impact of a treatment on an outcome, but also support for the application of the evidence to meet a specific intervention need

Experiment – a specific research design consisting of manipulating an independent variable and measuring a dependent variable

Experimental Design – utilizes random assignment and purposely introduces a manipulation to observe an effect

Experimenter Expectancies – construct validity threat. Expectancies from the researcher may influence the responses of the participants.

Exploratory Factor Analysis – a multivariate statistical technique utilized to examine underlying structure of a data set

Extraneous Variance in Experimental Setting – statistical conclusion validity threat. When conducting studies, the possibility exists that there is some variability within the experimental design. This variability may make it more challenging to be able to detect a statistical significant relationship.

Fabrication – the creation of data that were not collected through the actual research study

Falsification – the distortion of data that were collected in a research study in order to appear a certain way

Family Educational Rights and Privacy Act (FERPA) – federal law that protects the privacy of student education records

Field Notes – used in observational research to develop a comprehensive picture of a specific area or phenomenon of interest through interpretation of data collected

Fishing and Error Rate – statistical conclusion validity threat. Every study should be conducted with a specific purpose. Additional unplanned analyses that are conducted may result in an inflation of statistical significance.

Forced Choice Question – a question in survey research that provides respondents with a short list of items from which to select the most appropriate response to that item

Generalizability Theory – a measurement error theory extending the principles of classical test theory with the exception of not assuming a raw score is combined of a true and random error component, but rather the distinction is between the reliability and validity of a measure

Generalize or Generalization – the process whereby the results of the current research study can be extended to the population

Health Insurance Portability and Accountability Act (HIPAA) – a law signed into effect in 1996 that ensures compliance to maintain patient and client information privacy

Heterogeneity of Units – statistical conclusion validity threat. Most parametric statistics require that the sample is normally distributed, which means that the participants in the sample are homogenous. When a sample is heterogeneous, the possibility exists that this increased variability may impact the ability to detect a significant relationship.

History – internal validity threat. An event that may occur during the beginning, middle, or end of the experiment could have produced the effect in the absence of a treatment.

Hypothesis – a scientific prediction that is suspected to occur in a study based on previous research findings

Hypothesis, Alternative – opposite of null hypothesis. A statement that a study is trying to prove. States that there is a relationship or effect within the population.

Hypothesis, Causal – a statement driven by theory, data, or direction that specifies a cause and effect relationship between variables

Hypothesis, Data-Driven – a statement using inductive reasoning to predict a phenomenon on the basis of previous results

Hypothesis, Descriptive – a statement driven by theory, data, or direction that specifies a relationship between variables

Hypothesis, Directional – also known as one-tailed hypotheses. A statement of the relationship between variables focused on implying the direction of the relationship.

Hypothesis, Nondirectional – also known as two-tailed hypotheses. A statement of the relationship between variables where the direction of the relationship is not known.

Hypothesis, Null – opposite of alternative hypothesis. A statement that a study is trying to disprove. States that there is no relationship or effect within the population.

Hypothesis, Theory-Driven – a statement using deductive reasoning to predict a phenomenon on the basis of theory

Inaccurate Effect Size Estimation – statistical conclusion validity threat. Some statistical procedures may inherently over or under estimate the size of the effect within the study.

Inadequate Explication of Constructs – construct validity threat. Researcher does not adequately explain the construct that may lead to incorrect conclusions about the variable and the construct it is meant to measure.

Induction – using common sense as a way of learning

Inferential Statistics – statistical analyses used to draw conclusions beyond the data by testing hypotheses or research questions

Informed Consent – provide potential research subjects with adequate information regarding a study, including what to expect and its risks and benefits, in order to make an informed decision regarding whether or not to participate

Institutional Review Board – examines a study's procedural elements, such as subject selection and assignment to conditions, informed consent, and methodology, and may review the scientific rigor, quality, and value of potential benefits of the research before allowing researchers to use funds, time, and other resources to proceed

Instrumentation – internal validity threat. An instrument used to measure how a variable may change over the course of time even in the absence of the treatment.

Interval Scale – a quantitative scale of measurement that has equal numeric intervals between values that do not have a true 0

Interview – a technique used to gather information from a face-to-face interaction with a participant

Introduction – designed to provide the reader with the information necessary to fully understand the existing body of research in a particular topic area and the rationale for the present study before moving into the Method section

Jargon – terminology that is specific to a population, industry, organization, or group and is not well known or understood by anyone outside that entity

Levels of Evidence – relevant research findings are identified as pieces of evidence and each is weighted and categorized into one of seven categories

Likert Scale – developed by Rensis Likert in 1932, it is an interval scale with anchors that are numbered or coded and each anchor represents a degree of attitude that ranges from extremely favorable on one end to extremely unfavorable on the other end of the scale

Low Statistical Power – statistical conclusion validity threat. The study does not have an adequate power to be able to detect a cause and effect relationship.

Manuscript – an entire research report that includes all components necessary to publish a research article or submit to a conference

Maturation – internal validity threat. Natural changes over the course of time occur regardless of the presence of a treatment.

Mean – a measure of central tendency that measures the average value in a given distribution

Median – a measure of central tendency that measures the middle value in a given distribution

Meta-Analysis – a nonexperimental research technique utilizing statistics to compare and contrast various articles on a particular topic

Method – a detailed section of a research paper that includes all the information necessary to re-create a research study that consists of participants, variables, and procedure

Mode – a measure of central tendency that measures the value that appears the most in a distribution

Mono-Method Bias – construct validity threat. Researchers using one method to measure the dependent variable.

Mono-Operation Bias – construct validity threat. One operationalization of the independent variable may underrepresent the construct of interest and measure irrelevant constructs.

Multidisciplinary – an approach in research that involves a variety of diverse disciplines

Multimodal – a measure of central tendency where more than two values in a distribution appear the same number of times in a distribution

Multitrait-Multimethod Analysis – a technique used to establish construct validity by examining correlations of two or more traits by two or more methods

Naturalistic Observation – a research study that occurs in the context of their natural setting; the *picture* a researcher gets through the observation

Nominal Scale – a qualitative scale of measurement used to provide a categorical response to a variable

Nonexperimental Design – utilizes primary analysis, secondary analysis, or meta-analysis to describe data, examine relationships or covariation between variables, and compare groups

Nonparametric Statistics – statistical analyses where the data distribution is not a normal distribution

Nonprobability Sampling – a category of sampling techniques where a researcher cannot determine the probability of any one member of the population being included in the sample

Normal Distribution – also referred to as a bell shaped curve. A symmetrical probability distribution.

Novelty and Disruption Effects – construct validity threat. Participants may respond well to a novel idea or poorly to one that interferes with their routine.

Nuremberg Code – recommended by an international court in the late 1940s and adopted by the United Nations General Assembly and is comprised of 10 principles for researchers

Obtrusive Observation – individuals in the setting are aware of the researcher's presence, whether or not the researcher is actually in the setting or observing from outside the setting

Open-Ended Question – a question in survey research in which the respondent may answer freely and provide a response in any length or detail

Order Effects – occurs when a participant is exposed to more than one condition and the results from one condition can influence the next condition

Ordinal Scale – a qualitative scale of measurement used to rank order categorical responses

Outcomes – part of the UTOS acronym; the element in the study pertaining to the effects demonstrated through the data that were collected

Outlier – an extremely high or low value that is in a dataset

Parametric Statistics – statistical analyses where the data distribution is considered a normal distribution

Parsimonious – a term used to state that "simpler is better," which indicates that categories should consist of either too many or too few

Participant Burnout/Overuse – a situation where the same sample is used in multiple research studies over time

Passive Voice – a sentence where the object of the action is made the subject

Plagiarism – the act of copying the writing of another author verbatim and submitting it as your own original work

Population – an entire group of individuals that comprise all characteristics of a phenomenon

Power – a statistical term in research that determines the extent to which a statistically significant effect can be found

Primary Analysis – term used to describe the analysis of data that was collected by the actual researcher

Privacy – similar to anonymity where an individual decides to withhold information from the public

Probability Sampling – a category of sampling techniques where a researcher can determine the probability of any one member of the population being included in the sample

Purposive Sampling – a nonprobability technique where a researcher specifically selects the cases judged to be most typical of the population and should be included in the sample

Qualitative Data – a type of data that offers a richness and depth of detail in the information that are not characteristics of quantitative data

Quasi-Experimental Design – utilizes other design features to account for lack of random assignment to study the impact of a cause and effect relationship

Questionnaire – also known as a survey, it is a document that contains a list of questions that a participant is asked to provide responses to

Quota Sampling – a nonprobability technique where a population is divided into subgroups, similar to stratified sampling, but the researcher gathers individuals for the sample's subgroups based on a defined number of participants required to select for a research study

Random Assignment – a technique in experimental designs used after a sample is selected to increase internal validity by assigning participants to conditions by chance

Random Error – a type of error in measurement where any factor or variable randomly has an impact of the measured variable

Random Selection – a sampling technique used in research to select participants from a population based on chance before a sample is determined

Range – a measure of variability of a data set calculated by the difference between the highest and lowest value

Ratio Scale – a quantitative scale of measurement that has equal numeric intervals between values that does have a true 0

Reactive Self-Report Changes – construct validity threat. Participants required to respond to measures may be influenced when researchers ask participants to self-report measures.

Reactivity – a participant response when they believe or know they are being observed

Reactivity to the Experimental Situation – construct validity threat. Participants may engage in a behavior to anticipate what the researcher is trying to study.

Recall – a technique where a participant is asked to remember an event or detail that occurred in the past

References – the last part of a research paper that provides a reader with the full citation of every source used in the current research study

Regression to the Mean – internal validity threat. Participants selected to participate based on extreme high (low) scores on a measure will likely decrease (increase) to the average score on the measure.

Reliability – the extent to which a measure in a study is consistent, dependable, precise, or stable

Reliability, Coefficient Alpha – also referred to as internal consistency reliability. Measures the consistency of the same items on a test that measure the same construct.

Reliability, Equivalent Forms – also referred to as parallel forms reliability. The extent to which two tests are developed to measure the same construct of interest.

Reliability, Internal Consistency – also referred to as internal consistency. Measures the consistency of the same items on a test that measure the same construct.

Reliability, Interrater – the extent to which measurement ratings are consistent across different raters

Reliability, Intrarater – the extent to which measurement ratings are consistent among the same raters

Reliability, Parallel Forms – also referred to as equivalent forms reliability. The extent to which two tests are developed to measure the same construct of interest.

Reliability, Split Half – measures the internal consistency of items on a test when different items assessing the same construct throughout the test are compared

Reliability, Test-Retest – the consistency to which the test scores are similar when participants are given the same test more than once

Repeated Measures Design – also known as a within subjects design. A research design component where participants are exposed to all conditions of a study.

Research Question – a question developed based on a problem where limited knowledge or research exists

Resentful Demoralization – construct validity threat. Participants not receiving the treatment may become resentful and change their responses to the outcome measures.

Response Rate – percentage of individuals selected for a sample that actually completes a questionnaire or interview

Response Scale – used in forced choice questions where respondents are provided with options that fall along a continuum

Restriction of Range – statistical conclusion validity threat. Generating a sample with a small range of participants may weaken the results.

Results – the section of a research paper where the statistical analysis of the hypothesis or research question is written

Running Head – located in the upper left hand of a research paper that contains an abbreviated version of the full title that is written in all uppercase letters

Sample – a subset of a population that a researcher wants to select participants from to participate in a research study

Sampling Error – an error that may occur when a researcher has not randomly selected an adequate number of representative individuals from the population and the sample does not represent the population

Science-Practice Gap – a gap that exists between scientists and practitioners

Secondary Analysis – examination of data collected by someone other than the researcher

Selection – internal validity threat. Participants differ from each other at the start of the experiment.

Settings – part of the UTOS acronym; the element in the study pertaining to the specific environment or context in which the findings from the study will be applied

Snowball Sampling – a nonprobability sampling technique where a researcher requests referrals of additional individuals to contact from existing respondents because the desired respondents are difficult to locate within the population based on scarcity or lack of identifying information

Stakeholder – an individual within an organization that is seen as a key player to ensuring an intervention is carried out

Standard Deviation – a measure of variability or spread of a data set around the mean that is measured in the same units as the calculated measure. It is calculated by the square root of the variance.

Stratified Sampling – a probability sampling technique where the population is divided into subgroups, or strata, and a researcher selects members from each subgroup to be included in the sample

Structural Equation Modeling (SEM) – an advanced statistical technique involving hierarchical linear regression modeling used to derive data models for forecasting trends and needs

Survey – also known as a questionnaire, it is a document that contains a list of questions that a participant is asked to provide responses to

Systematic Error – a type of error in measurement where any factor or variable that is not random that has an impact of the measured variable

Testing – internal validity threat. Test scores on a posttest may be influenced by pretest scores.

Thurstone Scale – developed by L. L. Thurstone in 1929, this type of scale is used to assess attitudes and is constructed using a method of equal-appearing intervals

Title VII – part of the Civil Rights Act of 1964 that prohibits discrimination on any employment decisions including hiring, promotion, compensation, training and development opportunities, and termination based on race, color, religion, sex, and national origin

Trade-Off – a situation in research where the researcher is unable to deal with all validity threats in a research design

Treatment Diffusion – construct validity threat. Participants not within the treatment group may receive parts of the treatment.

Treatments – part of the UTOS acronym; the element in the study pertaining to the independent variable(s) and their respective levels selected to manipulate. They must be relevant to the research question and the field settings in which findings will be applied.

Treatment Sensitive Factorial Structure – construct validity threat. Change in structure of the measure may be a result of the treatment.

Triangulation – collecting data in different ways using different research designs or methodologies to examine a research question or hypothesis

True Score Theory – also referred to as Classical Test Theory. A measurement error theory derived from the thought that a raw score consists of a true and random component.

Type I Error – related to alpha; an error in decision making where it is stated that the cause and effect covaries when there is no relationship

Type II Error – related to beta; an error in decision making where it is stated that the cause and effect does not covary when there is a relationship

Unexplained Variance – variability within the criterion variable that the predictor variables do not account for

Uniquely Explained Variance – variability within the criterion variable that the predictor variables do account for

Units – part of the UTOS acronym; the element in the study pertaining to the participants that are either assigned to the different conditions or levels of the independent variable(s) or are being examined in the presence of a specified variable or context

Unobtrusive Observation – individuals in the setting are not aware of the researcher's presence or that they are being observed

Unreliability of Measures – statistical conclusion validity threat. Every measure taken has some degree of measurement error. When measures are unreliable, then the validity of the results is decreased.

Unreliability of Treatment Implementation – statistical conclusion validity threat. Any variation in the way a study is conducted from participant to participant may impact the reliability of the treatment that is implemented.

Utility – the usefulness of a research design or research results

Validity – the accuracy of the results of a research study

Validity, Concurrent – a type of criterion-related validity. Extent to which data is collected from the same sample at one point in time to predict a criterion.

Validity, Construct – generalizability that the variables used in a study represent the variables they intend to measure

Validity, Content – related to construct validity and often confused with face validity. It is the extent to which the items on a test or measure represent the content of the material that is being measured.

Validity, Convergent – a type of criterion-related validity. Extent to which multiple items measuring theoretically similar constructs are expected to be related to each other.

Validity, Criterion-Related – extent that the current test or measure is related to some specified criteria

Validity, Discriminant – a type of criterion-related validity. Extent to which multiple items measuring theoretically different constructs are expected to not be related to each other.

Validity, External – generalizability of the cause and effect relationship across changes in the participants, settings, treatments, or the outcomes

Validity, Face – related to construct validity and often confused with content validity. It answers the question of does this test or measure appear to look like it is accurate.

Validity, Internal – covariation of the cause and effect relationship

Validity, Predictive – a type of criterion-related validity. Extent to which data is collected from the one sample at one point in time and used to predict a criterion for a different sample at another point in time.

Validity, Statistical Conclusion – covariation of the cause and effect relationship through the appropriateness of the statistical procedure used for the analysis

Variable – construct, measure, or object that can be studied

Variable, Confounding – similar to extraneous variable. A variable that may influence the relationship between the independent and dependent variable.

Variable, Continuous – a variable that is generally quantitative in nature. These variables often utilize an interval or ratio scale of measurement.

Variable, Control – a variable in research that is designed to remain constant

Variable, Covariate – a variable that is known to interact with the independent and dependent variable and is measured in the study

Variable, Criterion – similar to dependent variable. A variable in regression that is measured.

Variable, Dependent – a variable in research that is measured

Variable, Dichotomous – a variable that has two levels often denoted as a 1 and 0

Variable, Extraneous – similar to confounding variable. A variable that may influence the relationship between the independent and dependent variable.

Variable, Independent – a variable in research that is manipulated or changed

Variable, Predictor – similar to an independent variable. A variable in regression that is manipulated by the researcher.

Variance – a measure of variability or spread of a data set around the mean that is not in the same units as the calculated measure

Variance Partitioning Analysis – a technique based on generalizability to examine different sources of variance

Variation in Outcomes – external validity threat. An effect found in an experiment may not hold if other outcome observations are used.

Variation in Participants – external validity threat. A cause and effect relationship with the participants in the experiment may not hold when different participants are included in the experiment.

Variation in Settings – external validity threat. A cause and effect relationship in one setting may not hold in another setting.

Variation in Treatments – external validity threat. A cause and effect relationship with one treatment may not hold if the treatment is varied or combined with other components of different treatment.

Violated Assumptions of Tests – statistical conclusion validity threat. Every statistical analysis procedure has specific assumptions associated with each test that much be met in order to conduct the analysis. Researchers that violate these assumptions may lead to an inaccurate result.

Weighting – a technique whereby research results are categorized to give a value that is more meaningful to differentiate levels of evidence

Within Subjects – a research design component where participants are exposed to all conditions in a study

Z Score – a statistical term to indicate a normal or standardized score based on a normal distribution

References

Aamodt, M. G. (2007). *Industrial/organizational psychology an applied approach* (5th ed.). Belmont, CA: Thomson Wadsworth.

Alnuaimi, O. A., Robert, L. P., Jr., & Maruping, L. M. (2010). Team size, dispersion, and social loafing in technology-supported teams: A perspective on the theory of moral disengagement. *Journal of Management Information Systems, 27*(1), 203–230.

American Psychological Association. (2010). *Publication manual of the American Psychological Association* (6th ed.). Washington, DC: Author.

Anderson, C. A., Lindsay, J. J., & Bushman, B. J. (1999). Research in the psychological laboratory: Truth or triviality? *Current Directions in Psychological Science, 8*(1), 3–9.

Arthur, W., Day, E. A., & Woehr, D. J. (2008). Mend it, don't end it: An alternate view of assessment center construct-related validity evidence. *Industrial and Organizational Psychology, 1,* 105–111.

Arthur, W., Woehr, D. J., & Maldegen, R. (2000). Convergent and discriminant validity of assessment center dimensions: A conceptual and empirical re-examination of the assessment center construct-related validity paradox. *Journal of Management, 26*(4), 813–835.

Aryee, S., Walumbwa, F. O., Seidu, E. Y. M., & Otaye, L. E. (2012). Impact of high-performance work systems on individual- and branch-level performance: Test of a multilevel model of intermediate linkages. *Journal of Applied Psychology, 97*(2), 287–300.

Babbie. (2004). *The practice of social research* (10th ed.). Belmont, CA: Wadsworth/Thomson Learning Inc.

Banki, S., & Latham, G. P. (2010). The criterion-related validities and perceived fairness of the situational interview and the situational judgment test in an Iranian organization. *Applied Psychology: An International Review, 59*(1), 124–142.

Barrick, M. R., Mount, M. K., & Judge, T. A. (2001). Personality and performance at the beginning of the new millennium: What do we know and where do we go next? *International Journal of Selection and Assessment, 9,* 1–2, 9–30.

Bauer, T. N., Truxillo, D. M., Sanchez, R. J., Craig, J. M., Ferrara, P., & Campion, M. A. (2001). Applicant reactions to selection: Development of the selection procedural justice scale (SPJS). *Personnel Psychology, 54,* 387–419.

Belmont Report. (1979). *The Belmont Report: Ethical principles and guidelines for the protection of human subjects of research.* Retrieved January 1, 2013, from hhs.gov/ohrp/humansubjects/guidance/belmont.html

Berry, C. M., Sackett, P. R., & Landers, R. N. (2007). Revisiting interview-cognitive ability relationships: Attending to specific range restriction mechanisms in meta-analysis. *Personnel Psychology, 60,* 837–874.

Berry, L. M. (2002). *Employee selection.* Belmont, CA: Wadsworth Publishing.

Bezrukova, K., Jehn, K. A., & Spell, C. S. (2012). Reviewing diversity training: Where we have been and where we should go. *Academy of Management Learning & Education, 11*(2), 207–227.

Bing, M. N., Steward, S. M., & Davison, H. K. (2009). An investigation of calculator use on employment tests of mathematical ability: Effects on reliability, validity, test scores, and speed of completion. *Educational and Psychological Measurement, 69*(2), 322–350.

Borman, W. C. (1978). Exploring the upper limits of reliability and validity in job performance ratings. *Journal of Applied Psychology, 63*, 135–144.

Borman, W. C., & Hallam, G. L. (1991, February). Observation accuracy for assessors of work-sample performance: Consistency across task and individual-differences correlates. *Journal of Applied Psychology, 76*(1), 11–18.

Bowler, M. C., & Woehr, D. J. (2009). Assessment center construct-rated validity: Stepping beyond the MTMM matrix. *Journal of Vocational Behavior, 75*, 173–182.

Brown, K. G., Le, H., & Schmidt, F. L. (2006). Specific aptitude theory revisited: Is there incremental validity for training performance. *International Journal of Selection and Assessment, 14*(2), 87–100.

Brutus, S., & Duniewicz, K. (2012). The many heels of Achilles: An analysis of self-reported limitations in leadership research. *The Leadership Quarterly, 23*, 202–212.

Brutus, S., Gill, H., & Duniewicz, K. (2010). State of science in industrial and organizational psychology: A review of self-reported limitations. *Personnel Psychology, 63*, 907–936.

Chan, D., Schmitt, N., DeShon, R. P., Clause, C. S., & Delbridge, K. (1997). Reactions to cognitive ability tests: The relationships between race, test performance, face validity perceptions, and test-taking motivation. *Journal of Applied Psychology, 82*(2), 300–310.

Chandon, P., Smith, R. J., Morwitz, V. G., Spangenberg, E. R., & Sprott, D. E. (2011). When does the past repeat itself? The interplay of behavior prediction and personal norms. *Journal of Consumer Research, 38*, 420–430.

Cheng, Y., Huang, H. Y., Li, P. R., & Hsu, J. H. (2011). Employment insecurity, workplace justice and employees' burnout in Taiwanese employees: A validation study. *International Journal of Behavioral Medicine, 18*(4), 391–401.

Cohen, J. (1988). *Statistical power analysis for the behavioral sciences* (2nd ed.). Mahwah, NJ: Erlbaum.

Cojuharenco, I., Patient, D., & Bashshur, M. R. (2011). Seeing the "forest" or the "trees" of organizational justice: Effects of temporal perspective on employee concerns about unfair treatment at work. *Organizational Behavior and Human Decision Processes, 116*, 17–31.

Connelly, B. S., & Ones, D. S. (2010). Another perspective on personality: Meta-analytic integration of observers' **accuracy** and predictive validity. *Psychological Bulletin, 136*(6), 1092–1122.

Conway, J. M., & Huffcutt, A. I. (1997). Psychometric properties of multi-source performance ratings: A meta-analysis of subordinate, supervisor, peer, and self-ratings. *Human Performance, 10*, 331–360.

Cook, T. D., & Campbell, D. T. (1979). *Quasi-experimentation: Design and analysis for field settings*. Chicago, IL: Rand McNally.

Corrigan, P. W., & Salzer, M. S. (2003). The conflict between random assignment and treatment preference: Implications for internal validity. *Evaluation and Program Planning, 26*(2), 109–121.

Cozby, P. C. (2001). *Methods in behavioral research* (7th ed.). Mountain View, CA: Mayfield Publishing Company.

Cronbach, L. J. (1951). Coefficient alpha and the internal structure of tests. *Psychometrika, 16*(3), 297–334.

Cronbach, L. J. (1955). Processes affecting scores on understanding of others and assumed "similarity." *Psychological Bulletin, 52*, 177–193.

Cronbach, L. J. (1982). *Designing evaluations of educational and social programs*. San Francisco, CA: Jossey-Bass.

Cronbach, L. J., Gleser, G. C., Nanda, H., & Rajaratnam, N. (1972). *The dependability of behavioral measurements. Theory of generalizability for scores and profiles*. New York, NY: Wiley.

Damitz, M., Manzey, D., Kleinmann, M., & Severin, K. (2003). Assessment center for pilot selection: Construct and criterion validity and the impact of assessor type. *Applied Psychology: An International Review, 52*(2), 193–212.

De Lange, A. H., De Witte, H., & Notelaers, G. (2008). Should I say or should I go? Examining longitudinal relations among job resources and work engagement for stayers versus movers. *Work & Stress, 22*(3), 201–223.

Deloise, F. A., & Kolb, J. A. (2008). The effects of an ethics training program on attitude, knowledge, and transfer of training of office professionals: A treatment- and control-group design. *Human Resource Development Quarterly, 19*(1), 35–53.

Denton, F. T. (1985). Data mining as an industry. *The Review of Economics and Statistics, 67*(1), 124–127.

Derous, E., Ryan, A. M., & Nguyen, H. D. (2012). Multiple categorization in resume screening: Examining the effects of hiring discrimination against Arab applicants in field and lab settings. *Journal of Organizational Behavior, 33*, 544–570.

DeTienne, K. B., Agle, B. R., Phillips, J. C., & Ingerson, M. C. (2012). The impact of moral stress compared to other stressors on employee fatigue, job satisfaction, and turnover: An empirical investigation. *Journal of Business Ethics, 110*(3), 377–391.

Dierdorff, E. C., & Wilson, M. A. (2003). A meta-analysis of job analysis reliability. *Journal of Applied Psychology, 88*(4), 635–646.

Dillman, D. A. (2007). *Mail and internet surveys The Tailored Design Method* (2nd ed.). Hoboken, NJ: Wiley.

Dirani, K. M., & Kuchinke, K. P. (2011). Job satisfaction and organizational commitment: Validating the Arabic satisfaction and commitment questionnaire (ASCQ), testing the correlations, and investigating the effects of demographic variables in the Lebanese banking sector. *The International Journal of Human Resource Management, 22*(5), 1180–1202.

Duriau, V. J., Reger, R. K., & Pfarrer, M. D. (2007). A content analysis of the content analysis literature in organizational studies: Research themes, data sources, and methodological refinements. *Organizational Research Methods, 10*, 5–34.

Edwards, J. E., Scott, J. C., & Raju, N. S. (2003). *The human resources program-evaluation handbook.* Thousand Oaks, CA: Sage.

Edwards, J. R., & Bagozzi, R. P. (2000). On the nature and direction of relationships between constructs and measures. *Psychological Methods, 5*(2), 155–174.

Egan, T. B., & Song, Z. (2008). Are facilitated mentoring programs beneficial? A randomized experimental field study. *Journal of Vocational Behavior, 72*, 351–362.

Erceg-Hurn, D. M., & Mirosevich, V. M. (2008). Modern robust statistical methods: An easy way to maximize the accuracy and power of your research. *American Psychologist, 63*(7), 591–601.

Field, A. (2009). *Discovering statistics using SPSS* (3rd ed.). Thousand Oaks, CA: Sage.

Finch, W. H., & Davenport, T. (2009). Performance of monte carlo permutation and approximate tests for multivariate means comparisons with small sample sizes when parametric assumptions are violated. *European Journal of Research Methods for the Behavioral and Social Sciences, 5*(2), 60–70.

Fredrickson, B. L. (2001). The role of positive emotions in positive psychology: The Broaden-and-Built theory of positive emotions. *American Psychologist, 56*, 218–226.

Frisque, D. A., & Kolb, J. A. (2008). The effects of an ethics training program on attitude, knowledge, and transfer of training of office professionals: A treatment- and control-group design. *Human Resource Development Quarterly, 19*(1), 35–53.

Gatewood, R. D., & Field, H. S. (2001). *Human resource selection* (5th ed.). Mason, OH: South-Western.

Glass, G. (1976). Primary, secondary, and meta-analysis of research. *Educational Research, 5*, 3–8.

Gotsi, M., Andriopoulos, C., Lewis, M. W., & Ingram, A. E. (2010). Managing creative: Paradoxical approaches to identity regulation. *Human Relations, 63*, 781–805.

Grant, A. M. (2008). The significance of task significance: Job performance effects, relational mechanisms, and boundary conditions. *Journal of Applied Psychology, 93*(1), 108–124.

Hahn, V. C., Binnewies, C., Sonnentag, S., & Mojza, E. J. (2011). Learning how to recover from job stress: Effects of a recovery training program on recovery, recovery-related self-efficacy, and well-being. *Journal of Occupational Health Psychology, 16*(2), 202–216.

Hardre, P. L., & Reeve, J. (2009). Training corporate managers to adopt a more autonomy-supportive motivating style toward employees: An intervention study. *International Journal of Training and Development, 13*(3), 165–184.

Harris, M. M., & Heft, L. L. (1993). Preemployment urinalysis drug testing: A critical review of psychometric and legal issues and effects on applicants. *Human Resource Management Review, 3*(4), 271–291.

Heller, J. (1972, July 26). Syphilis victims in U.S. study without therapy for 40 years. *The New York Times,* pp. 1, 8.

Helzer, E. G., & Dunning, D. (2012). Why and when peer prediction is superior to self-prediction: The weight given to future aspiration versus past achievement. *Journal of Personality and Social Psychology, 103*(1), 38–53.

Hogan, T. P., Benjamin, A., & Brezinski, K. L. (2000). Reliability methods: A note on the frequency of use of various types. *Educational and Psychological Measurement, 60*(4), 523–531.

Hulsheger, U. R., Alberts, H. J. E. M, Feinholdt, A., & Lang, J. W. B. (2012). Benefits of mindfulness at work: The role of mindfulness in emotion regulation, emotional exhaustion, and job satisfaction. *Journal of Applied Psychology, 98*(2) 310–325 .

Hunter, J. E., Schmidt, F. L., & Le, H. (2006). Implications of direct and indirect range restriction for meta-analysis methods and finding, *Journal of Applied Psychology, 91*(3), 594–612.

Jeanneret, P. R., & Strong, M. H. (2003). Linking O*Net job analysis information to job requirement predictors: An O*Net application. *Personnel Psychology, 56,* 465–492.

Jiang, K., Liu, D., McKay, P. F., Lee, T. W., & Mitchell, T. R. (2012). When and how is job embeddedness predictive of turnover? A meta-analytic investigation. *Journal of Applied Psychology, 97*(5), 1077–1096.

Johnson, R. E., & Chang, C. H. (2008). Relationships between organizational commitment and its antecedents: Employee self-concept matters. *Journal of Applied Social Psychology, 38*(2), 513–541.

Kamen, J. M., & Toman, R. J. (1971, May). Psychophysics of prices: A reaffirmation. *Journal of Marketing Research,* 252–257.

Kravitz, D. A., & Brock, P. (1997). Evaluations of drug-testing programs. *Employee Responsibilities and Rights Journal, 10*(1), 65–86.

Kunin, T. (1955). The construction of a new type of attitude measure. *Personnel Psychology, 8,* 70–71.

Lance, C. E. (2008). Why assessment centers do not work the way they are supposed to. *Industrial and Organizational Psychology, 1,* 84–97.

Lance, C. E., Woehr, D. J., & Meade, A. W. (2007). Case study: A monte carlo investigation of assessment center construct validity models. *Organizational Research Methods, 10,* 430–448.

Latham, G. P., Ford, R. C., & Tzabbar, D. (2012). Enhancing employee and organizational performance through coaching based on mystery shopper feedback: A quasi-experimental study. *Human Resource Management, 51*(2), 213–230.

Law, M. (Ed.). (2002). *Evidence-based rehabilitation.* Thorofare, NJ: Slack.

Le Maistre, C., & Pare, A. (2004). Learning in two communities: The challenge for universities and workplaces. *Journal of Workplace Learning, 16*(1), 44–52.

Lievens, F., & Sanchez, J. I. (2007). Can training improve the quality of inferences made by raters in competency modeling? A quasi-experiment. *Journal of Applied Psychology, 92*(3), 812–819.

Likert, R. A. (1932). A technique for the measurement of attitudes. *Archives of Psychology, 140,* 1–55.

Lofland, J., & Lofland, L. (1995). *Analyzing social settings: A guide to qualitative observation and analysis* (3rd ed.). Belmont, CA: Wadsworth

London, M., Mone, E. M., & Scott, J. C. (Winter, 2004). Performance management and assessment: Methods for improved rater accuracy and employee goal setting. *Human Resource Management, 43*(4), 319–336.

Luthans, F., Rhee, S., Luthans, B. C., & Avey, J. B. (2008). Impact of behavioral performance management in a Korean application. *Leadership & Organization Development Journal, 29*(5), 427–443.

Mael, F. A. (1994). If past behavior really predicts future, so should biodata's. In M. G. Rumsey, C. B. Walker, & J. Harris (Eds.), *Personnel selection and classification* (pp. 273–291). Hillsdale, NJ: Erlbaum.

Martell, R. F., & Borg, M. R. (1993). A comparison of the behavioral rating accuracy of groups and individuals. *Journal of Applied Psychology, 78*(1), 43–50.

Masick, K. D., Shapiro, T., & O'Neal, J. C. (2010). *Satisfaction as a mediator between explanations and organizational outcomes.* Poster presented at the Annual Conference of the American Psychological Association, August 15, 2010, San Diego, CA.

May, D. R., Reed, K., Schwoerer, C. E., & Potter, P. (2004). Ergonomic office design and aging: A quasi-experimental field study of employee reactions to an ergonomics intervention program. *Journal of Occupational Health Psychology, 9*(2), 123–135.

Mayo, E. (1949). *Hawthorne and the Western Electric Company: The social problems of an industrial civilization.* London, UK: Routledge.

McAuliff, B. D., Kovera, M. B., & Nunez, G. (2009). Can jurors recognize missing control groups, confounds, and experimenter bias in psychological science? *Law and Human Behavior, 33*(3), 247–257.

McBride, D. M. (2010). *The process of research in psychology.* Thousand Oaks, CA: Sage.

McElroy, J. C., & Crant, J. M. (2008). Handicapping: The effects of its source and frequency. *Journal of Applied Psychology, 93*(4), 893–900.

McFarland, J. (2001, September). Margaret Mead meets consumer fieldwork. *Harvard Management Update.* Retrieved from http://hbswk.hbs.edu/archive/2514.html

Melnyk, B., & Fineout-Overholt, E. (2005). *Evidence-based practice in nursing and healthcare: A guide to best practice.* Philadelphia, PA: Lippincott, Williams & Wilkins.

Meyers, L. S., Gamst, G., & Guarino, A. J. (2006). *Applied multivariate research design and interpretation.* Thousand Oaks, CA: Sage.

Milgram, S. (1963). Behavioral study of obedience. *Journal of Abnormal Social Psychology, 67,* 371–78.

Mitchell, G. (2012). Revisiting truth or triviality: The external validity of research in the psychological laboratory. *Perspectives on Psychological Science, 7*(2), 109–117.

Mone, M. A., Mueller, G. C., & Mauland, W. (1996).The perceptions and usage of statistical power in applied psychology and management research. *Personnel Psychology, 49,* 103–120.

Morgeson, F. P., Campion, M. A., Dipboye, R. L., Holenbeck, J. R., Murphy, K. R., & Schmitt, N. (2007). Reconsidering the use of personality tests in personnel selection contexts. *Personnel Psychology, 60,* 683–729.

Morris, R. (1994). Computerized content analysis in management research: A demonstration of advantages & limitations. *Journal of Management 20*(4), 903–931.

Mugge, R., & Schoormans, J. P. L (2012). Product design and apparent usability. The influence of novelty in product appearance. *Applied Ergonomics, 43,* 1081–1088.

Murphy, K. R. (2009). Content validation is useful for many things, but validity isn't one of them. *Industrial and Organizational Psychology, 2,* 453–464.

Murphy, K. R., & Balzer, W. K. (1989). Rater errors and rating accuracy. *Journal of Applied Psychology, 74,* 619–624.

Murphy, K. R., Garcia, M., Kerkar, S., Martin, C., & Balzer, W. K. (1982). Relationship between observational accuracy and accuracy in evaluating performance. *Journal of Applied Psychology, 67,* 320–325.

Murray, H. A., & MacKinnon, D. W. (1946). Assessment of OSS personnel. *Journal of Consulting Psychology, 10,* 76–80.

National Commission for the Protection of Human Subjects of Biomedical and Behavioral Research. (1979). *The Belmont report: Ethical principles and guidelines for the protection of human subjects of research* (OPRR Report; FR Doc. No. 79–12065). Washington, DC: U.S. Government Printing Office.

Ng, T. W. H., & Feldman, D. C. (2012). A comparison of self-ratings and non-self-report measures of employee creativity. *Human Relations, 65*(8), 1021–1047.

Nunnally, J. C., & Bernstein, I. H. (1994). *Psychometric theory* (3rd ed.). New York, NY: McGraw-Hill.

Nuremberg Code. (1949). *Trials of war criminals before the Nuremberg Military Tribunals under Control Council Law No. 10* (Vol. 2). Washington, DC: U.S. Government Printing Office.

Oostrom, J. K., Bos-Broekema, L., Serlie, A. W., Born, M. P., & Van der Molen, H. K. (2012). A field study of pretest and posttest reactions to a paper-and-pencil and a computerized in-basket exercise. *Human Performance, 25,* 95–113.

Orne, M. T. (1962). On the social psychology of the psychological experiment: With particular reference to demand characteristics and their implications. *American Psychologist, 17*(11), 776–783.

Oswald, F. L., Saad, S., & Sackett, P. R. (2000). The homogeneity assumption in differential prediction analysis: Does it really matter? *Journal of Applied Psychology, 85*(4), 536–541.

Ouellette, J. A., & Wood, W. (1998). Habit and intention in everyday life: The multiple processes by which past behavior predicts future behavior. *Psychological Bulletin. 124* (1), 54–74.

Ozminkowski, R. J., Mark, T., Cangianelli, L., & Walsh, M. J. (2001). The cost of on-site versus off-site workplace urinalysis testing for illicit drug use. *Health Care Manager, 20*(1), 59–69.

Pawar, B. S. (2009). Some of the recent organizational behavior concepts as precursors to workplace spirituality. *Journal of Business Ethics, 88,* 245–261.

Peterson, S. J., & Luthans, F. (2006). The impact of financial and nonfinancial incentives on business-unit outcomes over time. *Journal of Applied Psychology, 91*(1), 156–165.

Pierce, H. R., & Maurer, T. J. (2009). Linking employee development activity, social exchange, and organizational citizenship behavior. *International Journal of Training and Development, 13*(3), 139–147.

Ployhart, R. E., Ziegert, J. C., & McFarland, L. A. (2003). Understanding racial differences on cognitive ability tests in selection contexts: An integration of stereotype threat and applicant reactions research. *Human Performance, 16*(3), 231–259.

Porath, C., Spreitzer, G., Gibson, C., & Garnett, F. G. (2012). Thriving at work: Toward its measurement, construct validation, and theoretical refinement. *Journal of Organizational Behavior, 33,* 250–275.

Randall, R., Nielsen, K., & Tvedt, S. D. (2009). The development of five scales to measure employee's appraisals of organizational-level stress management interventions. *Work & Stress, 23*(1), 1–23.

Roch, S. G. (2006). Discussion and consensus in rater groups: Implications for behavioral and rating accuracy. *Human Performance, 19*(2), 91–115.

Rogelberg, S. G. (2004). *Handbook of research methods in industrial and organizational psychology.* Malden, MA: Blackwell Publishing Ltd.

Rogelberg, S. G., & Brooks-Laber, M. E. (2004). Securing our collective future: Challenges facing those designing and doing research in industrial and organizational psychology. In S. G. Rogelberg (Ed.), *Handbook of research methods in industrial and organizational psychology.* London, UK: Blackwell.

Rogers, W. N., Schmitt, N., & Mullins, M. E. (2002). Correction for unreliability of multifactor measures: Comparison of alpha and parallel forms approaches. *Organizational Research Methods, 5*(2), 184–199.

Rosenthal, R. (1979). The "file drawer problem" and tolerance for null results. *Psychological Bulletin, 86*(3), 638–641.

Rosnow, R. L., & Rosenthal, R. (1997). *Beginning behavioral research: A conceptual primer.* New York, NY: Macmillan Publishing Company.

Rupp, D. E., Thornton, G. C., & Gibbons, A. M. (2008). The construct validity of assessment center method and usefulness of dimensions as focal constructs. *Industrial and Organizational Psychology, 1,* 116–210.

Sackett, D. L., Rosenberg, W. M., Gray, J. A., Haynes, R. B., & Richardson, W. S. (1996). Evidence-based medicine: What is it and what isn't it. *British Medical Journal, 312,* 71–72.

Salgado, J. F., Moscoso, S., & Lado, M. (2003). Test-retest reliability of ratings of job performance dimensions in managers. *International Journal of Selection and Assessment, 11*(1), 98–101.

Saunders, M. N. K. (2012). Web versus mail: The influence of survey distribution mode on employees' response. *Field Methods, 24*(1), 56–73.

Scandura, T. A., & Williams, E. A. (2000). Research methodology in management: Current practices, trends, and implications for future research. *Academy of Management Journal, 43*(6), 1248–1264.

Schippmann, J. S., Prien, E. P., & Katz, J. A. (1990). Reliability and validity of in-basket performance measures. *Personnel Psychology, 43,* 837–859.

Schmidt, F. L., & Hunter, J. E. (1996). Measurement error in psychological research: Lessons from 26 research scenarios. *Psychological Methods, 1*(2), 199–223.

Schmidt, F. L., Oh, I., & Le, H. (2006). Increasing the accuracy of corrections for range restriction: Implications for selection procedure validities and other research results. *Personnel Psychology, 59,* 281–305.

Schmidt, F. L., Shaffer, J. A., & Oh, I. (2008). Increased accuracy for range restriction corrections: Implications for the role of personality and general mental ability in job and training performance. *Personnel Psychology, 61,* 827–868.

Schriesheim, C. A., Wu, J. B., & Cooper, C. D. (2011). A two-study investigation of item wording effects on leader-follower convergence in descriptions of the leader-member exchange (LMX) relationship. *The Leadership Quarterly 22,* 881–892.

Schwab, D. P. (2005). *Research methods for organizational studies.* Mahwah, NJ: Erlbaum.

Sekerka, L. E. (2009). Organizational ethics education and training: A review of best practices and their application. *International Journal of Training and Development, 13*(2), 77–95.

Seva, R. R., Gosiaco, K. G. T., Santos, C. E. D., & Pangilinan, D. M. (2011). Product design enhancement using apparent usability and affective quality. *Applied Ergonomics, 42*(3), 511–517.

Shadish, W. R., Cook, T. D., & Campbell, D. T. (2002). *Experimental and quasi-experimental designs for generalized causal inference.* Boston, MA: Houghton Mifflin.

Short, J. C., Broberg, J. C., Cogliser, C. C., & Brigham, K. H. (2010). Construct validations using computer-aided text analysis (CATA): An illustration using entrepreneurial orientation. *Organizational Research Methods 13*(2), 320–347.

Silzer, R., & Jeanneret, R. (2011). Individual psychological assessment: A practice and science in search of common ground. *Industrial and Organizational Psychology, 4*(3), 270–298.

Sitzmann, T., & Ely, K. (2010). Sometimes you need a reminder: The effects of prompting self-regulation on regulatory processes, learning, and attrition. *Journal of Applied Psychology, 95*(1), 132–144.

Sitzmann, T., & Johnson, S. K. (2012). The best laid plans: Examining the conditions under which a planning intervention improves learning and reduces attrition. *Journal of Applied Psychology, 97*(5), 967–981.

Smither, J. W., Reilly, R. R., Millsap, R. E., Pearlman, K., & Stoffey, R. W. (1993). Applicant reactions to selection procedures. *Personnel Psychology, 46,* 49–76.

Stone-Romero, E. F. (2002). The relative validity and usefulness of various empirical research designs. In S. G. Rogelberg (Ed.), *Handbook of research methods in industrial and organizational psychology* (pp. 77–98). London, UK: Backwell.

Sturman, M. C., Cheramie, R. A., & Cashen, L. H. (2005). The impact of job complexity and performance measurement on the temporal consistency, stability, and test-retest reliability of employee job performance ratings. *Journal of Applied Psychology, 90*(2), 269–283.

Suazo, M. M., & Stone-Romero, E. F. (2011). Implications of psychological contract breach: A perceived organizational support perspective. *Journal of Managerial Psychology, 26*(5), 366–382.

Sun, S., Pan, W., & Wang, L. L. (2011). Rethinking observed power concept, practice, and implications. *European Journal of Research Methods for the Behavioral Social Sciences, 7*(3), 81–87.

Taylor, P. J., Pajo, K., Cheung, G. W., & Stringfield, P. (2004). Dimensionality and validity of a structured telephone reference check procedure. *Personnel Psychology, 57*, 745–772.

Terrion, J. L. (2006). The impact of a management training program for university administrators. *Journal of Management Development, 25*(2), 183–194.

Thurstone, L. L. (1929). *The measurement of social attitudes*. Chicago, IL: University of Chicago Press.

Tippins, N. T. (2011). What's wrong with content-oriented validity studies for individual psychological assessments? *Industrial and Organizational Psychology, 4*, 327–329.

Tolman, R. S. (1946). Six years after: A study of predictions. *Journal of Consulting Psychology, 10*(3), 154–160.

Trials of War Criminals Before the Nuremberg Military Tribunals Under Control Council Law No. 10, Vol. 2 (pp. 181–182). Washington, DC: U.S. Government Printing Office, 1949. Retrieved from http://www .hhs.gov/ohrp/archive/nurcode.html

Van Hooft, E. A. J., & Born, M. P. (2012). Intentional response distortion on personality tests: Using eye-tracking to understand response processes when faking. *Journal of Applied Psychology, 97*(2), 2, 301–316.

Van Iddekinge, C. H., Putka, D. J., & Campbell, J. P. (2011). Reconsidering vocational interests for personnel selection: The validity of an interest-based selection test in relation to job knowledge, job performance, and continuance intentions. *Journal of Applied Psychology, 96*(1), 12–33.

Van Iddekinge, C. H., Roth, P. L., Raymark, P. H., & Odle-Dusseau, H. N (2012). The criterion-related validity of integrity tests: An updated meta-analysis. *Journal of Applied Psychology, 97*(3), 499–530.

Vecchio, R. P. (2007). *Leadership: Understanding the dynamics of power and influence in organizations* (2nd ed.). Notre Dame, IN: University of Notre Dame Press.

Vevea, J. L., Clements, N. C., & Hedges, L. V. (1993). Assessing the effects of selection bias on validity data for the General Aptitude Test Battery. *Journal of Applied Psychology, 78*(6), 981–987.

Viswesvaran, C., Ones, D. S., & Schmidt, F. L. (1996). Comparative study of job performance ratings. *Journal of Applied Psychology, 81*, 557–574.

Wanous, J. P., Reichers, A. E., & Hudy, M. J. (1997). Overall job satisfaction: How good are single-item measures? *Journal of Applied Psychology, 82*(2), 247–252.

Wilcox, R. R. (1995). ANOVA: A paradigm for low power and misleading measures of effect size? *Review of Educational Research, 65*(1), 51–77.

Wilcox, R. R. (1998). How many discoveries have been lost by ignoring modern statistical methods? *American Psychologist, 53*(3), 300–314.

Yan, J., Wu, Y., & Zhang, W. (2010). Biodata as a personnel recruitment selection approach in China: Assessment and its validity. *Acta Psychologica Sinica, 42*(3), 423–433.

Zhao, S. (2009). The nature and value of common sense to decision making. *Management Decision, 47*(3), 441–453.

Zijlstra, W. P., Van der Ark, L. A., & Sijtsma, K. (2011). Outliers in questionnaire data: Can they be detected and should they be removed? *Journal of Educational and Behavioral Statistics, 36*(2), 186–212.

Zimbardo, P. G. (1971). The power and pathology of imprisonment. *Congressional Record*. (Serial No. 15, 1971–10–25). Hearings before Subcommittee No. 3, of the Committee on the Judiciary, House of Representatives, Ninety-Second Congress, *First Session on Corrections, Part II, Prisons, Prison Reform and Prisoner's Rights: California*. Washington, DC: U.S. Government Printing Office.

Index

selection and, 66
testing effect, 69
Interrater reliability, 46, 48
Interval scale, 16–17, 172
Interview, 158–159
Intrarater reliability, 46, 48
Introduction, report, 225–228
Item quantity and progression, 154

J
Jargon, 149
Jeanneret, P. R., 89, 90 (box)
Jehn, K. A., 86
Jiang, K., 87
Johnson, R. E., 101, 102, 109, 180
Johnson, S. K., 101, 179
Judge, T. A., 6, 47
Justice, 32

K
Kamen, J. M., 205
Katz, J. A., 50 (box)
Kleinmann, M., 46, 50
Kolb, J. A., 82
Kovera, M. B., 108
Kravitz, D. A., 69
Kuchinke, K. P., 51
Kunin,T., 154

L
Lado, M., 46, 47
Lance, C. E., 78 (box), 81
Landers, R. N., 180
Lang, J. W. B., 106
Latent variables, 13 (table)
Latham, G. P., 92, 123, 124, 180
Law and ethics, 28
Le, H., 59
Learning through induction and deduction, 6–7
Lee, H., 89
Lee, T. W., 87
Lewis, M. W., 82
Li, P. R., 46
Lievens, F., 48, 85
Likert, R., 152
Likert-type scale, 16–17
Lily Ledbetter Fair Pay Act, 37
Lindsay, J J., 76, 77, 103
Liu, D., 87

Lofland, J., 131, 132
Lofland, L., 131, 132
Low statistical power, 63
Luthans, B. C., 117–118, 122
Luthans, F., 117–118

M
MacKinnon, D. W., 78 (box)
Mael, F. A., 6
Mail-based surveys (MBS), 22
Maldegen, R., 87
Manifest variables, 13 (table)
Manipulation in experimental design, 101
Manzey, D., 46, 50
Mark, T., 69
Market research, 84 (box)
Maruping, L. M., 204
Masick, K. D., 81
Maturation and internal validity, 68
Maurer, T. J., 23
May, D. R., 125, 126
Mayo, E., 134 (box)
McAuliff, B. D., 108
McBride, D. M., 43
McElroy, J. C., 107, 108
McFarland, L. A., 89, 212
McKay, P. F., 87
Meade, A. W., 81
Mean, 180–181
    regression to the, 68–69
Measurement
    descriptive and inferential statistics, 180–183,
        184 (table)
    error, 161
    in experimental design, 101–102
    statistical analysis and scales of, 184–190
    variability, 181–183, 184 (table)
Median, 180–181
Mediating variables, 14 (table)
Memory and recall of respondents, 160
Meta-analysis, 6, 21, 130, 138–140
Method section of reports, 228–230
Meyers, L. S., 58, 63
Milgram, S., 30
Millsap, R. E., 88
Mirosevich, V. M., 64, 65
Mitchell, G., 77, 103
Mitchell, T. R., 87
Mode, 180–181

⑨SAGE research**methods**

The essential online tool for researchers from the world's leading methods publisher

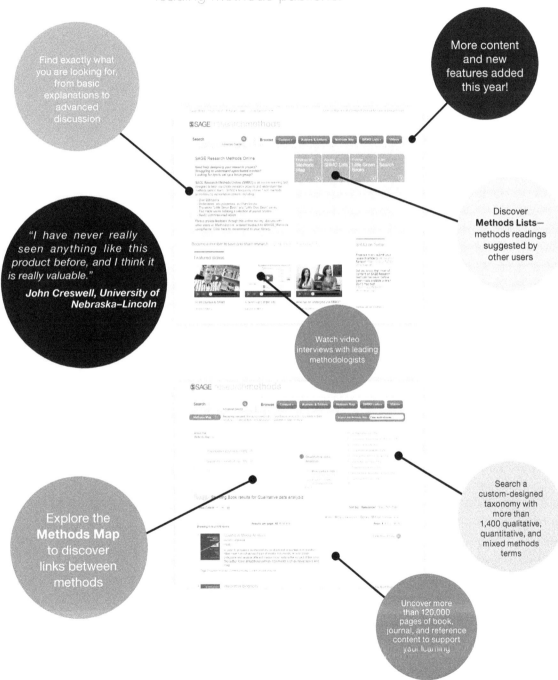

Find exactly what you are looking for, from basic explanations to advanced discussion

More content and new features added this year!

"I have never really seen anything like this product before, and I think it is really valuable."

John Creswell, University of Nebraska–Lincoln

Discover **Methods Lists**— methods readings suggested by other users

Watch video interviews with leading methodologists

Search a custom-designed taxonomy with more than 1,400 qualitative, quantitative, and mixed methods terms

Explore the **Methods Map** to discover links between methods

Uncover more than 120,000 pages of book, journal, and reference content to support your learning

Find out more at
www.sageresearchmethods.com

Lightning Source UK Ltd.
Milton Keynes UK
UKHW011015110123
415159UK00006BA/110